GOD
AND
HUMAN
ANGUISH

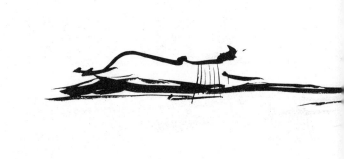

GOD AND HUMAN ANGUISH

S. Paul Schilling

Abingdon   Nashville

God and Human Anguish

Copyright © 1977 by Abingdon

Library of Congress Cataloging in Publication Data
Schilling, Sylvester Paul, 1904–
God and human anguish.

Includes indexes.
1. Theodicy. 2. Good and evil. I. Title.
BT160.S33   231'.8   77-5857

ISBN 0-687-14909-6

Twenty-nine lines (*passim*) from *J.B.* by Archibald MacLeish, copyright © 1956, 1957, 1958 by Archibald MacLeish, reprinted by permission of Houghton Mifflin Company. Poem "And, Behold, It Was Very Good" by Wayne Leiser, copyright 1975 Christian Century Foundation, reprinted by permission from the August 6-13, 1975, issue of *The Christian Century*. Poetry quotation on page 204 is taken from "The Black Christ," contained in *On These I Stand* by Countee Cullen. Copyright 1935 by Harper & Row, Publishers, Inc.; renewed 1963 by Ida M. Cullen; by permission of the publisher. Six lines from "A New Song" by Langston Hughes, published in *A New Song*, are reprinted by permission of Harold Ober Associates Incorporated. Copyright 1938 by Langston Hughes, Renewed. Quotations from T. S. Eliot's *Murder in the Cathedral* are reprinted by permission of Faber and Faber Ltd., Publishers. These same lines from *Murder in the Cathedral*, taken from Eliot's *Complete Poems and Plays*, are reprinted by permission of Harcourt, Brace, Jovanovich, Inc. Quotation from "A Prodigal Son" is reprinted from *God's Trombones* by James Weldon Johnson, copyright 1935 by The Viking Press, Inc. Four lines from the poem "Optimist" are reprinted from the *Collected Poems* of James Stephens, copyright 1909 by Macmillan Publishing Co., Inc. Permission is also extended by Mrs. Iris Wise and Macmillan London and Basingstoke, as well as by The Macmillan Company of Canada Limited.

Scripture quotations unless otherwise noted are from the New English Bible. © the Delegates of the Oxford University Press and the Syndics of the Cambridge University Press 1961, 1970. Reprinted by permission. Scripture quotations noted RSV are from the Revised Standard Version of the Bible, copyrighted 1946, 1952, © 1971, 1973.

MANUFACTURED BY THE PARTHENON PRESS AT
NASHVILLE, TENNESSEE, UNITED STATES OF AMERICA

Contents

To Lois

**who has responded to anguish
with fortitude and active trust**

Preface

"There's always someone playing Job," declares Mr. Zuss in Archibald MacLeish's drama *J.B*. He might have added that all people play Job some of the time, though with different scripts, since many suffer in other ways—less severely, perhaps, or without Job's religious faith.

Suffering is universal. All human beings do everything possible to diminish or overcome it, and the more thoughtful try to make sense of the contradiction between the impact of evil and the opportunities for the realization of good in human existence. Job's problem was still more acute. As a man of religious faith he was forced to ask how the God he trusted could send or permit the pain and desolation that engulfed him. This is the primary question confronted by this book: How can we reconcile the devastating effects of evil with faith in the goodness, power, and wisdom of the God believed in as Creator and Sustainer of our lives?

Our central focus will be philosophical and theological. However, the suffering that raises the troublesome theoretical questions occurs in concrete experience. Therefore, we shall deal constantly with the anguish of real people, assuming the practical need for its reduction. Yet again and again sensitive persons are forced to cry out, "Why?" and their search for answers cannot be suppressed or lightly dismissed. This book is an effort to deal with the hard *why* questions.

The heart of the inquiry interprets and evaluates nine major responses to the problem of harmonizing evil, both natural and moral, with theistic faith. These responses, the main ones I have encountered in a lifetime of personal relationships, study, and reflection, come to light in historical and contemporary thinkers and in the sufferings of ordinary people. The proposals found most constructive are those stated in chapters 8 through 11 and, in part, chapter 7. The closing chapter, after summarizing the major conclusions reached, seeks to relate them as a whole to our human situation. Despite our best intellectual explanations, human beings still suffer and die. If we can say that God is present in their sufferings, what does this mean? How does he "keep" them?

The meaning of evil cannot be understood apart from its relation to good. We regard as good those experiences that we desire, cherish, and seek to conserve and enhance; as evil, those that we try to avoid because they impair attainment of goods or values. Normatively, *good* refers to experiences that are really desirable because they enrich and fulfill life, while *evil* refers to those that thwart such fulfillment and impede the actualization of value. It is not easy to distinguish between real and apparent goods and evils, though we dare never forget that events perceived as evil by the one experiencing them must be treated seriously because they are evil for him.

Suffering overlaps with evil, but is not synonymous with it. To suffer is to undergo physical or mental pain, distress, injury, or loss. Not all evil entails suffering for the person most directly concerned. Karen Anne Quinlan, existing in a comatose state for more than two years, apparently does not suffer, nor does an individual who dies instantly through heart attack or accident. Yet the potentialities of such persons are not realized, and the contributions they might make are lost to associates and society. Thus evil is evil whether or not it causes pain. However, most evil does involve distress, because those who experience it are at least marginally, and often keenly, aware of the goods they are denied. Conversely, not all suffering is evil, or at least wholly evil, for those centrally concerned. Pain may contribute in some degree to the achievement of values, such as heightened sensitivity and concern for others. Yet most suffering is evil, hindering the realization of experiences of worth for all involved. Thus evil and suffering are not interchangeable; yet in our total experience they overlap and interpenetrate, and probably most frequently they coincide.

If the title of this book were to specify either evil or suffering, it would be the latter, since it is centrally concerned with evil as experienced—existential evil. We know evil primarily as suffering. But I have chosen instead the term *anguish,* for two reasons. First, words like *suffering* and *pain* appear repeatedly in book titles, and a variant seems preferable. Secondly, *anguish* connotes more vividly the extremity and depth of the suffering encountered by people today. The word comes from the Latin *angustus,* "narrow," which roots in *angere,* "to press together." The word therefore conveys the feeling of being radically constrained, forced into narrow confines where freedom is stifled. Is this not what suffering often means to people who face the ills of contemporary existence?

This book attempts to deal realistically and forthrightly with the full scope and intensity of human anguish and the problems it raises, with no hostages given to traditional answers. It is concerned to examine the evidence found in the natural, biological, and social sciences, and in the day-by-day experience of individuals and groups, past and present. It likewise seeks to listen to the affirmations of faith as found in the scriptures of various religions and in garden-variety believers. It makes no attempt to prove the goodness of God, nor does it simply assume that God is known to be good without reference to our total experience. Obviously, evil is part of the experience that counts against such belief—for some people decisively. But these chapters do assume the existence of religious faith. The problem is to discover to what degree two givens may be harmoniously related: (1) suffering and (2) belief in the goodness, power, and wisdom of God. The results of our explorations may affect both our attitudes toward pain and our conceptions of the truth of Christian or other religious faith.

In these pages, especially in the closing chapters, many statements are made about God. They speak of his goodness, love, care, knowledge, and judgment. God is described as exercising power, seeking certain ends, creating human beings for fellowship with one another and himself, and sharing in our suffering. Though such assertions may sometimes sound as though the author claims some inside knowledge of the divine, this is not the case. I frequently speak of God as having qualities "somewhat akin to" or "broadly consonant with" what we find in our own existence, or refer to him "by critical analogy with" human experience. I point out that everything we say of God has a nonliteral, symbolic quality, making use of images and models drawn from what we know. When such cautions are not expressed, they are implied. In discussing the ultimate Ground of all our being and becoming, our best thinking is inadequate. Nevertheless, we are entitled to find in our experience, critically interpreted, reliable clues to the reality on which we depend. In our interpretations we must use human ideas and words—the only ones we have. In this sense all our thinking is unavoidably anthropomorphic, but it is not for that reason untrue.

This book owes much to the constructive criticisms of several faculty colleagues who are also cherished longtime friends. Walter G. Muelder read the entire manuscript with painstaking care and made many perceptive and valuable suggestions. L. Harold DeWolf and Peter A. Bertocci, representing different perspectives on central emphases of chapter 11, gave this chapter their exacting attention, contributing thereby to clarification of the issues and sharpening of the conclusions. Jannette E. Newhall, asked to comment on one chapter, read five, and offered helpful recommendations regarding both content and style. Most of all I am indebted to my wife, Mary, who devoted innumerable hours to editing, typing, discriminating evaluation of content, proofreading, and indexing. The net effect of all this effort has been, I am sure, marked improvement in quality. For the defects that remain I accept full responsibility.

S. Paul Schilling

PART ONE • THE PROBLEM

1   The Many Faces of Evil

The lives of human beings are a blend of varying measures of good and evil, value and disvalue, joy and sorrow, happiness and suffering, fulfillment and frustration. We are constantly being enriched by experiences we find worthful. From past centuries we have received a priceless heritage of literature, music, painting, architecture, creative ideas, scientific discovery, ethical insight and action, and religious awareness and devotion. Moreover, the manifold process of the creation and realization of values moves forward today.

Motivated as always by curiosity and wonder, fertile minds explore new dimensions of truth and push back the horizons of knowledge. Amazingly accurate mathematical calculations and scientific technology make possible human explorations of the moon and sophisticated photography on the planets Venus and Mars. The songs of birds, the loveliness of spring flowers, and the majesty of mountains ablaze with autumn color delight modern beholders as they did Wordsworth and Thoreau. Music is being composed, performed, and appreciated, and electronic reproduction makes it accessible to more people than ever before. Unprecedented means of communication and travel increase the possibility of understanding and cooperation among peoples. Men and women reach out in loving concern for others and join responsibly in the struggle for justice in society. Colonial peoples have achieved independence and won new opportunities for personal growth and national development. Hundreds of millions find strength, meaning, and wholeness as they seek to relate their lives to a cosmic ground of existence and value.

Evil as We Encounter It

We all know, however, that there is another side of the human story, often frightening and grim. Our lives contain numerous experiences we regard as evil because they prevent the enjoyment of cherished values, cause physical pain or mental anguish, disrupt social relations, or thwart the attainment of worthy ends. No sensitive person can live today, facing the demands of his own existence, sharing the lives of others, and maintaining contact with human events through newspapers, radio, and television, without being vividly aware of the vast amount of suffering, much of it intense, that people are called on to endure.

Disasters in which natural forces play a considerable role have brought death or injury to incalculable numbers of people. Some of these, like strokes of lightning, may involve only one or two persons; others, such as tidal waves, volcanic eruptions, drought, and floods, may claim the lives of many thousands, while plagues and other epidemics may bring suffering and death to millions. But all entail unfulfilled potentialities, and grief and hardship for surviving relatives and friends. Since the first recorded shipwreck on Cape Cod, Massachusetts, in 1626, storms off the great outer beach have spelled destruction for some three thousand vessels. The earthquake that struck Lisbon, Portugal, on the morning of November 1, 1755, accompanied by mountainous waves and huge fires, destroyed nine thousand buildings and wrought colossal losses of paintings, books, and priceless records of explorations. Out of a population of about two hundred seventy-five thousand, between ten and fifteen thousand people lost their lives. Many died in churches, where they were either attending All Saints Day masses or seeking refuge from the havoc without. The Quanto earthquake of 1923 destroyed almost the whole of Tokyo and Yokohama and killed one hundred thousand persons. In June, 1975, four young American Peace Corps volunteers and two aides died in Liberia when their taxibus was crushed by a tree felled by lightning. In the early 1970s, several million people died of starvation, malnutrition, and related illnesses in India, Bangladesh, Pakistan, Ethiopia, the Sahel region of northern Africa, and other lands. The world hunger crisis continues, with many millions facing famine and starvation.

14

Accidents of many kinds bring loss and tragedy to countless persons. Alfred Wallace, who arrived at the theory of natural selection independently of Charles Darwin, lost all the results of four years of collecting in tropical South America when fire gutted the ship on which he was returning with his specimens to England. In a church in Baltimore in 1952, an eight-year-old girl, reaching to light a candle near the altar, was fatally burned when her dress caught fire from a burning candle. In 1952, two small children drowned when the family car in which they were playing in front of their family's summer cottage on Lake Sunapee, New Hampshire, plunged down the driveway into the lake. In July, 1966, in a beautiful spot near Limburg, West Germany, a bus hurtled off the Autobahn to a road fifty feet below, killing thirty-two passengers returning from a vacation in the Alps. In June, 1975, four members of one family on a camping trip in Maine perished when their camper became stuck in a stream at night and the exhaust filled the interior with deadly carbon monoxide gas. In Rijeka, Yugoslavia, in March, 1975, a flash fire in a hospital maternity ward killed twenty-four newborn babies. In April, 1975, two hundred Vietnamese orphans and helpers, having survived years of warfare, were killed when their plane crashed as it left Saigon on the way to the United States. Events like these could be multiplied almost *ad infinitum*.

All human beings are exposed to suffering from a wide variety of diseases. Many babies are born with deformities such as blindness, deafness, misshapen members, or mental deficiencies. Children with irreparable brain defects or other severe handicaps are condemned to spend years in lonely emptiness, sometimes in pain, incapable of anything resembling normal development. At the other end of life, the elderly often spend their closing years in helplessness and misery amid drab surroundings, with little remaining capacity for any kind of enjoyment, wishing for life to end but unable to die. Thousands of persons die of cancer, often in the prime of life, after months of suffering. In a letter of Sigmund Freud to his friend Pfister, dated January 27, 1920, he tells of his daughter's being suddenly "snatched away" by influenzal pneumonia from her full life as a capable mother and loving wife. The heartache of the Freuds was compounded by their inability to go to their stricken daughter in Hamburg, since in this early postwar period no trains were running to other lands from ruined Austria. To the distress of physical disease must be added the torments suffered by the mentally ill. To the hundreds of thousands of persons confined in mental hospitals, often with little or no therapy, must be joined the far greater numbers of the emotionally disordered who somehow manage to exist outside institutions, alienated within themselves and from other people. The isolation of individuals and groups, graphically portrayed by the exhibit of the Christian Pavilion at Expo '70 in Osaka, is stressed also in the plaintive song by Malvina Reynolds about the "little boxes," which "all look just the same." Part of the sameness lies in the bitterness of estrangement and aloneness that so many of us know at first hand.

Closely akin to physical and mental sickness is the spiritual malaise that appears variously as a deep sense of meaninglessness, an unrelieved sense of failure and unrealized dreams, apprehension of the emptiness of material possessions and the futility of much human striving, and a consciousness of the transience of earthly existence and the certainty of approaching death. The more tightly organized social life becomes, the greater seems to be the lostness experienced by the individual in relation to society and the cosmos. Marriages launched with sincere commitments and high expectations are dashed to pieces on the rocks of misunderstanding, self-seeking rivalry, and shifting aims. Many aged persons, bereft of faculties they once enjoyed and without families or friends who care, live out their closing years in loneliness and despair. Even characters of true nobility like Henry Pitney and Elizabeth Van Dusen choose to covenant to end their lives by their own action rather than face years of helplessness and pain. The judgment of Ecclesiastes, "Vanity of vanities, all is vanity," is echoed in the complaint of the chorus in T. S. Eliot's *Murder in the Cathedral:*

> Here is no continuing city, here
> is no abiding stay.
> Ill the wind, ill the time, uncertain
> the profit, certain the danger.
> O late late late, late is the time,
> late too late, and rotten the year;
> Evil the wind, and bitter the sea, and
> grey the sky, grey grey grey.[1]

Many of the evils so far considered are traceable wholly or largely to nonhuman factors in our natural or cosmic environment—though the causative influence of human attitudes and choices has become increasingly evident. We now turn to sources of suffering that are primarily the result of human decisions and deeds. This is the realm of what is ordinarily called moral evil and religiously and theologically designated as sin. Here belong those individual ways of thinking and acting that hamper the realization of values and prevent the attainment of full personhood. Accompanying them are the feelings of guilt that paralyze constructive action and cry out for healing and renewal. Here appear also the social ills that wreak havoc in the lives of millions of victims. "Man's inhumanity to man," wrote Robert Burns, "makes countless thousands mourn." In the letter previously cited, in which Freud bewails the war-caused disruption that prevented him and his wife from journeying to their critically ill daughter, he writes, "The undisguised brutality of our time weighs heavily on us." This can hardly fail to be the mood of any sensitive person who looks unblinkingly at the world we know more than a half century later.

"I saw the tears of the oppressed, and I saw that there was no one to comfort them." These words from Ecclesiastes 4:1 are echoed by the psalmist when he deplores the oppression of the poor and the orphans by the powerful wicked, who assume that God does not exist or does not care (Ps. 10; cf. Ps. 73; Hab. 1:13). Sin has collective dimensions, appearing in oppressive social structures as in relations between individuals. In the twentieth century, people of limited capacity or opportunity are often exploited mercilessly by powerful and aggressive men. The weak are victimized by the strong. One "slumlord" who recently died in a large eastern city left an estate of more than thirty million dollars, accumulated in part through sharp practices in buying and selling real estate, exorbitant rentals, and shabby maintenance of hundreds of units of substandard housing. Millions of ordinary people are forced to pay for necessities like food and energy exorbitant prices determined by those who own and control a disproportionate share of the world's resources, which they manage entirely for their own profit: huge multinational corporations, oil cartels, and the like. People living in the United States, for example, comprise only 6 percent of the world's population but consume 35 percent of the world's food and 40 percent of its total consumer goods.

Almost unbelievable horrors are perpetrated by human beings on other human beings. Paintings like Picasso's *Guernica* and Goya's *Junta of the Philippines* depict the fierce cruelty that often lurks beneath the veneer of supposedly civilized society. Helpless, innocent children are harshly abused by parents who resent their existence and project on their offspring their own pent-up frustration and guilt. Gifted leaders like the Kennedys and Martin Luther King, Jr., seem at the mercy of warped and sick minds with power to kill. On a larger scale, the wars of our time have seen humanity sink to new depths of violence and destruction. The bombings of Coventry, London, and Rotterdam, the saturation bombings of Dresden and Tokyo, and the atomic bombings of Hiroshima and Nagasaki during World War II were surpassed in volume and ferocity by the mass destruction of the Vietnam War, with its use of antipersonnel and napalm bombs, its wholesale killing of civilians at My Lai and elsewhere, its defoliation, its ruination of a vast acreage of rice paddies and resulting starvation, and its tiger cages near Saigon.

With the memory of our American Bicentennial still fresh, it is salutary to recall not only those events in our history to which we can point with pride, but also those which we must confess with sorrow and shame. During King Philip's War in 1675, colonial troops burned the fort of the Narragansett Indians under Metacomet, destroyed their grain stores, killed a thousand men, women, and children, and left the rest to starve in the dead of winter.

The witch craze in seventeenth-century New England, as in Europe, sometimes engulfed whole communities—all ages, both sexes, and ignorant and learned alike. In Salem, for instance, fear and panic led in 1692 to the indiscriminate accusations that resulted in the execution of many innocent people.

From 1619 to the eve of the Civil War in 1860, the number of black slaves in the territory that became the United States increased to 4,441,830. Those brought from Africa were tightly packed in the hulls of the slave ships, often chained to prevent rebellion or escape overboard, with inadequate food, water, and ventilation, and no sanitary facilities, so that at least 20 percent died en route. Though conditions of slave labor varied according to the nature of the work and the character of the master, slavery was itself at best degrading, and it imposed on its victims intense suffering and hopelessness. Emancipation brought legal servitude to an end, and court decisions, civil rights legislation, vigorous action by black people, and attitudinal changes in the white majority have radically expanded the opportunities open to the black minority. Yet subtle and not-so-subtle oppression continues. Segregation in education and housing and discrimination in jobs, income, and the administration of criminal justice are daily ingredients of the black experience; the goal of an unsegregated society is far from realization; and the call for "freedom now" remains unfulfilled.

In recent years our national record contains such disgraces as the slaughter of unarmed students at Kent State and Mississippi State; inhuman conditions in the prison system, highlighted by the riots in the "correctional institution" at Attica, New York, in 1971; clandestine interference in the internal affairs of other countries, including the expenditure of six million dollars by the Central Intelligence Agency to overthrow the Allende government in Chile; planned assassinations; and the obscenities of Watergate.

No other man-caused evils can compare in extent and brutality with the genocidal massacres of the Armenians in Turkey and the Jews by Adolf Hitler or the persecutions and purges carried out by Josef Stalin in the Soviet Union. In 1894–96 about three hundred thousand people, one-eighth of the Armenian population of the Ottoman Empire, were put to death under Sultan Abdul-Hamid. Much of the killing was done in remote sections, with little news finding its way into the outside world. During three days of killing in Urfa alone, ten thousand died. Many persons, especially women and children, took refuge in their church. The Turks nailed heavy wooden beams across the doors, so that they could not be opened from inside, and set fire to the building. No one escaped from the all-night blaze, and about two thousand perished. In the persecutions of 1915–16, according to careful estimates, about one million Armenians, more than half the Armenian population of Turkey, disappeared. Most of them were murdered by police or soldiers, or died as a result of roadside massacres, forced marches, starvation, sickness, or conditions in concentration camps.[2]

During the Russian civil conflicts of 1917–20 approximately one hundred thousand lost their lives in pogroms. But these deaths were only a prelude to those caused by Stalin's actions to consolidate his power in the U.S.S.R. Between 1928 and 1934 it is probable that close to ten million peasants died in the dictator's program of forced industrialization and collectivization, followed by famine in the Ukraine, when Stalin continued to export grain desperately needed by the farmers who had raised it. In the middle and late 1930s Stalin carried out a bloody purge of high-ranking Communist party members, some of whom had aided materially in his rise to power, and others whom he viewed as potentially dangerous to the state. Several million were either executed or died in prison.[3]

Stalin's excesses were matched by the bestial cruelty of the persecutions perpetrated by Hitler and the Nazis between 1933 and 1945, culminating in the infamous extermination camps such as Belsen, Buchenwald, and Auschwitz. In Buchenwald during a period of eight years, fifty-six thousand men, women, and children perished—either shot, beaten to death, drowned, starved, poisoned, or mortally infected with toxic injections. Their crimes were not *acting* in antisocial ways, but *being*—being social democrats, communists, Jews, priests, pastors, scientists, artists. The height of this diabolical fury was reached in the concerted effort to wipe out the Jewish population of Europe. The Nazis removed seventy thousand Jews from Amsterdam alone, and today only one thousand remain. Jews were herded into cattle and freight cars and shipped to centers like Auschwitz to be murdered in gas chambers or by firing squads. In this holocaust a total of about six million were massacred—35 percent of all Jews alive in the world between 1933 and 1945.[4]

One of the saddest and most complicated forms of human evil is that which springs from the faulty understanding, wrong choices, and competitive striving of basically high-minded persons. Many marriages founder on the rocks of discord because partners who genuinely desire harmony cannot comprehend or control their own emotions and are unable to reconcile their differences. Educational communities, including theological seminaries, are sometimes wrecked because the efforts of administrators, faculty, and students who are truly committed to the enhancement of human values are undermined by ambition, defective personal relations, misunderstanding of motives, struggle for power (seen as necessary for the attainment of worthy ends), and search for financial stability. The result may be the disintegration of distinguished institutions with many decades of conspicuous service, bringing profound suffering to large numbers of participants and supporters whose hopes for an enterprise they love are dashed to earth.

Any listing of the ills that flesh is heir to must include the pain that afflicts a large part of the animal world. As Tennyson has reminded us, nature is "red with tooth and claw," and few animals indeed are free from the threat of being attacked and devoured by stronger animals. My wife and I observed a small but moving example of such torture when we saw, behind our house in the Philippines, a small snake writhing in pain while being bitten to death by an army of ants—torment we were able to end only by killing the reptile. Yet it is probable that human beings exhibit more cruelty toward animals than the animals themselves in the methods widely used in trapping and hunting. No "brute" is more insensitively brutal than men who employ leghold traps to catch fur-bearing animals; trapped creatures often suffer for days or weeks before being found and killed by trappers making their rounds, frequently dying slowly from lacerated legs or lack of food or water. In the same category is the annual clubbing to death of baby seals—highly valued for their white fur—in the Pribilof Islands of Alaska.

Without doubt, one of the greatest evils of all is the indifference to evil that characterizes enormous numbers of people who do not want to be disturbed as they pursue their parochial interests. Michael J. Arlen writes of his conversation in Istanbul with two American professors of English from an American college up the Bosporus. One of them admitted that the Armenian massacres were "a pity," but added that the Armenians were "a great nuisance" to the Turkish population, and, after all, the country belonged to the Turks. "Those things are probably brutal, but they're life. . . . The truth that seems to emerge . . . is that the Armenians basically provoked them. . . . Actually, even the massacres weren't as terrible as they were made out to be." Later that evening Arlen's wife commented to him, "The Turks don't admit to anything. And nobody else still gives a damn." Arlen himself sums up the incident: "The Armenians were once a great nuisance. The sounds of a dance band floated up to us from the hotel garden.'' [5] The sad truth of this observation is underlined by a cynical question of Adolf Hitler in 1939. According to documents presented at the Nürnberg trials in 1945, in discussion with Goering about the imminent invasion of Poland, Hitler asked, ''Who talks nowadays of the extermination of the Armenians?'' Much of the response to the holocaust has been marked by somewhat similar apathy. At least some Germans knew what was happening to the Jews, but very few acted in their behalf. Little was done to intercede for them by leaders or agencies outside Germany. The Allied Command knew of the gas chambers at Auschwitz and could have knocked out the railroads hauling prisoners to their deaths, but they were so intent on winning the war that none of the bombs rained on cities and industrial centers were diverted to the humanitarian end of saving Jewish lives. Today, human awareness of Hitler's ''final solution of the Jewish problem'' is not so dim or unconcerned as that regarding the decimation of the Armenians, but neither is there clear evidence that memory of the holocaust is vivid enough to generate wide or deep sensitivity to infringements on the rights of today's minorities. Millions of blacks, Indians, Puerto Ricans, and Chicanos are victims of racist attitudes and practices in American society, and most white Americans seem content to look the other way. Continued acceptance of a subordinate status for women is evidenced in the number of states opposing ratification of the Equal Rights Amendment.

Humanitarian groups so far have had very limited success in either state legislatures or the U.S. Congress in their efforts to bar leghold traps and inhumane seal-hunting. In 1974, in the face of unprecedented world hunger, one member of the United States National Security Council, looking for political advantage for the U.S. from distribution of foreign aid, asserted: ''To give food aid to countries just because people are starving is a pretty weak argument.'' [6]

Some of the most disturbing evidences of indifference have to do with failures to extend aid to individuals near at hand. Many readers will recall the tragedy of Kitty Genovese, who was stabbed to death in a street in Queens while neighbors watched from their apartment windows. She screamed for help and was heard, but no one responded. A less dramatic but equally fatal failure is disclosed in a recent incident in Marshfield, Massachusetts. The report in the press speaks for itself: ''The bodies of an elderly Marshfield man, who had been dead about three months, and his wife, who died about two weeks ago, were found in their Plain Street home yesterday afternoon. Death was believed due to natural causes." A two-months' accumulation of mail finally led the postal service to notify police that something might be wrong. Two people, aged eighty-one and seventy-seven, were so completely alone and friendless that no one was close enough or cared enough to discover their predicament.

In the above account I have tried to report as objectively and candidly as possible concrete illustrations of some of the major varieties of evil and suffering that are to be found in our world. However, my role is not that of a disinterested spectator watching from the sidelines. In a fairly long life I have had often enough firsthand experience of the numbing reality of mental and physical pain. During my graduate studies the wife of a beloved fellow student, after only six months of marriage, was killed in a gas explosion in their apartment in Massachusetts, plunging him into a serious emotional disturbance. A dear friend and ministerial associate in Maryland died of cancer in his middle forties after six months of courageous suffering, leaving his widow with three children to provide for. Leukemia has claimed the lives of a twelve-year-old grandnephew and an intimate friend and teaching colleague, aged seventy-six, both after more than two years of alternate remissions and agony. A grandniece, now aged fourteen, in a home for retarded children, and afflicted with cerebral palsy and degeneration of the central nervous system, is slowly deteriorating, unable to walk or crawl or care for herself, and completely unaware of the world around her, but deeply loved by her parents who have done everything conceivable for her well-being. A valued friend barely survived an attempted suicide, later having to endure the amputation of a leg because her life was further endangered by a massive blood clot. Another close friend, a woman of eighty, who for years devoted herself to a loving ministry to the handicapped, but now deaf, unable to read, and almost helpless in the infirmary of a home for the aged, confided to a friend, "If I weren't a Christian I'd have committed suicide." I myself have undergone major surgery six times; three of these were for the same ailment that had twice thwarted the surgeon's efforts; and one, following several months of illness, probably saved my life.

Kinds of Evil

This fairly lengthy, though by no means exhaustive, sampling of forms of evil and suffering has been offered here for two reasons. First, it provides an empirical basis and point of reference for the discussion that follows. When the term *evil* is used, it will refer to concrete experiences like these, never to an abstraction. Secondly, this background survey may serve to underline the urgency of the problem of evil and the importance of confronting it unflinchingly, with eyes open to its terrors. Suffering is a stern reality in our world, and nothing is to be gained, and much lost, by evading the enigma it poses.

Various forms of suffering have been listed more or less at random, because this is the way in which they occur in human life. Though the account exhibits a rough continuum from evils attributable mainly to natural forces to those springing primarily from human actions, there has been no attempt to classify them. Experiences of evil do not come neatly organized, but helter-skelter. However, understanding of the nature of suffering will be enhanced if we make some effort to group its chief forms. If classification is not too rigid or compartmental, it should help us to see the relationship between various types and so to deal with them more intelligently.

Historically, the division accepted by the majority of philosophers and theologians has been that between natural and moral evil. Natural evil refers to undesirable experiences of sentient beings due to events in the physical world not subject to human control. Moral evil designates unwanted experiences referable to human agency, such as wrongdoing, ignorance, or complacency. Viewed religiously, moral evil is sin, comprising choices and actions that are regarded as contrary to the purpose of God. Natural evils occur independently of human volition, whereas moral evils are caused by voluntary actions of human beings.

C. J. Ducasse prefers a division that identifies four classes of evil: (1) *physical,* comprising "all the pains and discomforts which arise from disease, from accidents, or from duress upon the body"; (2) *psychological,* including conditions due to separation from loved ones by forced absence or death, loneliness, anxiety, fear, and frustration—all states "not traceable to causes in or accidents to the body of the suffering person" or to wickedness in him or others; (3) *moral,* comprising character defects such as selfishness, greed, malice, hatred, and cruelty, which cause suffering to persons who have them as well as others; and (4) *intellectual,* including irrationality, stupidity, poor judgment, and defective perception, which lead to ineffective handling of many situations.[7]

It may be noted that Ducasse's physical evil is essentially what has traditionally been called natural evil, while the other three forms are largely subdivisions of moral evil as earlier understood. There is value in this further breakdown of forms. However, it is partly vitiated by incomplete division; the subforms are not mutually exclusive. The psychological evils are primarily emotional, and should therefore include the disorders of insanity, which are listed as intellectual. Stupidity and defective perception are sometimes physically or genetically rooted, and in such instances would be forms of physical or natural evil. However, these difficulties serve chiefly to point up the fact that any classification is bound to involve some degree of overlap.

Langdon Gilkey suggests the value of substituting for the distinction between natural and human or moral evil that which exists between "manageable" and "unmanageable" evils. We have learned that many forms of evil—even those regarded as natural—can be studied, understood, and increasingly controlled. Thus such occurrences as floods, diseases, plagues, economic maladjustments, and even wars have definite natures and modes of behavior. As we learn more about how to deal with them, they yield to human efforts to conquer them and become more manageable. On the other hand, there are evils that no scientific skill or devotion of will can master. Such is the mystery of historical life that often our very efforts to destroy evil and advance good embroil us in the very conflicts we try to end, and in actions that cause further immediate suffering and tragic results in the more distant future. This is true because there are facets of evil that function within us, so that in opposing it, we sometimes become part of the evil we seek to destroy. This baffling reality appears in three guises: fate, sin, and death, all unmanageable.

Fate consists of those political, economic, intellectual, and technological forces within history that, beyond all of our individual intentions, seem to drive us irresistibly toward social conflicts, wars, and depressions. Such forces provide the context and the conditions within which we act; hence we cannot control them but instead are determined by them. Sin is a powerful force within us that "subtly twists each of our acts and intentions into a glorification of self." We lack the power to control it precisely because the self-centeredness is a quality of our own wills, tainting even our best efforts to change. Death is ultimately beyond all human control. When it occurs prematurely, it destroys every possibility of fulfillment for the individual; and if it is the final word for the human race, it means the final dissolution of all human creativity.[8]

This shifting of the criterion for distinction between evils from causation to control sheds important light on our understanding. It is clear, however, that the differentiation is relative. Increased knowledge does indeed diminish the scope and seriousness of many evils, but few are subject to complete human control. Scientific warning systems and wise precautions reduce the impact of storms and earthquakes, and gratifying progress has been made in the struggle against disease; but natural disasters continue to wreak havoc, and leukemia and congenital deformities still exact a frightful toll, while new inventions often introduce new dangers. On the other hand, of the unmanageable evils listed by Gilkey, it may be that only death is in the last analysis—except as regards the time and manner of its occurrence—completely unmanageable. When the resources of Christian faith are fully utilized, for example, trust in the power of God and his forgiving, transforming grace may make it possible to deal with fate and sin as effectively as increased knowledge helps to control natural ills. Thus the boundary between manageable and unmanageable evils is seen to be variable and blurred.

On balance, it seems to me unwise to dispense with the traditional division between natural and moral evil, as long as we recognize fully that these also overlap. The sinking of the "unsinkable" *Titanic* in 1912 was due partly to natural forces like the freezing and thawing that produce floating icebergs, but partly also to human carelessness and irresponsibility in navigation. In many crimes of violence, unethical disregard of human life and rights is partly the result of, or is compounded by, physical and psychological limitations due to hunger, malnutrition, or other aspects of human finitude not chargeable to specific human choices. Poverty, which is desperate in many regions of the world, and which in 1975 afflicted about 12 percent of the population of the United States, as determined by the U.S. government index, is attributable to both natural circumstances and complex human factors. Therefore, even as we ascribe a certain primacy to the distinction between natural and moral evil, we shall recognize that the two are not mutually exclusive, but comprise intersecting circles. Moreover, we shall find value in discerning within each varying degrees of manageability and unmanageability.

We also need to recognize the existence of some evils that are not clearly either natural or moral, but that spring from impersonal social structures and processes. These reflect, not wicked desires or intentions, but limitations in the behavior of massive groups. Even where a group intention is good, the outcome may be evil because social reality is not understood or taken seriously enough. The world market, for example, is a reality that no one can fully grasp, but which affects everyone. Evil implicit in complex group processes, though not traceable to physical nature, might be termed natural in that it is not willed by persons; yet it is moral in the sense that we can control it to some degree when we become conscious of it.

In the chapters that follow we shall maintain a continuing awareness of the distinctions just noted. However, we shall not undertake separate discussions of the problems related to the major types of evil or the suffering arising from them. In concrete human life natural and moral evil occur in close relation. Hence in our search for answers to the questions they occasion, we shall deal with evil as it is actually experienced. In the process we may discover that much that can be said in response applies to both kinds of evil.

Weighty voices have been raised to declare that much more suffering springs from human beings themselves than from the forces of nature. Thus Thomas Aquinas asserts, "Things which are generated and corrupted, in which alone there can be natural evil, are a very small part of the whole universe." Similarly, John Hick maintains that "by far the greatest bulk of human suffering is due either wholly or in part to the actions and inactions of other human beings.'' C. S. Lewis estimates that human wickedness accounts for four-fifths of human sufferings. Radoslav A. Tsanoff, pointing out that Christianity, in stressing salvation from sin, put the problem of evil in the center of its concern, goes on to identify the essential evil as sin, which he finds far more important than hunger, disease, or poverty.[9] Such judgments, I believe, are basically sound. They are reinforced by the illustrations of suffering cited earlier in this chapter, and they will find further confirmation in ensuing chapters.

Nevertheless, there remains much suffering that cannot be imputed to human beings, and no discussion of evil that expects to be taken seriously can evade the problems that it raises. Such evasion has been all too often the resort of pious people, a circumstance that underlines the importance of facing squarely the tragedies wrought by events that men and women are often powerless to prevent: cancer, diseases of old age, tornadoes, disastrous fires caused by lightning, and comparable afflictions. Many atheists have been led to or confirmed in their unbelief by the impact of natural evils, as was Albert Camus by his sensitive awareness of the suffering caused by bubonic plague. On the theistic side, the same New Testament that cares so much about salvation from sin is also concerned with freeing people from disease. The salvation it proclaims includes the healing of human bodies and minds. With respect to sin itself, serious minds have often insisted that recognition be given to the grave difficulties that finite existence imposes on persons as they try to fulfill what they accept as the divine purpose. Further, as C. S. Lewis observes, ''Even if all suffering were man-made, we should like to know the reason for the enormous permission to torture their fellows which God gives to the worst of men.''[10] Such concerns require us to reckon with our nature as creatures, which extends beyond human responsibility. Accordingly, we shall need to confront as a whole the evils that beset us, natural as well as human, unmanageable as well as manageable, and inquire how best to resolve the problems they raise.

2 The Problems of Evil

Evil not only exists in a variety of forms; its very existence constitutes an urgent problem—or, more accurately, problems. The remainder of this book will be an attempt to deal critically with the insistent questions raised by the scope and intensity of human suffering, and with some of the answers that may be given.

At the outset it is obvious that there are two main problems: (1) all human beings face the practical question of how to reduce, control, or alleviate evil, so that suffering may be diminished; (2) more thoughtful persons confront also the theoretical problem of reconciling the desolating reality of evil with other aspects of their experience and belief. Even relatively unreflective individuals are troubled at times by this question, though they may not formulate it clearly or deal with it explicitly.

The Practical Problem

Those who address the practical problem of evil approach it differently, depending on whether their perspective is religious or nonreligious. The person whose orientation is wholly secular or humanistic will bring to bear all the resources of human knowledge and intelligence as he exerts his best efforts to remove or restrict the impact of evil. In company with others he will seek to understand the manner of operation of the forces that produce earthquakes, floods, droughts, famines, and other natural events that threaten human life, and will draw up proposals for controlling or mitigating the effects of such occurrences as far as possible. Results may include warning populations of impending danger, or demonstrating flood control, different agricultural methods, and the like. Concerned individuals, well-endowed foundations, and governmental agencies like the National Institutes of Health in the United States carry on medical research on tuberculosis, cancer, heart ailments, muscular dystrophy, and other diseases; as a result of such scientific work, paralytic poliomyelitis can now be prevented by means of the Salk vaccine, and smallpox, long a dreaded scourge, is on the verge of elimination. Psychiatrists, mental health clinics, family counseling centers, schools, juvenile courts, and—at least theoretically—state "correctional" institutions try to help people deal with ethical questions and problems of interpersonal relations. A wide variety of social agencies exist to aid persons who cannot cope with their physical or social environment by themselves. Vast governmental operations deal with such problems as health, welfare, education, unemployment, and social security, which affect tens of millions of citizens. A complex network of educational institutions for all age levels and with many types of specialization attempt constantly to reduce the sway of ignorance, to prepare persons to confront intelligently the needs, opportunities, and hazards of human existence, and to participate responsibly in the creation and enhancement of human values. Within nations, laws and provisions for the enforcement of laws seek to protect lives and property, while internationally the United Nations acts to settle differences between governments, promote world peace, and advance human welfare.

Persons who view suffering from a religious perspective ordinarily participate fully in efforts to ameliorate evil by activities like those just cited. However, to their humanitarian motivation they add the desire to relate their lives harmoniously to an activity beyond themselves that they regard as supremely worthful. They are thus moved by what Tillich called an ultimate concern, and they testify to the availability of resources that provide strength for the struggle.

The Christian, for example, asks the same question raised by other men and women, "How can evil be overcome?" But from the vantage point of his faith he pushes on to ask, "Is there a creator and sovereign who rules over these powers that rule over us?" [1] The answer he finds in the God proclaimed in the Christian gospel, who is constantly acting to conquer evil, and who summons his worshipers to work with him to eradicate it. The Christian stance toward evil is therefore two-faceted: it involves trust in a power that far exceeds our highest human capacities, a power that can be relied on because God is ultimately and supremely good; and it arouses in those who have this trust a commitment to become co-laborers with God in the struggle against the negativities of existence.

A striking summary of the Christian approach to the practical problem of evil is found in the prayer with which Alan Paton closes one of his meditations on a famous prayer of St. Francis of Assisi:

O God, Creator of mankind, I do not aspire to comprehend You or Your creation, nor to understand pain or suffering. I aspire only to relieve the pain and suffering of others, and I trust that in doing so, I may understand more clearly Your nature, that You are the Father of all mankind, and that the hairs of my head are numbered.[2]

Already in these words is a hint of the theoretical problem—the desire for understanding. But the understanding sought is seen as a by-product of faithful action, and it is itself more a part of an ultimate trust than the result of critical reflection.

The Philosophical Problem

Many people who are one with Paton in their desire to relieve pain do not share his willingness to forgo the quest for understanding. They seek rather the greatest attainable comprehension of suffering. Such minds note that in all other areas we do all we can to make our experience intelligible; why should this not be true, they ask, for the question of suffering, which touches and threatens every human life? The theoretical or philosophical problem may be approached from three main perspectives, each of which has its own ways of formulating the question and responding to it: (1) that of the sensitive thinker, whether or not he is religious in his world view, who wants if possible to make sense of human existence; (2) that of the atheist; and (3) that of the theist or religious believer.

1. As pointed out in chapter 1, the world as we know it offers both rich opportunities for the realization of value and devastating experiences of disvalue, often in close juxtaposition. Inevitably the question arises, How can we conceive reality in such a way as to account for these apparently contradictory manifestations of good and evil?

The admixture of opposites in human existence is emphasized by the author of the book of Ecclesiastes: "In the day of prosperity be joyful, and in the day of adversity consider; God has made the one as well as the other" (6:14 RSV). "All is vanity and a striving after wind," and the best enjoyments open to human beings are eating, drinking, and toil; nevertheless, "to the man who pleases him God gives wisdom and knowledge and joy" (Eccl. 2:17, 24, 26 RSV). Though there is here to be sure a nominal reference to God, this is incidental to the assertion of contradictories that marks the entire book. The Letter of James asks, "Does a fountain gush with both fresh and brackish water from the same opening?" (James 3:11). In this passage James is stressing that a person's words should consistently express his basic character, and he therefore implies a negative answer. But if we broaden his question to relate it to the source of the total reality we confront, our answer would have to be affirmative. Whatever the ultimate nature of that reality may be, it does bring forth both sweet and bitter water, summer gardens and cholera epidemics, Michelangelos and Mansons, selfless struggle for human rights and brutal oppression. Good overlaps evil, and evil, good—in the impact of nature on human existence, in human society, and in the lives of individuals. There is much truth in the words uttered by T. S. Eliot's Thomas Beckett just before he is murdered:

> For every life and every act
> Consequence of good and evil can be shown.
> And as in time results of many deeds are blended
> So good and evil in the end become confounded.[3]

What, then, are we to make of this conjunction? If we seek maximum understanding of our experience—however limited that maximum may be—this question must be asked of the universe. Every persistent thinker looks for some coherent account of the apposition and frequent interpenetration of good and evil.

Some philosophical realists and naturalists regard the universe as indifferent or neutral toward good and evil and therefore maintain that the problem is artificial. If reality is indeed disinterested with respect to our value judgments, then the presence of evil and good together should occasion no surprise. David Hume reaches somewhat similar conclusions. Arguing against the theistic argument from design, he contends that the phenomena we observe are too diversified to justify selecting any one aspect as the basis for an analogy. It would be sounder simply to affirm some principle of order, a generative force, or a blind, purposeless vitality. Moreover, the extent of pain and suffering would oblige us to postulate either two cosmic powers (working respectively for good and evil) or one source that is both incomprehensible and morally neutral. Of these suppositions, Hume regards the latter as more probable.[4] A third alternative, not mentioned by Hume but seriously advanced recently by Frederick Sontag, proposes that the ultimately real is one, but is two-sided, combining good and evil.[5] These hypotheses—that of a metaphysical dualism and that of a single creative ground of reality that is either morally neutral or two-faceted—will be examined later. For the present, it will suffice to point out that the ultimate neutralism asserted by some naturalists, and suggested by Hume, in effect writes off the whole realm of value experience as irrelevant to the human attempt to understand reality. This is at best a dubious procedure for thinkers who claim to give a serious interpretation of experience.

2. The problem of reconciling the competing influences of good and evil in human experience becomes more urgent when the good is related to God as its source or ground and the evil is seen as antagonistic to divine intention. Those who are most profoundly affected by the power and extent of suffering and injustice are often led to adopt an atheistic or at least nontheistic stance toward reality. On the other hand, those who are impressed primarily by the potentialities for the conservation and advancement of values, in spite of manifest impediments, commit themselves to a theistic position.

Probably no one circumstance contributes more to the unbelief of the serious atheist than the magnitude of human suffering caused by the forces of nature and the injustices of human beings. Such atheism runs the gamut of sorrowful assertion of a vast cosmic silence in face of the pathos and tragedy of earthly existence (indicating that the universe is ultimately indifferent to or unaware of our plight) to a vehement, bitter, cynical rejection of any divine presence in a world as absurd as ours.

During the fourteenth and fifteenth centuries the Armenian plateau was overrun by Turkish, Mongol, and Arab invaders. Appended to Armenian manuscripts from this period are many colophons, brief explanatory notes by the scribes telling of the persecutions, slaughter, and destruction suffered by the inhabitants of various monasteries and villages at the times the copies were made. Michael J. Arlen writes that these despairing messages were "stuffed into the shipwreck bottles of history, actually buried in cellars—uncommunicated to anyone save God (who never answered)," and scholars who learned of them only hundreds of years afterward.[6] Five centuries later the works of Samuel Beckett portray eloquently his view of the bleakness, emptiness, and meaninglessness of human existence. *Waiting for Godot,* for example, records the conversation of two characters who illustrate the fundamental human situation of being in the world but not knowing why. They are waiting for someone, but they are not sure that someone has made an appointment, and they have no definite evidence that he even exists. Roger Garaudy, eminent French Marxist, reverses the relationship in denying categorically any divine presence: "For us atheists nothing is promised and no one is waiting."[7]

In 1966 in Prague I talked with Milan Machoveč, a Marxist teacher of philosophy at Charles University, about the major bases of his atheistic position. He cited first of all "the depth of evil in the world. I can't combine faith in God with Auschwitz." The brutalities perpetrated on the Jews by the Nazis elicited no divine intervention. "Either there is no God," concluded Machoveč, "or I don't belong to him." In an article written in 1967, Elie Wiesel describes the spiritual agony experienced by many Jews who felt forced to conclude that God, in failing to provide protection, had broken his promises to his covenant people.[8]

In *The Blood of the Lamb,* Peter De Vries voices a vivid protest against a God who permits suffering in his creation. At one point the chief character, Wanderhope, is a patient in a tuberculosis sanitarium. There he befriends another patient, Rena Baker, who asks whether he prays for her. "That would mean," he replies, that "the one I was addressing had done this to you to begin with, which I find hard to believe anybody would.'' When she fails to understand, he elaborates: ''I simply mean that asking Him to cure you—or me, or anybody—implies a personal being who arbitrarily does us this dirt. The prayer then is a plea to have a heart. To knock it off. I find the thought repulsive. I prefer to think we're the victims of chance to dignifying any such force with the name of providence.'' [9]

Wanderhope recovers from tuberculosis, but later lives through the suicide of his wife and the long, agonizing sufferings of his only daughter Carol, who dies of leukemia at the age of twelve. She is the lamb referred to in the title of the book, since the final stages of her illness bring much bleeding at the gums. In conversation with other parents of leukemia victims at the hospital, Wanderhope tries to uphold a kind of theistic belief, but under the impact of his daughter's excruciating pain he finally rebels completely. In anger he hurls a cake, prepared by his housekeeper for Carol's birthday, at the statue of Christ in front of St. Catherine's Church, hitting it in the face. [10]

This kind of response to the silence of God in the presence of unjust suffering finds poignant expression in the lines of Alfred de Vigny:

> If in the Holy Garden of Gethsemane
> The Son of Man did pray to God, and
>   prayed in vain;
> Deaf, blind, and unresponsive to our misery,
> If Heav'n did spurn our misbegotten
>   world of pain,
> This scorn Divine my mortal honor will defy
> With scorn, and silence cold will be
>   my one reply
> To God's eternal silence and to God's disdain. [11]

Many black novelists and poets have responded similarly to the horrors inflicted on their race long after slavery was legally abolished. Thus W. E. B. DuBois cried out against the slaughter of black people in Atlanta on ''the Day of Death'' in 1906:

O Silent God, . . . bewildered we are . . . mad with the madness of a mobbed and mocked and murdered people. . . . *What meaneth this?* Tell us the Plan, give us the Sign!

Sit no longer blind, Lord God, deaf to our prayer and dumb to our dumb suffering. Surely Thou too art not white, O Lord, a pale, bloodless, heartless thing?[12]

Some later black writers, finding such appeals worthless, have concluded that black religion has frequently served as an opiate, strengthening a spirit of passive acceptance and submission amid oppression. Langston Hughes laments the day when blacks through their "sorrow songs" sought relief in "the precious Name of Jesus," but found instead only forgetfulness of their plight—"humble life and silent death." He then lifts his own voice in strident protest:

> That day is past.
> I know full well now
> Jesus could not die for me—
> That only my own hands,
> Dark as the earth,
> Can make my earth-dark body free.[13]

Most of the utterances just cited reflect the attitudes of sensitive thinkers influenced by cultures and traditions in which belief in God has been nominally assumed. In view of the incongruity of such belief with the evils of the world as they observe and experience them, they break through the accepted belief-structure of their societies to a rejection of religious faith. But because of the social and religious environment out of which they come, they tend to state the problem of suffering much as it is formulated by theistic thinkers: How can an all-powerful and loving God allow such things to happen? Obviously he can't; therefore his reality must be denied in deference to the empirical facts that cannot be refuted. However, once this conclusion has been reached, there is no philosophical problem of evil.[14] In a universe with no divine creator or sustainer and no ultimate ground of values but only a cold indifference or unawareness to the pains and sorrows of human beings, there can be no occasion for surprise when evils appear. On the contrary, such occurrences can be reasonably expected in a world that is blind and deaf to human aspirations.

Yet this does not mean that the atheist has no problem—far from it. Whether or not he recognizes his situation, he is confronted by the problem of good, which is at least as difficult for him as the pervasiveness of evil is for the theist. In a godless universe, how are we to account for the manifest fact that high values are sought and realized? How can we reconcile with an absurd, meaningless cosmos that cares nothing for human striving the patent reality in human experience of the pursuit and discovery of truth, the creation and appreciation of beauty, and the quiet strength of self-sacrificial love? Harry Emerson Fosdick offers an imposing list of values integral to the daily lives of countless numbers of men, women, and young people, many of them quite ordinary folk:

> sunsets and symphonies, mothers, music, and the laughter of children at play, great books, great art, great science, great personalities, victories of good over evil, the long hard-won ascent from the Stone Age up, and all the friendly spirits that are to others a cup of strength in some great agony.[15]

If the ground of our world in no way corresponds to the activity that religious faith has called God, the emergence in human existence of values like these is an impenetrable mystery, and probably a greater mystery than is the presence of evil in a world viewed ultimately as rooted in the work of supreme power and infinite goodness.

Strangely, few atheists seem to acknowledge the reality of the problem of good from their perspective. At least, in a fairly wide reading of the literature of the main varieties of atheistic thought, though I have found much discussion of the contradiction between religious belief and evil, I have seldom encountered any admission of a similar incongruity between materialism, nontheistic naturalism, or scientific humanism and the undeniable richness of our human experience of value. Although some religious believers are guilty of superficial handling of evil in relation to their theistic claims, most of them admit that the problem exists. This circumstance suggests that in this respect they may be after all more realistic in interpreting the experienced world than their opponents, who sometimes accuse them of hopeless naïveté. Possibly some light may be shed on this question by our later discussion.

3. Just as the reality of evil has provided one of the weightiest arguments for atheism, it is probably also the strongest theoretical root of perplexity and doubt among religious believers. Confronted by the greed and arrogance of the wicked in their oppression of the poor, the psalmist cries,

> Why stand so far off, LORD,
> hiding thyself in time of need?
>
> (Ps. 10:1)

His plaintive query is echoed by Habbakuk:

> O mighty God, . . .
> thou whose eyes are too pure to look upon evil,
> and who canst not countenance wrongdoing,
> why dost thou countenance the treachery of the wicked?
> Why keep silent when they devour men more righteous than they?
>
> (Hab. 1:13)

The same kind of response has often been evoked by natural catastrophes. Following the Lisbon earthquake, many of the faithful who survived asked whether the city had not suffered more than it deserved, and wondered whether, in view of such occurrences, God really is a loving Father. Similar questions were raised by sympathizers outside Portugal. The halting, unconvincing replies of many of the clergy no doubt reflect their own bewilderment.

Implicit in the questions occasioned by such events is the assumption that God is both perfectly good and unlimited in power. The problem is therefore that of reconciling the divine character with the evils permitted in a world presumably created and controlled by God. A classic formulation of the question is that of Epicurus as reported by the Christian Lactantius (died *ca.* 330). Logically, says Epicurus, there are four possibilities: (1) God wants to remove evil but is unable; (2) he is able but unwilling; (3) he is neither willing nor able; (4) he is both willing and able. Only the fourth option is appropriate to the God of religious faith. But then where do evils come from, and why doesn't God eliminate them?[16]

Augustine posed the question with similar forthrightness and precision, though less systematically:

> Behold God, and behold what God hath created; and God is good, most mightily and incomparably better than all these; but yet He, who is good, hath created them good. . . . Where, then, is evil, and whence,

and how crept it in hither? What is its root, and what its seed? Or has it no being at all? Why, then, do we fear and shun that which has no being? . . . He, indeed, the greatest and chiefest Good, has created these lesser goods; but both Creator and created are all good. Whence is evil?[17]

Augustine goes on to explore other questions that hinge mainly on his belief in the power and eternity of God. For example, as Plato believed, did God create the world out of some preexistent matter? Did this matter contain evil, some of which God did not change to good? "But why was this? Was He powerless to change the whole lump, so that no evil should remain in it, seeing that He is omnipotent? . . . Such things did I revolve in my miserable breast, overwhelmed with most gnawing cares lest I should die ere I discovered the truth."[18]

Epicurus, finding it impossible to account for evil if God is both willing and able, concludes that there is no God. Among those who have followed his lead was John Stuart Mill, who is emphatic in asserting the "absolute contradiction" entailed in affirming both infinite power and infinite benevolence and justice "in the Creator of such a world as this." To attempt to do so involves also "the revolting spectacle of a jesuitical defence of moral enormities."[19]

In contrast to this line of thought, Augustine goes on from his own searching statement of the problem to a belief in divine providence that unabashedly combines almighty power and perfect goodness. This he does through his conception of evil as privation of being, his judgment that the absolute authority he affirms is a mystery that human minds are unable to comprehend, and his faith in God's revelation in Jesus Christ as proclaimed by the Catholic Church.[20] This affirmation of both omnipotence and unsullied goodness continues to be the orthodox response to the problem, although its advocates differ considerably from Augustine, and from each other, in the arguments they present and the implications they draw.

On the contrary, to some theologians and philosophers of religion it now seems axiomatic that either absolute power or unlimited goodness in human thought of God must be surrendered or modified. Most of these, believing that a God worthy of worship cannot be less than good, conceive of God as finite in power, though infinite in goodness.

For the present, however, our concern is not to explore proposed solutions, but to shed as much light as possible on the nature of the problem. In this connection it should be pointed out that historic Christian thought has usually presupposed that God is one and that he is personal Spirit. Unity seems to be implied in the notion of omnipotence, since a God who lacked it could hardly be all-powerful.[21] Likewise, to ascribe goodness and volition to God assumes that he possesses characteristics somewhat akin to what we experience as self-consciousness, reason, purposiveness, discrimination among and ability to realize values, and capacity to enter into and sustain relations with other persons. To conceive of God in these terms obviously accentuates the problem of harmonizing the existence of evil with the divine character.

In the twentieth century, increased attention has been given to the bearing of the divine knowledge on the problem of suffering. Omniscience, affirmed by traditional theism, is often linked with omnipotence and perfect goodness as a further quality in God needing somehow to be reconciled with evil if faith in God is to be maintained. If the Creator is all-wise, the question arises, Could he not have devised a world involving less evil, better suited to his ends? The problem is particularly acute if omniscience is interpreted to include foreknowledge. We then must face the circumstance that God created a world which he knew beforehand would cause vast misery to innumerable creatures, and which he sustains in full knowledge of their plight. These considerations are drawn together by C. J. Ducasse in a formulation of exceptional succinctness and clarity:

> If men and all other things in the world were created by an omnipotent, omniscient, and infinitely good God, then, because omniscient, he knew *ab initio* that there would be evil in the kind of world he was creating; because omnipotent, he could have prevented this evil and indeed could eliminate it even now; and, because perfectly good, he would not have willed to create the kind of world in which evil would exist, and he would not allow it to persist. Yet evil is rampant on earth.[22]

An especially troublesome aspect of the problem of evil is its inequitable distribution—a question that comes to the fore in the book of Job and in other biblical writings (see Pss. 10:5-11; 94:3, 6;

Hab. 1:2-4). Why do some people suffer and not others? More poignantly, why do the wicked often prosper while those who trust in God and seek to do his will are called on to endure hardship? Good and evil fortune are parceled out indiscriminately and erratically, with no correlation between the ills visited on individuals and their need for the moral growth that sometimes results from suffering patiently endured.

Trouble does not strike human beings in proportion to their capacity to endure it. Unforeseeable events like the collapse of the tower of Siloam (Luke 13:4) befall the selfish and the altruistic alike. A given event may have widely different results for different people. Some persons succumb to epidemics or contract incurable diseases, while others in apparently similar circumstances do not. A drunken driver speeding down the wrong side of the road is unhurt, while a whole family in the car he hits is killed. Some travelers change their plans at the last minute and board a plane that crashes, while others booked for the ill-fated flight are forced by unexpected circumstances to cancel, and escape with their lives. A brownskinned child in India or the Philippines may suffer irreversible brain damage from malnutrition during her earliest years and enter adulthood dwarfed in body and mind, while a white child in the United States grows up enjoying every advantage and equipped for the fullest realization of her potentialities.

Like questions arise regarding the sufferings of groups, graphically illustrated by the experiences of various ethnic groups. The injustice involved in the murder of six million Jews by the Nazis, for no other reason than that they were Jews, provides a glaring example. The slavery of black people in America offers another. Thus Bishop Daniel Payne of the African Methodist Episcopal Church shortly before the Civil War voiced his deep agony over black suffering:

> I began to question the existence of the Almighty, and to say, if indeed there is a God, does he deal justly? Is he a just God? Is he a holy Being? If so, why does he permit a handful of dying men thus to oppress us? . . . Thus I began . . . to murmur at the administration of his providence. And could I do otherwise, while slavery's cruelties were pressing and grinding my soul in the dust?[23]

The bishop's questions have been repeatedly on the lips of black people in the century and a quarter since he spoke. Martin Luther King, Jr., tells of the agonizing query of his five-year-old son in 1963: "Why do white people treat colored people so mean?"[24] James H. Cone gives eloquent theological expression to the same question. Referring to the liberating activity of the God who freed Israel from Egyptian slavery, who in Jesus' ministry healed the sick and helped the poor, and who is disclosed today as the Holy Spirit of liberation, he asks why blacks are still forced to live in wretchedness without the economic and political power needed to control their own destiny. "Why does the Holy One of Israel permit white people to oppress helpless black people when the Scripture says God came in Jesus Christ to set the captives free?"[25]

Another form of inequitable distribution of suffering appears when comparisons are made between threats to human well-being in different historical periods. It is sometimes pointed out that suffering often stimulates research that results in effective control and even elimination of specific evils. Thus formerly dangerous diseases are eradicated, and sophisticated methods of weather forecasting minimize damage to life and property from hurricanes and other storms. Such challenges also lead to intellectual and moral growth in those who meet them. Augustine possibly had in mind fifth-century counterparts of such developments when he wrote that God "judged it better to bring good out of evil, than not to permit any evil to exist."[26]

Yet advances like these do not blot out the pains and sorrows of the millions who lived and died before the conquests were achieved, and who were no less deserving of deliverance than those now alive. It was not until the mid-nineteenth century that the use of ether and chloroform as anesthetics became possible, and only in 1864 did Joseph Lister begin his work in antiseptic surgery, utilizing the earlier discoveries of Louis Pasteur. Obviously the lack of such knowledge occasioned a staggering total of suffering and death in earlier generations, who needed relief as much as those who now take it for granted. My wife survived an attack of bronchial pneumonia in 1974, largely because of the prompt administration of penicillin, but our brother-in-law died of the same disease twenty-eight years earlier, before research in World War II discovered how to isolate the drug in a stable form from the mold in which it was formed. I myself suffer from a serious deficiency of vitamin B-12 (cyanocobalamin), which is essential to digestion and nutritional absorption. It is kept under constant control by monthly injections of the vitamin, which was isolated only in 1948/49. Prior to that date many persons with symptoms similar to mine but not knowing either the cause or the cure, contracted pernicious anemia, which was frequently fatal; yet they wanted to be cured as much as I. In the area of social injustice, one need only contrast the present outlook of European Jews with those of their predecessors, who were victims of Hitler's "final solution," or the lot of black people now, grim though it often is, with that of those who lived during the 244 years of American slavery, or of those who until a few decades ago faced the constant threat of lynching by bloodthirsty mobs. Keenly aware of such contrasts, many of us would join Augustine in the query that raises doubts about his own assurance, already quoted, that God has planned a gradual overcoming of evil. If evil "were from eternity," he asks, "why did He permit it to be so for infinite spaces of times in the past, and was pleased so long after to make something out of it?"[27]

The Importance of Both Problems

Many interpreters regard the philosophical and theological problems raised by suffering as much less important than the practical question of how to diminish or overcome it. This assertion of the priority of the practical approach ranges all the way from relative subordination to outright dismissal of the theoretical.

James H. Cone finds that theoretical wrestling with the problem of evil often takes the place of responsible struggle to reduce or eliminate it. Thus the Augustinian and Irenaean approaches, in spite of marked differences, both focus on the origin of evil rather than on the social and political structures that produce suffering.[28] Following Gabriel Marcel, Cone distinguishes between objectively considering evil and suffering it. Evil that is only observed is not really evil. Truly to understand evil means to be personally involved in it. Theologians who are only spectators and not victims of suffering may devote their energies to the attempt to explain it, yet actually contribute to "the religious justification of unjust structures that oppress the poor."[29]

Other writers who view the practical solution of the problem as more insistent than the intellectual have in mind not so much the removal of evil as the overcoming of it. The crucial question is then, Can evil be conquered, and how? Christian faith, says Harry Emerson Fosdick, is less concerned with explaining evil than with furnishing power to surmount it. "Jesus himself never said, I have explained the world, but he did say, I have overcome it."[30] E. Stanley Jones agrees. In his last book, writing out of his own deep experience of physical infirmity occasioned by illness, he declares that if Christ had attempted to explain suffering, "his message would have been merely another philosophy." Instead, he gave us a gospel, good news. "A philosophy explains, but it does not change. The Gospel may not explain, but it does utterly change. Jesus transforms suffering by using it. The victim may become victor."[31] O. Fielding Clarke offers his interpretation as to how this victory may be won. Instead of offering a speculative answer to the problem of evil, Christ bore its full impact and, finally, by his death and resurrection, destroyed death. We can understand his answer only by incorporation into Christ's body and a life of creative and redemptive love. There is "no answer to evil except by facing it in Christ's way—by overcoming evil with good, and by the readiness to die for love if need be."[32]

Other statements go beyond these by rejecting, even deriding, the possibility that reason can make any significant contribution to the problem of evil. "There can be no rational answer," writes Clarke, "as to why a perfect God should make an imperfect world." Hence "in terms of the philosophy of the past and traditional systems of logic there is no answer to the problem of evil." This does not matter to the Christian, however, since in this area, as in all other fundamentals, he does not *search* for truth. A non-Christian may seek, but a Christian "has already found and *been found*." Already committed to one who is the Way, the Truth, and the Life, he cannot now start thinking as though he were not so committed.[33]

George A. Buttrick is impatient with efforts, however serious, to deal intellectually with the enigma of God's permission of evil. Referring to two recent books that make the attempt, he declares,

"Both leave me not only unconvinced but rebellious, for not even a toothache can be intellectualized." Neither helps the man whose six children have been killed at a railroad crossing. In such crises human wisdom is of no avail. Pain and death must be approached, not as problems, but as existential events; they can be answered only by another "Event." The decisive Event is God's self-revelation in Christ, above all in his resurrection. This "Breakthrough" does not tell us "why the devil has so much power in our world." But in its light, we know that God has borne and conquered our pains, of both sin and death. This awareness ushers us into a new age. By sharing Christ's sufferings we enter into the creative purpose of pain as our redemptive vocation. Then we no longer care about neat answers. "Why waste time on rationalistic 'reasons' when you have been surprised by joy?" [34]

If a choice were necessary, most thoughtful persons would probably perceive removing and overcoming suffering as more urgent than finding a sound interpretation of it. If evil could be eradicated, there would be nothing left to interpret, while for those who have discovered how to surmount its impact, understanding the *why* of suffering declines in importance. Moreover, James H. Cone is altogether justified in opposing metaphysical speculation that becomes a substitute for struggle against oppression and other forms of evil.

However, when serious efforts by thoughtful, searching minds to relate our encounters with evil as coherently as possible to faith in God and our experience as a whole are denigrated as sterile reliance on human reason instead of revealed truth, I must protest. Such disdain toward any search for reasonable answers may cover an unwillingness to undertake the hard mental labor of critical thinking on the issues. However that may be, there are several weighty grounds for affirming the worth and importance of earnest philosophical and theological examination of the problems raised by suffering.

First, the plea for exclusive attention to the reduction of evil forgets that even our most strenuous efforts fall short of removing it. People continue to get sick and die, to suffer from natural disasters, to face hunger and poverty, to be victimized by injustice. This recognition provides no justification whatever for giving up our attempts to combat and mitigate evil. It rather calls for a realistic facing of our human situation. It reminds us that the theoretical and theological questions persist even as we struggle to lessen the impact of the forces that occasion suffering. Indeed, the claim that only the reduction of evil is important is just as one-sided as sole interest in philosophical speculation without concern for people who are hurting.

Second, people who are intellectually troubled are looking for answers to the fundamental questions. Proclamation to them of the Good News as experienced by believing Christians is likely not to be heard unless it is accompanied by a direct facing of the contradictions that disturb them. The eloquent testimony of witnesses like Fosdick, Jones, and Buttrick cannot be dismissed. However, their words are addressed primarily to convinced—or almost convinced—Christians, while others have little background for receiving them. The Christian may declare with Buttrick, that in the light of the Resurrection "pain is transitory, parasitic, and doomed." [35] Yet it is real, often excruciatingly real, while it lasts, and sometimes it lasts a lifetime. What comfort would these words bring to a Jew at Auschwitz? [36]

The penetrating questions that serious searchers for truth are asking dare not be evaded. "How can we believe in the justice of God," asks Archibald MacLeish, "in a world in which the innocent perish in vast meaningless massacres, and brutal and dishonest men foul all the lovely things?" MacLeish's answer may possibly be found in his play *J.B.*, where Nickles asserts:

> If God is God He is not good,
> If God is good He is not God. [37]

If Christians, in opposition to this reply, simply offer their own assurance that God *is* good, and fail to deal head-on with the troublesome questions that elicit the answer, they arouse the suspicion that they shrink from a genuinely critical examination of the issues and that their professed faith will not bear scrutiny. They thereby lose the opportunity to help the sincere doubter.

It is only a truncated faith in God that will not bear being related critically to our experience as a whole and what we know of the cosmos created and sustained by the God affirmed by faith. It is true, as Buttrick maintains, that evil is first of all an existential event rather than a topic for discussion. But why does this make thoughtful discussion irrelevant or useless? Honest doubt is also an event, as is thinking about it. All events demand our best possible effort to understand them, and therefore the most incisive thinking of which we are capable. As the apostle Paul, no mean exponent of faith, puts it, "Brethren, do not be children in your thinking; be babes in evil, but in thinking be mature" (I Cor. 14:20 RSV).

These words suggest a third consideration. Christians and other religious believers are themselves disturbed by questions aroused by suffering. In some moods we respond sympathetically to the words of Maude Royden: "The Faith does not give us the reasons for tragedy: it gives us power to meet it and to transform it. Then it gives us the reasons, or, rather, it would, if we any longer cared about them." [38] These are noble words, but they are too simplistic. I have known a great many men and women of Christian faith, but I know few who have risen above caring about reasons. Alert Christians are neither immune to questions nor unconcerned with answers. Like other people, they are buffeted by suffering and sorrow, and face periods of perplexity and doubt. If a St. John of the Cross can be engulfed in a "dark night of the soul," it is hardly surprising that persons less capable of vivid mystical experiences than he should have problems with evil. This is true of those of deep faith as well as those of more nominal belief. Indeed, the former may sometimes be especially exposed to the problem, since the evils they see around them and themselves experience are so contradictory to their personal faith in the divine goodness, and since their personal belief makes them more sensitive to the suffering of others.

In this respect, the Christian community has a solemn responsibility to stimulate its members to think clearly and avoid ambiguity concerning the truths they hold. Unfortunately, some of the hymns and prayers used in worship help to spread confusion rather than clarity. In Isaac Watts's stirring hymn, "O God, our help in ages past," congregations address God as "our shelter from the stormy blast." Yet for most worshipers, as for Watts also, the physical stormy blast is the work of God himself. The hymnal used by the Lutheran congregations of Württemberg, West Germany, contains a prayer headed "Bei schwerem Gewitter" (in severe storms). In it

47

God is addressed as the almighty Father in heaven, before whom tremble the heights and depths—that is, the God who is in control of nature, and hence the source of storms. He is entreated not to be terrible, and not to destroy his worshipers in anger, but to "guard body and soul, house and stable, village and city, and all who travel." He is asked to "protect the crops in the field, trees, and vineyards from hail and flood." In short, the congregation calls on him who sends the storm to guard them from the harm it causes.[39] Such liturgical expressions carry theological implications which at least for some worshipers seem incongruous. They therefore call for critical examination if sound conclusions are to be reached.

An advertisement recently placed in many American newspapers by Religion in American Life contains the following appeal:

> Some Asians need your prayers during the bicentennial—and your help. . . . Millions of them are starving to death. Floods and earthquakes have left others homeless and penniless. The God we worship expects us to help them. Join with others at your local church or synagogue and help make this world—and this country—a better place. Welcome God to America's bicentennial. Practice what you pray.[40]

Some thoughtful readers who are rightly sympathetic to this worthy request may still be brash enough to ask, "If God wants us to help them, why did he allow the earthquakes and floods that destroyed their homes?" Persons of serious religious faith must come to terms with such questions.

A fourth ground for serious struggle with the theology of evil is the plain fact that the theoretical and practical problems are so intertwined they cannot reasonably be separated. On the one hand, careful theological interpretation may shed on our lives the kind of light that helps them to gain victory over the threat of evil. On the other, the practical question is at bottom partly that of the perplexity aroused by the contradictions of our existence.

The theoretical question is itself practical. James Cone, arguing for the priority of the latter, states that black suffering in slavery "was not so much a conflict in rational theory as a contradiction in black life." But realistic theological discussion of evil is precisely an effort to deal with this conflict—not with one imagined to exist somewhere in the clouds. Elsewhere Cone writes that the problem of evil emerges "out of the struggle of faith with the negative dimensions of human experience."[41] Exactly! Some theologians unfortunately journey far from the empirical circumstances out of which their problem arose, but if they are true to their vocation, they do not speculate in a vacuum or an ivory tower out of all relation to concrete existence. Rather, as Cone insists, they confront the contradictions encountered within human experience. Resolution of those contradictions entails arduous mental effort as well as courageous struggle to reduce or eradicate specific evils.

During the time of the Jewish holocaust, Judah Leon Magnes, founder and first president of the Hebrew University in Jerusalem, spoke at the beginning of the fall semester. He quoted these words ascribed to Rabbi Levi Yitzhak of Berdichev: "I do not ask, Lord of the World, to reveal to me the secrets of Thy ways—I could not comprehend them. I do not ask to know *why* I suffer, but only this: Do I suffer for Thy sake?" President Magnes concluded his address with the same prayer: "Teach us only this: Does man suffer for *Thy* sake, O Lord?"[42] What does it mean to suffer for God's sake? Is it because suffering is his will that we are called on to accept, placing his purposes above ours? Or is it because suffering relates us to God and his purposes, enabling us somehow to share in his creative work? If the latter, Dr. Magnes's question becomes a form of the practical problem of suffering, since an affirmative answer would identify the sufferer with the ultimate values cherished by God himself and thus help him to surmount evil. But if the question, "Do I suffer for Thy sake?" means "Does my suffering have meaning for God?" it merges with the other question, "Why do I suffer?" An affirmative reply to it is an answer to the *why* question as well. If we regard God as the ultimate reality of our existence, the two questions coalesce. This should become clearer as we proceed to examine the theological problem of evil, always keeping in mind the relevance of our search for our daily lives in the midst of suffering.

Guidelines

Before undertaking the investigation that will occupy us in the remainder of this book, it seems wise to make plain the chief premises or principles that will underlie and guide the discussion.

First, the problem of suffering will be approached from the third of the three perspectives already considered in this chapter, that of the theist or religious believer. I should be less than honest if I claimed to come to the search for possible solutions without presuppositions. As Kierkegaard (1813–1855) made unmistakably clear, they are unavoidable. We all bring to our quest for truth on philosophical and theological issues certain assumptions, whether conscious or unconscious, that influence our perception of the data. The whole background from which I approach any consideration of fundamental questions is infused with religious, particularly Christian, faith. Hence the form of the theoretical problem of evil that I shall address is the theological one of inquiring whether and how the patent reality of evil can be reconciled with belief in God—with particular reference to God's goodness, power, and wisdom. However, in using the word *God* I do not mean a being who stands over against the world and acts upon it from outside, but rather the creative activity that underlies, permeates, relates, and sustains all finite realities. Thus the world exists in and through him. I think of God as the dynamic personal Spirit who is the ultimate ground of all being and becoming, and who through manifold interrelationships seeks the maximum realization of value.

This theistic orientation does not mean, however, that I begin the discussion with a rigid system of belief so sacrosanct that it cannot be questioned. Even long-standing assumptions can be critically examined, and sometimes such examination compels modification or even abandonment of once-cherished beliefs. How free we really are to make such changes is a moot question, but they occur often enough to justify the hope that persons who seek light with complete seriousness will be open to possible correction.

This brings us to a second important guideline: the inquiry will be carried out with constant attention to the evidence provided by our human experience as a whole and concern to find the most cogent interpretation of that experience. Some writing on the problem of evil seems to proceed on *a priori* premises, assuming that we know in advance what or who God *must* be. On the basis of supposedly revealed truths, declarations of church councils, official creedal formulations, or abstract reasoning by individual thinkers, a given conception of God is accepted as definitive and untouchable. This doctrine is then placed over against the realities of suffering as empirically observed, and the problem becomes that of harmonizing dogma with the phenomena of experience as these are rationally understood.

The theistic standpoint from which I start has not been adopted in isolation from the sufferings of humanity. Rather, my convictions concerning God have been fashioned through the years in full awareness of the presence of evil. The order has not been first faith in God, *then* a look at the evil in life in an effort to reconcile the latter with the former at all costs. Rather, the chronology has been the forging of faith in the midst of diversified experiences, including encounters with evil as well as good, and always combined with attempts at rational interpretation, *then* repeated examination of such questions as whether theistic faith is really harmonious with all the data, what kind of faith may be most harmonious, and what modifications may be demanded. Such changes might conceivably include even the possibility that some form of atheism might better account for the facts.[43] Following this kind of procedure, some writers have proposed modifying traditional theism by rethinking divine omnipotence, omniscience, or goodness. Some of these proposals will be examined in later chapters of this book.

Thomas Huxley's conception of the scientific attitude is pertinent here:

> Science seems to teach in the highest and strongest manner the great truth which is embodied in the Christian conception of entire surrender to the will of God. Sit down before the fact as a little child, be prepared to give up every preconceived notion, follow humbly wherever and to whatever abysses nature leads, or you shall learn nothing.[44]

Considering the source of the norm accepted by Huxley for the work of the scientist, it is not surprising that it provides equally appropriate guidance for seekers of truth in religion. As we attempt to relate evil and religious faith, we need a resolute willingness to look unflinchingly at the evidence of our total experience, reaching those conclusions that make it most intelligible.

Inevitably we bring to our consideration of evil certain ideas of

God reached in advance. However, these ideas are themselves interpretations of experience—its more specifically religious aspects and all other areas—and therefore subject to reexamination in the light of new and broader ranges of awareness. Further, our encounters with suffering often lead to conceptualizations that become hardened through removal from the life situations that produced them. We are likely to come closest to the truth if we continually reassess the meaning of our experience as a whole, seeking always the most coherent and illuminating understanding of the facts. As part of this process, we shall ask what truths concerning God are indicated by the diversified events of our lives when they are taken together: our realizations of ethical, intellectual, aesthetic, and religious value, and the circumstances that thwart such attainment; our greed and pride and our moments of selfless concern for others; our illnesses, pains, and sorrows, and our surges of strength to surmount them; our defeats and our victories; our failures and our successes; our sense of guilt and our awareness of forgiveness; our irresponsible and our responsible attitudes and actions; our feelings of aloneness and alienation, and our consciousness of divine support received in worship and prayer. Out of such searching will not come a neat, seamless garment of understanding with no loose ends or frayed edges, but there may appear one that fits our actual existence, a faith that is at home in the real world, and truths that will enable us to live with courage and meaning.

If we relate the experiential approach here favored to the theistic orientation previously affirmed, we discover a third presupposition that has an important bearing on the question of suffering. This is the reality of revelation. If God is personal Love who seeks in his world the fulfillment of ultimate values, he may be expected to act to make known his intention for humanity. If he has created persons for fellowship with himself and one another in the fulfillment of ultimate values, he will hardly leave them dependent solely on their own unassisted search for truth and meaning. In that case, prior to the human experiences that point to God is the initiative of God himself. As men and women struggle with evil and suffering, God does not leave them wholly in the dark, but seeks instead to shed light on their situation and give them guidance and loving support.

By revelation I mean the total activity by which God discloses his character and purpose to persons in order to lead them into a right relationship with himself. It may be general, comprising all those activities in which all human beings may discern the divine presence; notably, the phenomena of nature and history, as well as human experiences of truth, beauty, goodness, and holiness. Or it may be special, such as manifestations of God in particular events in the lives of particular individuals at particular times—for the Christian, in the events centering in and stemming from the coming of Jesus Christ.

Since for Christians the Bible is the record of special revelation at its highest, the biblical writings hold special significance for human knowledge of God's self-disclosure. Revelation is not the book, but the living reality of God's self-communication to which the Scriptures bear witness. Because of this revelation, however, the biblical writings speak with incomparable vividness and power to our human condition, including our experiences of evil. Hence as we examine various responses to the problem of suffering, we shall want to pay close attention to the biblical witness, relating it to its total context of history and experience. The divine Word always comes to us mixed with and in the form of human words. As soon as revelation is received, it is cast in the thought patterns and language of the recipient, colored by human understanding and inevitably subject to the distortion and error that characterize all finite knowledge. One result is found in the widely divergent interpretations by persons who believe they are declaring the self-authenticating Word of God attested by the Scriptures. Hence we have not only the right but the obligation to scrutinize all revelation claims—to "test the spirits, to see whether they are from God" (I John 4:1). We shall also refuse to limit God's revelatory deeds, but look for his illuminating activity also in extrabiblical events, including contemporary life.

In one sense, belief in revelation makes the problem of evil more acute, since it is hard to reconcile with the experiences of the divine hiddenness already noted. If God is really seeking to make himself known, why do so many people lament his absence? This circumstance must be frankly faced. But it then becomes all the more important to inquire what our human blindnesses, sins, and preoccupations may have to do with this sense of divine eclipse, and whether God himself may shed light on our darkness. Amid fearsome threats to our welfare, it becomes urgent for us to ask, as Zedekiah did of Jeremiah when Judah was menaced by the Babylonian army, "Is there any word from the Lord?" (Jer. 37:17 RSV) Human search must be supplemented by openness to divine wisdom.

PART TWO • PROPOSALS TOWARD SOLUTION

3 Acceptance of Mystery in Faith

Any attempt to come to grips with the theological problem of evil brings to mind the term coined by the German philosopher Leibniz in his influential *Theodicée* (1710). The English word *theodicy* is modeled after the French in Leibniz's title, which is based on the Greek words *theos* ("God") and *diké* ("right," or "justice"). A theodicy is an attempt to vindicate the justice or righteousness of God in ordering or permitting evil and suffering in his creation. In the words of Milton, it aims "to justify the ways of God to men."

Theodicies ordinarily take for granted the perfect goodness and almighty power of God and seek to show that evil is consistent with and involved in the intention of God for his world. In the strict sense, therefore, the chapters that follow do not purport to offer a theodicy. I am less concerned to defend God's righteousness in ordering or permitting evil than to inquire whether and how it may be possible to reconcile the goodness, power, and wisdom of God with the reality of evil in the world. Or—remembering that we are dealing throughout with human experiences and understandings—to what extent and in what way is it possible to harmonize human faith in God with the evil and suffering encountered in human life?

Moreover, these pages do not pretend to present a trim, systematic, airtight account that leaves no questions unanswered. They have a much more modest goal. They will examine critically some of the main proposals that have been advanced for reconciling evil and theistic faith, with two intentions: (1) to discover which suggestions have greatest validity and (2) to determine how far these, taken together, make possible the desired reconciliation. We begin with two responses that make much of the element of mystery in our encounters with suffering. Both of them accept the mystery as impenetrable; one finds an outlet in resignation or in positive devotion to duty and constructive work, the other responds with trust in the God found present within the mystery.

Acceptance of Mystery in Resignation or in Devotion to Work

In Samuel Beckett's novel *Watt,* the leading character enters the service of a mysterious employer, Mr. Knott. After working briefly for his superior without ever meeting him, he is discharged. For Beckett this story is clearly an allegory of human life in the midst of mystery, and it no doubt expresses accurately the perception that many people have of their own lives. They feel themselves subject to some power but have no dependable clues as to who or what it is. God, if he or it exists, is completely unknowable; hence no positive attributes can be assigned to the ultimate reality. God cannot be spoken of as good or powerful, so there is nothing that needs to be reconciled with the evils that afflict human beings. The source or ground of our being is so utterly transcendent that it is out of all relation to the moral lives of finite persons. Thus the problem of evil is solved—but only by a dichotomy that limits human values to purely subjective significance.

Somewhat similar is the belief in the wheel of fortune that continues to be influential in Filipino folk religion, including much popular Christianity. This involves a cyclical, fatalistic view of time and a sacral world of nature controlled by gods, spirits, and ancestors that man is powerless to change. The gods are not completely unknowable, but their purposes are obscure and arbitrary. Human beings tend to see reality and themselves as ruled by an inexorable fate that is seldom friendly to their interests. Hence the individual is likely to regard himself, in the words of Emerito P. Nacpil, as the "patient and pathetic victim of circumstance." He knows he is beset by typhoons, floods, droughts, disease, and poverty; but he does not

56

worry, because he is powerless to change his situation. In times of adversity he shrugs his shoulders and says to himself, "Bahala na!" "Let the future take care of itself!" If he has a bad year, he need not despair, for the wheel of fortune is turning, and next year will probably be better. If he has a good year, he should not become too hopeful, for next year is likely to be worse. On balance, however, he can face life with resigned fortitude, for his destiny is in the hands of mysterious powers that he cannot control.

In like manner, two of Voltaire's writings assert the opaqueness of reality and counsel the restriction of human concern to practical tasks near at hand. In a poem written shortly after the Lisbon earthquake of 1755, he points out the contradiction between belief in a benevolent God and the suffering and sorrow of the world, particularly that caused by the earthquake, in which the innocent suffered equally with the guilty. The original poem concludes that people know nothing of their origin, purpose, or destiny. "We know nothing; nature has no message for us; God does not speak." As mortals, we can only suffer, submit in silence to what occurs, worship, and die. In a later amended version, in response to objections and criticisms, he added hope to these verbs in the closing lines. Still later, in deference to friends who thought his change insufficient, he added a new ending, which included the lines:

> One day all will be well, that is our hope;
> All is well today, that is illusion.

In his most famous work, the fantasy *Candide* (1759), Voltaire recounts in a series of tales the misfortunes and calamities that befall the youth Candide, a disciple of Pangloss, who is a follower of the optimism of Leibniz. After the hanging of Pangloss, the terrified Candide asks himself, "If this is the best of all possible worlds, whatever must the others be like?" At the end of the book, Candide and his friends, including the recovered Pangloss and Martin, a pessimistic scholar from America, settle on a small farm near Constantinople. Martin observes, "Work without worrying; it is the only way to make life endurable." When Pangloss continues to claim that all is well, Candide replies, "That may be quite true.

Nevertheless, we have to cultivate our garden.'' The novel ends on this subdued note. In a mysterious world where there is no clear evidence of ultimate goodness there is room for a tough kind of optimism that no adversity can completely destroy. Our outlook is not hopelessly dark, as long as we abandon naïve idealism and perform our immediate tasks quietly and efficiently.

An eighteenth-century Portuguese poet, Faria Cordeiro, reaches similar conclusions in his *Defensam Apologetica,* expressing his views on the earthquake in conversations carried on by the shepherds Aonis and Menalio and their acquaintance Frondoso. Though they go beyond Voltaire in attributing the earthquake to divine power as well as natural causes, they make no pretense of understanding providence, and agree that their course should be that of full submission to what God sends. Life is not an opportunity to fulfill our ambitions, but a brief dream to be endured without complaint or question. Our lot is to be content with our sheep-tending and quiet village life.

Widely different from all of the above is Charles Darwin's reluctant acknowledgment of his inability to decide between design and chance, beneficence and amoral force, in his interpretation of nature. For him mystery took the form of contradictory evidence that he could not harmonize. In a letter to Asa Gray in 1860 he wrote:

> I own that I cannot see as plainly as others do, and as I should wish to do, evidence of design and beneficence on all sides of me. There seems to me too much misery in the world. I cannot persuade myself that a beneficent and omnipotent God would have designedly created the Ichneumonidae with the express intention of their feeding within the living bodies of caterpillars, or that a cat would play with mice. Not believing this, I see no necessity in the belief that the eye was expressly designed. On the other hand, I cannot anyhow be contented to view this wonderful universe, and especially the nature of man, and to conclude that everything is the result of brute force. . . .
>
> I cannot think that the world as we see it is the result of chance; and yet I cannot look at each separate thing as the result of design. . . . I am, and shall ever remain, in a hopeless muddle.
>
> If anything is designed, certainly man must be, yet I cannot admit that man's rudimentary mammae were designed. . . . I am in a thick mud yet I cannot keep out of the question.[1]

Just how insoluble the enigma seemed to Darwin is indicated by the fact that he, though as a scientist always open to new evidence, did not expect any that might extricate him from his quandary.

Acceptance of Mystery with Trust in God

In the instances just cited, human beings trying to make sense of evil confront a blank wall of mystery, with not even a crack allowing a glimpse of what lies on the other side. Belief in God is not rejected, but there is no assurance that the power or powers on which men and women depend care about human life, and no evidence that might yield light on this question. In our dark perplexity, however, we can find meaning in devotion to immediate pursuits, whether physical or intellectual.

In the attitudes now to be examined, the sense of mystery is equally great, but the uncertainty is accepted in trust that behind it is a God whose good purposes are in control of human events. The origin and purpose of evil are hidden in the will of God, which in such matters is not subject to human comprehension. Sometimes this limitation is ascribed to the essential pride of human reason, which because of self-centeredness can lead only to distorted, erroneous conclusions. Thus the Portuguese poet Pino e Mello in his *Parenésis* begins to question the mercy and justice of God in sending the Lisbon earthquake without warning. Was Lisbon more odious to God than Nineveh? But then he breaks off the inquiry, dismayed by his own audacity and fearing that he is presuming to comprehend the divine wisdom. More appropriate to his sinful condition is the humble prayer for mercy that he then offers to God and his plea for the intercession of the Blessed Virgin.

In other thinkers the renunciation of questions of theodicy is based simply on belief in the limitations of finite reason, which is seen as incapable of penetrating the infinite. According to Wolfgang Trillhaas, the very thought of a justification of God, directing toward him a moral question like those applied to men, goes beyond human competence. Such a procedure attempts to make comprehensible the incomprehensible world and to transform a religious need that can be met only in the subjectivity of faith into a question that can be resolved on the basis of a world view. Since all questions of faith tend to objectify themselves as questions relating to a world view, questions of theodicy are unquenchable, but by their very nature unanswerable.[2] T. B. Kilpatrick voices the same view much more briefly when he asks, "Did any serious thinker ever imagine a state of mind in which faith would rest on an argument?"[3]

The mystery which baffles all attempts at theoretical explanation may still be confronted in faith, which may take the form of simple acquiescence or that of a more active trust that seeks to lighten the burden of suffering. It should be instructive to examine examples of both forms.

Quiet Trust

Many people of quiet faith maintain that whatever happens, evil or good, is what God sends. But we can always trust him, even though we cannot understand. Radha, an illiterate Hindu woman of thirty-five in Delhi, endures bleak poverty and deprivation. She was a victim of an arranged marriage at the age of ten, and her husband left her when she was fifteen. She lives under a veranda with her daughter Chandra and an old bachelor named Pandit and ekes out a bare existence selling the betel leaves chewed by many laborers, shopkeepers, and taxi drivers around the center of the city. Yet she is able to say with a smile: "It's not bad; it could be worse. We live here, we wash here, we eat here. My child has grown up here. She sleeps next to me. I know the people here and they know me. It's my life. God has willed this and there's nothing I can say about it."[4]

A similar point of view may be found frequently in persons within the Christian tradition. For instance, the author of a weekly column on life in the agricultural community of Hooper's Delight in Carroll County, Maryland, comments as follows on the problems faced during a wet spring: "The farmers are very busy trying to get their potatoes and crops in, but it rains every other day. We have to take what God has in store for us and be thankful it is no worse."[5]

Essentially the same attitude seems to be implicit in the opening stanza of a well-known black spiritual:

> Over my head I see trouble in the air. . . .
> There must be a God somewhere.

I take this to mean, not that trouble demonstrates the reality of God, but rather that even in the midst of trouble God is real. Therefore, we can face the hardships that beset us in the realization that they are ultimately under God's control. More importantly, we are within God's care, so that we can face any situation with hope, assured that he will bring good out of it. Such an attitude is indicated by the references to music and glory in the air in the later stanzas. Here mystery is implied rather than explicitly affirmed, but the perplexity of the singer is evident. Also, there is no definite assertion that trouble is willed by God, but it is at least allowed by him, and though he may be only "somewhere" rather than close at hand, we can believe that he will disclose a solution to our predicament.

More sophisticated expressions of acceptance of God's will in spite of mystery are abundant. A classic example is of course the book of Job. Though Job remonstrates at length with both the Lord and his "comforters," arguing that his sufferings have been unjustly inflicted on him, when finally confronted by the evidences of the overwhelming greatness and awesome wisdom of God, he is forced to admit that he is far beyond his depth in problems that he cannot fathom. Asked where true understanding may be found, he has to confess,

> No man knows the way to it;
> it is not found in the land of living men.   (28:13)

Human beings can build houses, reproduce their kind, construct dams and irrigation ditches, and extract minerals from the earth, but they cannot begin to comprehend the complex marvels of the created universe, whether on earth or in the heavens. How then can one man expect to know enough to pass judgment on the Almighty? Job takes to himself the reprimand of the Lord:

> Who is this whose ignorant words
> cloud my design in darkness?   (38:2; cf. 38:4; 42:2)

Confounded by the utter contrast between his own ignorance and the infinite wisdom of his Creator, Job is reduced to silence:

> What reply can I give thee, I who carry no weight?
> I put my finger to my lips. (40:4)

> But I have spoken of great things which I have not understood,
> things too wonderful for me to know. (42:3)

In this mood, after all his bold questioning, it seems likely that Job would reaffirm the words spoken earlier to his wife: "If we accept good from God, shall we not accept evil?" (2:10). However, he is so impressed by the matchless power of God that he is confident of the fulfillment of the divine ends:

> I know that thou canst do all things
> and that no purpose is beyond thee. . . .
> I knew of thee then only by report,
> but now I see thee with my own eyes.
> Therefore I melt away;
> I repent in dust and ashes. (42:2-6)

In the light of all that has gone before, it is clear that Job does not "see" the nature and purpose of God. However, he does discern two truths that he had missed before: (1) that nothing can frustrate the will of the Most High and (2) that the divine intention is completely beyond human understanding, hence can only be accepted in the faith that God knows what is best and can be counted on to accomplish it. With these disclosures, Job repents of his effrontery and awaits whatever the Lord may have in store for him.

The willing—even cheerful—acceptance of whatever happens in the individual life as purposed by God is a recurring theme in Christian hymnody. Thus Georg Neumark (1621–1681) admonishes himself:

> Obey, thou restless heart, be still
> And wait in cheerful hope, content
> To take whate'er His gracious will,
> His all-discerning love, hath sent.

Two hymns from the nineteenth century, among others, sound the same note. In a hymn by Charlotte Elliott (1789–1871), the author moves from the opening prayer that on life's way she might seek to

fulfill the will of God to the plea that uncomplainingly she might
endure the ills that come as divinely ordained:

> Tho' dark my path, and sad my lot,
> Let me be still and murmur not,
> Or breathe the prayer divinely taught,
> "Thy will be done!"

Similarly, William H. Burleigh (1812–1871) adds to his prayer for
divine guidance and strength in the paths of peace, truth, and right an
appeal for further guidance that implies that God determines whether
we shall experience happiness or adversity:

> Lead us, O Father, to Thy heavenly rest,
> However rough and steep the path may be,
> Thro' joy or sorrow, as Thou deemest best,
> Until our lives are perfected in Thee.

That the theology of resignation has not been outgrown in the
twentieth century is amply attested by a variety of witnesses. In the
summer of 1973, a United Methodist missionary couple serving in
Rhodesia wrote to a friend in Tacoma, Washington, vividly
describing some of their experiences and observations. "This year,"
they reported, "our area is facing its worst drought, and the
catastrophe which was somewhere 'out there' is right here with us."
Even with normal rainfall some of the people needed to work as long
as three hours a day to secure water for family needs. Though one
large reservoir would probably provide sufficient water for those
dependent on it, it was clear that many of the smaller reservoirs,
wells, boreholes, and springs would be dry before the coming of the
rainy season. Following this information the writers offered their
interpretation: "This must be a part of God's plan, and although we
cannot always understand his purpose, in faith we know that if we do
our part he will see us through." [6]

An almost identical view was recently stated in a very different
situation by Ann Landers, syndicated columnist, whose answers to
all kinds of questions appear daily in hundreds of newspapers in the
United States. One questioner was deeply troubled by the murder of
his brother, aged twenty-one. He felt that if death comes as the result

of illness or accident, one can console himself by saying, "It was God's will. He had a reason." But how can one accept a horrible death by murder with this attitude? In her reply Ann Landers pointed out that there are many questions to which there are no answers, only more questions, such as, "Why him? Why would a good God allow such a thing to happen?" She then dealt specifically with the question raised: "You must accept death when it comes to a loved one, no matter how. Why? Because you have no choice. You must believe that God in His infinite wisdom had a reason—not known to you now, but it is there." Her only further suggestion to the surviving brother was that he undergo several months of grief therapy.[7]

Active Trust

The responses to mystery cited so far involve chiefly a more or less passive faith—sometimes because little or nothing can be done to change the situation. In such cases only one's inner attitude can be controlled, but when it is guided toward acceptance, therapeutic results often follow. Once a person recognizes that certain external events are not subject to his influence, he can turn his attention to those that he can affect. In other cases, however, passive resignation may involve evasion of responsibility for effecting really possible changes. Many people are therefore deeply concerned that all available avenues toward improvement be explored. In the absence of adequate theological explanations, they manifest a practical faith that commits them to whatever forms of action are open.

Something of this attitude is evident in three short papers on earthquakes published by Immanuel Kant in 1756, when he was only thirty-two. While he deals mainly with the scientific aspects, he does consider briefly the relation of earthquakes to God's government of the world. Kant decisively rejects the view that earthquakes are sent to punish sinners. This explanation impertinently pretends that human insight can perceive the intention of the divine will, and it forgets that human beings are not the only objects of God's concern. Many cities as blameworthy as Lisbon have never been shaken by earthquakes. In Peru, Christian no less than heathen regions have been devastated. Thus we are in the dark when we try to discern the purposes of God's governance. But there is no uncertainty as to how we should respond. We are not born to dwell forever on earth, and its goods cannot satisfy our desire for happiness. The misery caused by natural catastrophes should arouse our love for our fellows and move us to deep sympathy. Already apparent here is the nonmetaphysical stance of the *Critiques* of 1781 and 1788, as well as the seeds of Kant's mature view that the only defensible theodicy is practical faith in divine justice. If we can be assured that God is, and that he is good, we must live in absolute loyalty to him no matter how great our misfortunes.[8]

Active trust within a context of inadequate understanding characterizes the response of many black Christians to slavery and later oppression. The utterances and actions of two mid-nineteenth-century black preachers provide telling illustrations. Daniel Payne, a bishop of the African Methodist Episcopal Church, found quite mysterious God's ways of acting in the world but remained confident that he would yet vindicate the sufferings of the slaves: "Trust in him, and he will bring slavery and all its outrages to an end."[9] But this assurance was not for Payne a counsel of passivity. Already in 1839 he spoke out eloquently against the enslavement, not only of black people, but of all human beings, "because God, the living God, whom I dare not disobey, has commanded me to open my mouth for the dumb, and to plead the cause of the oppressed."[10]

Nathaniel Paul likewise focused attention on the mystery and sovereignty of God, whom he could hear proclaiming: "Be still, and know that I am God! Clouds and darkness are round about me; yet righteousness and judgment are the habitation of my throne. . . . It is my sovereign prerogative to bring good out of evil, and cause the wrath of man to praise me."[11] Consistently with this faith, Paul believed that the abolition of slavery in New York signified God's liberating activity. These views may not go so far as some twentieth-century Christians might wish, but they did not lead to inactivity and passive resignation in the presence of the sufferings of slavery. As James Cone has observed, "The black church and its ministers were the most visible activists against slavery."[12]

During the continuing oppression endured by black people in the decades since the Civil War, they have been repeatedly sustained by a positive faith that seemed to be contradicted by the social context.

Typically, they have felt unable to explain why God has permitted them to suffer so grievously. "The meaning of black suffering," writes Cone, "remains a part of the mystery of God's will." [13] Yet black Christians have been able to endure horrible indignities and injustices in the conviction of the living presence of God, particularly as he has made himself known in the cross and resurrection of Jesus Christ. In the light of these events they are confident that the wrongs foisted on them in a white racist society have been overcome in Christ, whose victory they can share. In this perspective Jesus becomes not an opiate, enabling suffering people to forget their troubles, but a motivating power. In him they perceive God's own concrete action in history, calling them out of bondage into freedom. They have responded with active struggle for liberation. [14]

What active trust in God can mean to an individual who faces crushing disappointment that he cannot understand is graphically illustrated by the experience of Père Albert Jamme, a fifty-nine-year-old Belgian-born priest. Father Jamme is one of only four living scholars who have sought to recover the Semitic languages and history of a people who lived in what is now Yemen about 1500 B.C., producing a civilization that antedated those of the Hebrews, Phoenicians, Greeks, Romans, and Arabs. He had labored for thirty-five years, ordinarily seven days a week, in the hot deserts of Yemen, and in Istanbul, Bombay, London, East Germany, and Saudi Arabia, ferreting out, photographing, and translating inscriptions and other records in order to build the foundation for a still unwritten dictionary of the languages of this ancient culture. On October 26, 1975, a fire swept through his office at Catholic University in Washington, D.C., where all the results of his research were stored. Many of his materials were destroyed, and thousands of his papers and cards were badly damaged by fire, smoke, or water. For ten days the faculty, students, and friends of the Department of Semitic Languages at the university set aside their own work to salvage everything possible from the wreckage. About sixty thousand charred index cards remained. Father Jamme estimated that it might cost close to forty thousand dollars and eight to nine years of work just to reorganize what remained and replace some of the lost items. Much was irreplaceable.

Father Jamme's theological response to what happened to him is instructive. In an interview he said, ''I know there is a great lesson in this. But I don't know what it is. What He wanted me to learn, I do not know. That He had a good reason, there is no doubt.'' Possessed of deep personal determination, he felt he must continue his labors. ''Besides, I have no right from a Christian point of view to give up anyhow.''

Pondering what God wanted him to do, he faced the question with faith. ''When I was ordained,'' he said,

> He gave me the most beautiful grace of the priesthood. And therefore I am His servant, and the servant is not above the master. And the master ends up on a cross. What do you expect me to do? End up in a limousine?
>
> It has been my philosophy that the Good Lord doesn't ask me for success. He only asks me to work. Work He is going to get. The rest is His business.[15]

Four weeks after the fire, Father Jamme learned that his application for a Ford Foundation grant for a new research trip to Yemen had been approved. By mid-December he was on his way, high-spirited again.

In Father Jamme's commitment to his work one detects echoes of Candide's decision to cultivate his garden. But the differences are much greater than the similarity. Though both confront mystery, the priest's action is informed by a positive, personal trust in God and a joyous dedication to his task that are completely missing in Candide. The work that calls him is the Lord's as well as his own.

Evaluation

Nicolas Berdyaev sharply criticized Christian thinkers who, when they reach a logical impasse, seek to escape into mystery. We should *begin* with mystery, he counseled, not end with it. The wisdom of this counsel regarding evil is hardly open to doubt, especially if it does not close the door to alert probing—as it did not for Berdyaev.

As finite human beings we *are* surrounded by mystery. The greatest scientists readily recognize its reality, admitting that their ignorance considerably exceeds their knowledge, yet carrying out their research with the humble desire to expand to some degree the frontiers of human understanding of natural, biological, or social phenomena. Our awareness of mystery is even greater as we confront metaphysical questions—those having to do with the ultimate character of the reality we experience. On such questions as the nature and destiny of human personality, the meaning of God or the ground of our existence, the nature of good and evil, right and wrong, and the trustworthiness and objectivity of human knowing, there are no answers convincing to all inquirers. Nobody can claim inside information in his or her attempts to answer questions like these, and no one can soundly pretend to arrive at definitive truth.

This judgment arises out of at least four circumstances familiar to us all: (1) the enormous complexity of the data to be interpreted; (2) the absence of any precise methods of measurement comparable to those available in the natural sciences; (3) the temporal and spatial limitations inherent in our finite human perspective; and (4) inevitable differences of opinion among those who seek answers, caused by their diverse personal, family, geographical, linguistic, social, and cultural backgrounds. No amount of conscientious concern for truth can counteract the influence of factors like these. All efforts to make sense of human suffering must therefore take account of them at the very start. The frank recognition that we all stand in the presence of mystery is a *sine qua non* of constructive thinking on this issue.

Also to be taken with full seriousness is the witness of those who have faced evil with trust. The simple, unquestioning faith of persons who yield themselves to a power they cannot fathom or control enables them to confront adversity without succumbing. Still more, those who in response to the Christian gospel entrust themselves to the God they find disclosed in Jesus Christ find power to overcome evil. The apostle Paul reports that when he prayed for deliverance from a "sharp pain" in his body, the Lord assured him: " 'My grace is all you need; power comes to its full strength in weakness.' . . . Hence I am well content, for Christ's sake, with weakness, contempt, persecution, hardship, and frustration; for when I am weak, then I am strong" (II Cor. 12:7-10). Feeling such support, many believers are able to face their sufferings with positive trust. Aware of a love from which nothing can separate them, they find little need for rational argument. They are assured that the basic meaning of their lives cannot ultimately be eroded. How this can be remains a mystery, but the conviction that it is so is enough.

Obviously this assurance is not open to many who have not had the experience which supports it. Such persons inevitably raise questions regarding the objective truth of such experiences. At the very least, however, the existence of this kind of faith must be seriously reckoned with. It is part of the evidence that needs to be weighed by all who try to form their judgments on the basis of human experience as a whole. Those who would summarily dismiss it as purely subjective are often more arbitrary and opinionated than those whom they accuse. Persons who are really looking for light on the mystery of pain dare not exclude the witness of those who are sustained by a dynamic personal faith.

Nevertheless, respect for and openness to the testimony of faith does not close the issue. Significantly, Berdyaev's counsel to begin with a recognition of mystery does not lead him to end there. There are weighty grounds for pushing on to a careful exploration of various facets of the problem that some men and women of faith find it necessary to consider.

1. As already indicated, there are many people whose experience does not enable them to confront bafflement with total trust, as well as others who feel the need to relate their faith to other experiences and beliefs that they deem important. It is not helpful, and may be disastrous, to say to such people, "Just trust and obey," or even to assert with T. B. Kilpatrick, "God is love. This we know. For the rest we can afford to wait."[16] For many this is precisely the question. *Is* God love? In the light of much contrary evidence, can we persuasively affirm God's goodness unless we demonstrate a willingness to relate the belief to those realities that for many sensitive and thoughtful minds seem to militate against it? If such circumstances are overlooked or suppressed, the declaration that God is love may become little more than a pious formula that expresses an understandable desire for reassurance, but which is not affected by actual human life and has no significant bearing on it.

Those who are unwilling to entertain questions about their faith raised by serious seekers after truth—or in their own minds—arouse the suspicion that their belief will not bear scrutiny. The main recommendation of such faith is that it is earnestly held. However, enough error is earnestly embraced that nonreligious persons who might be open to frank discussion of the problems they encounter will rightly look for stronger grounding. Hence persons who want to witness effectively to their experience of God amid suffering will strengthen rather than weaken their case if they listen receptively to the experiences that make faith difficult for others—and if they do their utmost to deal with the difficulties. It was a New Testament evangelist who counseled his fellow Christians: ''Be always ready with your defence whenever you are called to account for the hope that is in you'' (I Peter 3:15).[17]

2. Willingness to accept the mystery of suffering as the last word often seems equivalent to an attempt to dispose of the problem by forgetting it. But many thoughtful persons, while readily admitting the obscurities we face, are not content to renounce the quest for whatever degree of understanding may be accessible. To do so would mean abandoning the field to the atheist. He has scant respect for those who stress the insolubility of the problem; he interprets their attitude as a retreat, a manifestation of doubt concerning the reality of the God they profess to trust.

A related difficulty concerns the seeming inconsistency involved in asserting inscrutable mystery and at the same time claiming dependable knowledge. If the mystery is so great, some critics may ask, how do we know enough to say that God must have a reason, that God loves us, or that he wills good for his creation? If we insist that in spite of our lack of understanding we still know truths that are favorable to us, we lend support to the criticism of Feuerbach and others that believers simply project on the universe their own ungrounded human wishes and hopes. When religious people in the name of mystery refuse to examine data that threaten faith, they need not be surprised if critics suspect they are creating a void in human knowledge in order to fill it with a God who is only an illusory objectification of their own desires.

3. The counsel of resignation to the mysterious will of God sometimes—though by no means always—produces a passive trust that accepts evils as somehow sent by God, without acceptance of responsibility for removing or reducing them. Persons who are really ''content to take whate'er His gracious will . . . hath sent'' can hardly be expected to work actively to oppose that will by striving to undo the damage it has wrought. The fact that so many religious people do struggle heroically to diminish suffering shows that they do not really believe what they often thoughtlessly sing. But enough do believe it and act accordingly—or consistently fail to act—so that careful examination of what is meant by the will of God becomes imperative. To pray "Thy will be done" may mean to resign oneself to whatever occurs as divinely ordained. It may mean to accept what cannot be helped as the best possible in the given circumstances; such acceptance with appropriate action may be regarded as desired by God, even though God did not cause the circumstances. Or it may mean to pray for strength and wisdom to fulfill God's purpose in ethical decision or action. Which of these meanings applies in a particular situation cannot be decided without discriminating thought. To assume without such thought that trust in God always entails passive resignation is to disobey the first commandment, which calls on believers to love God with all their minds no less than with all their hearts and all their strength.

4. Uncritical acceptance of evil events as somehow mysteriously brought about by divine action fails to recognize the operation of other causative agencies. There are serious defects in a theology that regards a drought in Rhodesia, the murder of a young man, and a fire that vitiates thirty-five years of conscientious labor as planned or caused by God for "a good reason" unknown to us, without even hinting at the presence of other factors.

Two main difficulties in this interpretation may be pointed out. First, it overlooks completely the nature of the physical order, which functions according to uniform and discoverable patterns that can be formulated in what human observers call laws. In general, it may be sound to say that God "has a good reason" for creating a regular, dependable natural order that supports life but sometimes involves hardship; but this is very different from concluding that specific deaths from natural forces are divinely purposed.[18]

Secondly, the view that grounds human ills in an unknown divine plan implies an ultimate determinism that fails even to consider the part played by human agents operating with at least a measure of freedom. Droughts are frequently caused partly by overgrazing, overplanting, or other unwise agricultural methods, so that human actions—careless, ignorant, or intentional—contribute significantly to their occurrence. According to the District of Columbia Fire Department, the fire in Father Jamme's office was caused by a defective hot plate on which he had heated some stew; human failure or incompetence, therefore, had much to do with the disaster. Murders are perpetrated by human beings. The particular act that snuffs out another human life may be premeditated for some reason defensible to the murderer, or it may be the passionate deed of one driven by hate, jealousy, fear, or blind rage. But it is performed by a human being—not by God—though it is permitted by him. In creating men and women God presumably wants, not puppets, but persons capable of growing in the free realization of values. Such creative action on God's part entails the possibility of wrong choices and destructive deeds by his human creatures, but human agents alone translate the possibility into reality. If human beings have even a limited freedom, we cannot soundly trace human evil to the divine intention.[19]

In a broad sense, of course, the activity of God contributes something to every evil event. The laws of combustion that function when a handgun is fired and the properties of water that cause drowning when water replaces oxygen in the lungs belong to God's order of creation. However, neither murder nor death by drowning would occur apart from human volitions that operate within the natural order to produce these occasions of suffering. It is therefore grossly misleading and inaccurate to say of evil happenings that God planned them or had reasons for them that we cannot fathom, unless we indicate the other factors requisite to their occurrence.

4 Denial of Positive Reality to Evil

Strictly speaking, the view that evil is a mystery to be accepted in faith does not attempt to answer the theoretical question. Instead it dismisses the problem as unanswerable, while suggesting attitudes by which suffering may be confronted in practice. The views now to be examined also make an oblique approach to the problem, but instead of regarding it as insoluble, they shift the focus to the nature of evil, believing that removal of misunderstanding of what it is opens the way to handling it effectively. There are four main conceptions of evil that in effect deny its positive reality or aim to neutralize its impact. Evil may be seen as an erroneous idea; it may be traced to a finite self or order that has no real existence; it may be conceived as arising from a partial perspective, therefore not really evil when viewed in its total context or from God's standpoint; or it may be regarded as privation of good or being, hence nothing substantial in itself.

Evil as Error

In Christian Science, founded in Boston in 1879 by Mary Baker Eddy, evil is an illusion, a mistaken idea of mortal mind. According to Mrs. Eddy, God is infinite Mind, Spirit, Soul, divine Principle, Life, Truth, Love. Moreover, Mind is All-in-all, and the sole realities are the divine Mind and idea. Since God or Spirit is all, matter can have no reality; it "possesses neither sensation nor life." The belief that mind is in matter is false, an error of mortal mind—a term used by Mrs. Eddy to designate the flesh as differentiated from Spirit, the human mind in distinction from divine Mind. Actually, mortal mind is misnamed, since it refers to something that has no reality; only absolute, immortal Mind really exists.[1]

Once we recognize the unreality of the material body and the mortal mind, we have the clue to the status of evil in Christian Science. All forms of what human beings call evil—disharmony, sin, illness, suffering, death—spring from erroneous ideas; they occur because people harbor wrong perceptions of themselves and the world. Furthermore, they cannot be real, since God in his wisdom has called his creation good. Mrs. Eddy does not explain how or why human beings created by divine goodness fall away from their true being, but she insists that evil as the opposite of infinite Mind is not Truth, but error, lacking both intelligence and reality. Evil is a "suppositional lie," and its alleged power is "but a phase of nothingness."[2]

The combination of philosophical idealism and religious faith has enabled many Christian Scientists to find a way of dealing effectively with sin and some forms of illness and infirmity. There is no reason to disparage the testimony of earnest adherents to the genuineness of healings wrought through prayer and belief in and trustful commitment to the power of Spirit regarded as the sole reality. But there are serious weaknesses in the interpretation of evil offered by Christian Science. Two may be cited here.

In the first place, to ascribe evil to erroneous ideas of mortal minds offers no explanation at all of natural evils like hurricanes, volcanoes, or tidal waves. Christian Science, in spite of its claim to be scientific, cannot maintain that such events do not really occur, or that the universal belief—shared by Christian Scientists—that they do happen is a false idea rooted in a misunderstanding of the nature of reality. By what stretch of the imagination can a tornado be attributed to the failure of its victims to believe that atmospheric pressures, wind currents, and air temperatures have no reality since God alone exists?

Though faith in the curative activity of God can demonstrably contribute decisively to recoveries from many illnesses and even broken bones, the absence of such faith cannot reasonably be cited as causing the bacteria that produce tuberculosis or the accident that leads to the injury. It is not at all clear how an erroneous view of a femur as real can increase the likelihood of a fracture, while a practicing Christian Scientist under identical circumstances would be saved by his true conception of reality. Careful investigation would probably show that as many Christian Scientists as others—again, in similar circumstances—are injured in disastrous fires. Believers in Mind as All-in-all die physically in the same proportion as the rest of the population.

A second consideration is still more crucial. To treat evil as illusion does not get rid of it, but only redefines it, since it is still experienced as evil. The supposedly nonexistent toothache believed in hurts as much as a real one. On this point Mrs. Eddy gives away her own case. Since all that God creates is good, she argues, "the only reality of sin, sickness, or death is the awful fact that unrealities seem real to human, erring belief, until God strips off their disguise." [3] Thus she admits as an "awful fact" that human minds err in ascribing reality to unreality. If this error is really awful, it becomes itself evil, so that evil, thrust out of the door, comes back in by the window. It is actual—and awful—after all.

Mrs. Eddy does add a condition. Unrealities are real to erroneous belief "until God strips off their disguise." However, this exception raises again, in a slightly different form, the familiar theological problem of evil. If God is Good, Love, Spirit, why does he not strip the camouflage from all false ideas? Why does he wait? Why does he allow the deception in the first place? Mrs. Eddy does not seem to be aware of these questions, and she makes no effort to answer them. The problem of suffering in theistic faiths is that of reconciling experienced evil with the goodness, power, and wisdom of God. Little help in solving it is to be found in the conception of evil as an erroneous idea of mortal mind.

Evil as Rooted in Illusion

In Hinduism and Buddhism, as in Christian Science, illusion is an important element in a true understanding of evil, yet these religions offer interpretations of the nature of reality that are quite different from Mrs. Eddy's. In Brahmanism, evil is attributed to the soul's involvement in the finite realm, which is seen as an illusory manifestation of Brahman, the eternal, all-embracing principle of existence, the only ultimate reality. Since important aspects of Hindu thought will be examined in chapters 5 and 6, we shall confine the present discussion to Buddhism and particularly to the thought of the founder himself, Siddhartha Gautama (*ca. 563–ca.* 483 B.C.).

The central concern of Gautama was the pervasive actuality of suffering and salvation from it. His original insight is embodied in the Four Noble Truths: the existence of suffering (dukkha), its causes, its cessation, and the path that leads to its cessation. The term *dukkha* signifies not only particular experiences like sickness, despair, old age, grief, and death, but mainly the basic transitoriness and emptiness of all existence.

The Second Noble Truth of the causes of misery is in effect elaborated in Gautama's twelvefold law of dependent origination of the stages of life and understanding: suffering depends on birth, birth on existence, existence on attachment, attachment on desire, desire on sensation, sensation on contact, contact on the six organs of sense, the organs of sense on name and form, name and form on consciousness, consciousness on karma, and karma on ignorance. "Thus does this entire aggregation of misery arise."

It is attachment, with the thirst or craving to which it leads, that gives rise to repeated births in other existences, and hence to suffering. To be attached is to seize hold of some action in the hope that it will yield happiness or avoid hardship. Our desires cannot be satisfied: after each fulfillment the seeker looks for a new object that in turn is scorned as soon as it is attained. This frustrating circumstance reflects the impermanence of all existence. Both external things and the human individual represent a flowing together of matter and energy into the "aggregates of existence," which are perceived as real but do not constitute enduring essences. The fluctuation and dynamic becoming are real, but the I that is aware of it is not; the ego would be more truly called a not-self (anatta) than a self. Name, form, and consciousness, as in the individual named Nagasena, are only convenient terms or designations. Unfortunately, this transient center of awareness tries to cling to its apparent continuity and identity, with its promise of pleasure and prosperity; it resists change. Thus it becomes more deeply entangled in an unbroken chain of cause and effect (karma) in which every event depends on what precedes it. At the bottom of this series is ignorance, which prevents the self from breaking out of the process of "again-becoming" or rebirth.

The cessation of suffering can occur only when the illusion "I am" is dispelled and the thirst for continued identity is brought to an end. This happens when karma has been exhausted and the resultant series of births has been overcome. To realize completely the cessation of dukkha is to attain Nirvana, the extinction of "again-becoming," liberation from all craving. The way to this attainment is the Noble Eightfold Path—or the Middle Path—since it avoids the extremes of self-mortification and indulgence. It consists in right view, right thought, right speech, right action, right mode of living, right endeavor, right mindfulness, and right concentration. Following this path, one can be delivered from the chain of causation. This requires a long process of self-discipline, normally extending through numerous rebirths.[4]

Divisions among the disciples of the Buddha occurred soon after his death, and through the centuries many forms of Buddhism, with great variety in interpretation and application of the founder's teaching, have appeared. In the main, however, his essential ideas, including his understanding of suffering, are accepted by all Buddhists.

Clearly, the problem of suffering in Buddhism is different from that in Judaism and Christianity. In Gautama's agnostic thought there is no place for God. Theravada, or Hinayana ("Lesser Vehicle"), Buddhism is likewise nontheistic. Though Mahayana ("Greater Vehicle"), the major development in Buddhism, has accorded to the Buddha a transcendent status, making him in effect a god, it does not regard him as creator of the world. He has been joined by five other Buddhas, and by a multitude of Bodhisattvas, who have entered the path of enlightenment and have vowed to attain Buddhahood. On all of these is bestowed worship, love, and devotion. However, they are neither the ground nor the sustaining power of existence, but those who have learned how to terminate its suffering. Therefore Buddhism does not address the theological problem of evil faced by western theism, and it offers no direct help in the effort to reconcile evil with the power and goodness of God. Yet it does deal in depth with the nature, causes, and conquest of suffering, and it deserves to be evaluated in terms of its own intention.

Its psychological acuteness and philosophical profundity are unmistakable. No religion takes the insistent actuality of evil more seriously. Moreover, since Buddhists recognize the universality of pain and sorrow, most of them manifest a sense of responsibility for their fellow sufferers. Although Theravadins seem preoccupied with individual achievement of Nirvana, with little concern for the salvation of others, there is nothing inherently self-centered about the Buddhist view of evil. The great Buddha himself did not seek only his own enlightenment. He shared his teaching with a company of disciples and always showed deep compassion for human beings in the grip of dukkha. In Mahayana the Bodhisattva ideal is held before all people, and he who accepts the vocation compassionately identifies himself with those still in bondage, including animals. He unselfishly defers entrance into Nirvana so that he can remain in the world as long as others need salvation. Moreover, Buddhism makes no distinctions based on ethnic origin, caste, or social class.

Two difficulties may be briefly indicated. First, there seems to be something incongruous about asserting the actuality of suffering while denying the reality of the self that suffers. Buddhism accords a higher status to the changing flow of existence than to the consciousness in which the movement comes to a focus. Does not the perception of transitoriness depend on some center of awareness that endures and can experience the flow? What are the "aggregates" of existence if there is no aggregation—no totality that is at least as real as its parts? Empirically, assertions about the fluctuations and emptiness of the self are interpretations of the given concreteness of life; to regard impermanence or change as more real than the persons who experience it as they think, will, and feel is to give priority to an abstraction.

Secondly, Buddhism seems to overlook the positive values that are realizable in human life, or to sacrifice them in its proposal for bringing suffering to an end. If we gain deliverance from misery only through extinguishing the thirst for identity, we likewise must suppress the quest for experiences perceived as good, which require continuity. The desire for beauty, wisdom, or friendship, readily frustrated, is itself a source of anguish and must therefore be conquered. The attainment of values like these entails change and effort to actualize experiences now wanting. But if the pursuit of values is excluded—except the one value of overcoming all desires—the whole human venture is denigrated. The positive worth of life disappears along with the evil. Such a negation of the entire realm of values can hardly qualify as a coherent account of our human experience as a whole.

Evil as Element in the Good Whole

A number of able thinkers stress the inadequacy of our partial human perspective. What appears evil to our finite understanding, they contend, may be found to be actually contributory to the good when regarded from the standpoint of the whole or as seen by God. Why should we assume that the distinctions we make between good and evil apply equally to God? Repeatedly we must correct our limited perceptions by relating them to the ultimate and viewing them from the perspective of the divine perfection. When we do this, we discover that many attitudes and actions that seem to us bad find their place in the wholeness of the divine life. Let us look at some examples of this point of view.

One of the most forthright expressions of eighteenth-century optimism and the conception of evil we are now considering is found in six well-known lines of Alexander Pope:

> All nature is but art, unknown to thee;
> All chance, direction, which thou canst not see;
> All discord, harmony not understood;
> All partial evil, universal good;
> And spite of pride, in erring reason's spite,
> One truth is clear, Whatever is, is right.[5]

By "whatever is" Pope does not mean every particular entity or incident, but the universal cause, reality seen as a whole. His kinship with Leibniz appears in another passage of his poetic essay, where he declares that for a mere man to doubt that the universe in its totality is the best "of systems possible" is impious pride:

> All this dread order break—for whom? for thee?
> Vile worm! O madness! pride! impiety![6]

Human beings have no rights that reality must respect, but when they subordinate their interests to the "dread order" that enfolds them, they will see it as good.

Insistence on relating apparent evils to the universal whole comes to sharpest focus in the monism of absolute idealists like F. H. Bradley and Bernard Bosanquet. Against the background of Hegel's principle that "the true is the whole," they point out the limited nature of even our best finite judgments, hence the need for holding all our estimates of evil subject to rectification in the light of the total context.

Bosanquet, for example, stresses the priority of "the total harmony and perfectness" of reality and the importance of inquiring to what degree a particular experience may be seen as a constituent of that harmony. With respect to the more cruel forms of suffering, every one would pray that the cup might pass away from him. Yet in most instances the removal of the cup might be just as inimical to the truly good as it would have been in Gethsemane. In such instances "is it not clear that finite judgment would practically always be wrong?" One would refuse what alone could make him worthy or what imparts true value to an age or a nation. It should also be clear in principle that it is inherently contradictory to subject to the judgment of the finite spirit those depths of the universe that alone make it more than finite. Such a procedure would make futile the whole notion of a reference of the finite to infinity. "The whole point of the connection is that the finite is more than it knows. If we let it, taking itself as finite, lay down its own ultimate limits, why then, of course, all that it dreads is gone, and with it all that made life worth while." [7]

Josiah Royce also makes much of the relationship between part and whole, finite and infinite, but in a way that is both ingenious and closer to concrete moral experience. He distinguishes between two classes of evil: external apparent evil that we cannot understand or affect and the bad will itself. Evils of the former kind, such as pain, death, the disruption of cherished plans, and the cruelties of fate, are to us finite minds opaque, but to God who knows them fully, they must be "somehow clear and rational." He experiences them as elements in an absolutely perfect life. Therefore, though they are now inexplicable, "they are in themselves nothing that God vainly wishes to have otherwise, but they are organically joined with the rest of the glorious Whole." However, with regard to the moral evil that we experience as a present fact we are in a very different situation.[8]

The problem of moral evil is solved, Royce believes, if we proceed from the analogy between the overcoming of sinful impulses in the finite individual and God's eternal realization of goodness through his conquest of the injurious actions of sinful human wills. In human experience the will makes the evil tendency a part of its good consciousness in the very act of overcoming it. "The moral insight condemns the evil that it experiences; *and in condemning and conquering this evil it forms and is, together with the evil, the organic total that constitutes the good will.*" The moral person experiences at once "the partial evil of the selfish impulse . . . and the universal good of the moral victory." The goodness of the good will consists of its realization in struggle of this universal good, and both have their existence only in the experience of evil as a conquered tendency. True goodness is not mere innocence; it is realized insight.[9]

This moral experience provides for Royce the clue to the inclusion of the evil of finite wills in the total life of God. In him evil human impulses comprise parts of a total good will, as the evil tendencies of the good human being are elements in his actualization of goodness. "As the evil impulse is to the good man, so is the evil will of the wicked man to the life of God, in which he is an element"—a conquered element. In both instances the evil will is so included in the structure of the whole experience that the total act is good. "God's life includes, in the organic total of one conscious eternal instant, all life, and so all goodness and evil."[10]

Absolute idealists are in short supply in the thought world of the late twentieth century. Today we do not often encounter monistic interpretations of evil like those we have just examined. Yet in some quarters much is made of the radical difference between human and divine perspectives, the possibility that what we deem evil is not really or ultimately evil, the need of correcting the part by the whole, and the contributions that evils may make to the total good. Some evaluation of the monistic views before us should therefore be pertinent to our contemporary situation.

Royce's account of moral evil commands respect because of its perceptive understanding of human moral experience, especially the close connection between sinful tendencies and the good will that overcomes them. The moral life is indeed a struggle akin to that which Royce describes, and it is suggestive to think of God somewhat in these terms, conceiving him as conquering in his total life the evil finite wills that seek to go their own way. Something like this may have been in the mind of the psalmist, when he wrote that the Lord makes even the wrath of men to praise him (Ps. 76:10). But there are fatal difficulties in the pantheism of Royce's view, according to which all finite lives, including their good and evil motives, are elements in the eternal organic totality of the divine life. For one thing, there is an incongruity between the supposed timelessness of the infinite life of God and the real temporal succession of the finite events that, it is asserted, are somehow gathered up into his total good. Second, if finite spirits are truly elements in the wholeness of the life of God, each choice must be at one and the same time the action of a finite mind and of God himself. But how can the same violition both evil and good—evil for the sinful human part and good for the infinite divine whole? I do not see how this contradiction can be circumvented. Involved here also is the issue of the individual identity and freedom of the finite spirit, which requires consideration in any truly empirical account of human moral experience. Further definition of what it means for the finite to be an element in the infinite might shed light on this issue, but if the relationship is within one organic totality, as Royce says it is, there seems to be little scope for the free agency implied in ordinary moral experience.

What then shall we say of the broader theory that events that seem evil from our finite and partial perspective are really good when seen as elements in the total perfection of God? Unquestionably, this view expresses a sound insight. Only the most arrogant human mind would refuse to admit that God's knowledge of good and evil, as of other existents, must greatly exceed ours. The words of Second Isaiah utter a universal testimony of religious experience:

> For as the heavens are higher than the earth,
> so are my ways higher than your ways
> and my thoughts than your thoughts. (Isa. 55:9)

It is also important to relate the part, whether it is experienced as evil or as good, to the whole, as far as we are able to comprehend it. The more data we can consider in forming our judgments, the closer we are likely to come to the truth. However, it cannot be assumed that this procedure, if followed to the end, would always disclose the illusoriness of the evil and its actual participation in the good.

If we proceed empirically, we must take with full seriousness the distinctions we make between experiences that enrich life and those that frustrate the attainment of cherished values. Even Pope, who claims that discord is but "harmony not understood," writes elsewhere in the same essay, "What can we reason but from what we know?"[11] When our judgments concerning good and evil are critically examined, so that they become more than subjective wishes, we have a right to regard them as offering some indication of what these experiences might mean to God. If we maintain that God is good in something like the sense in which we understand goodness, when confronted by evil we cannot consistently change the meaning of terms to say that, after all, good and evil to God must be quite different from what they are to us. This is especially true if we surreptitiously include the assumption that the difference comes out in our favor. If evil is real only to our limited human understanding, may not the same be true of what we call good?

Moreover, it helps not at all to be assured that if we could adopt the perspective of God, or the eternal, or the whole, we should discern that what appears evil to us is not really so. The plain fact is that we cannot know as God knows. Our perspective is unavoidably human, partial, and temporal. We cannot remove the colored spectacles of our humanness and see reality with the undistorted clarity open only to another form of existence. Our perception of experiences that hurt is the one that arises out of our historical situation, the only kind of existence now accessible to us.

Thus the problem of evil remains: How can we reconcile what we experience as evil, these specific sufferings we live through here and now, with the presumed love, power, and goodness of our Creator? And if the solution is to be found in the holistic view available to

God, why has he created finite minds so incapable of seeing reality as a whole? As with Christian Science, where the imagined ill hurts as much as a real pain would, so here our inability to adopt the divine perspective leaves us trapped in an evil as great as an objectively real evil might be.

Evil as Privation of Good

Of the four main views that deny that evil has any positive reality, the one most influential in Christian tradition is that which regards evil as privation or absence of good. In this area early Christian thought was influenced by Platonism, which identified the good with being and interpreted evil negatively as the deprivation, lack, or corruption of the good. However, in Augustine and later theologians evil is traced not to nonbeing but to the human will, which by its own act becomes perverted.

In Augustine the good is identical with being or substance—that which really is. Every being is a good because it is created by God, the unchangeable, supreme good who has made all things "very good" (Gen. 1:31). Goodness therefore constitutes being; as long as created things *are,* or to the extent that they *are,* they are good. "Therefore whatsoever is, is good." [12]

Evil, then, is excluded from being. It can be understood only in relation to the good, as its absence. It is existentially real, exerting a limiting and perverse influence in our present experience, but it has no essence of its own, no ultimate reality. We call it evil, but it is simply the lack of good. In animal bodies, disease means nothing but the absence of health, as shown by the fact that when a cure occurs, the illness does not go away and take up residence somewhere else, but rather ceases to exist. The disease is not a substance but a defect. The flesh itself is a substance, hence good, but disease is a privation of the good of health. Human vices also are only privations of natural good, for when they are overcome they do not go elsewhere; they cease to be in the morally healthy person and cannot exist anywhere else.

These illustrations make plain that though all things that exist are good, their good is subject to diminution and increase; unlike their Creator, they are not unchangeably and supremely good. As long as they exist, some good must remain to constitute their being. Thus there can be evil only where there is some good. A vice injures by diminishing or taking away good. The good nature may be corrupted, in greater or less degree. When it is defiled, its corruption is evil, since it is deprived of some kind of good. But the evil can occur only in a being that is good. The good may be faulty or imperfect, but it alone has positive or substantial existence.[13]

What, then, leads human beings, basically good, toward evil? For Augustine the agent is the human will, and his discussion of the will provides further opportunity for the elucidation of his view. The evil act is preceded by an evil will. This originates in pride, "the craving for undue exaltation," which occurs when the soul deserts God, its only true end, and becomes its own end. When the will abandons the higher and turns to the lower, "it becomes evil—not because that is evil to which it turns, but because the turning itself is wicked." The will itself becomes perverse by its inordinate desire for an inferior thing. Iniquity is "not a substance, but a perversion of the will, bent aside from Thee, O God, the Supreme Substance, toward these lower things." Likewise, the perverted will is not "a nature"; it is "made of nothing." Thus the evil will itself illustrates Augustine's doctrine of evil as the privation of goodness. The extent of this deprivation may vary greatly, but it is never complete as long as the person has any being. When the individual turns from God and makes himself his own end, he does not quite become absolutely nothing, a nonentity, but he approximates to this condition.[14]

If we ask why the will becomes evil, there is no clear answer. All we can say is that one person sins because he is willing, while another does not sin because he is unwilling. The main reason for this inexplicability is that perverse will "is not efficient, but deficient, as the will itself is not an effecting of something, but a defect. For defection from that which supremely is, to that which has less of being—this is to begin to have an evil will." To seek the causes of these defections, says Augustine, is like trying to see darkness by not seeing, to hear silence by not hearing. Even so, we perceive the inscrutability of evil human volition by not perceiving it. We know deficient forms by not knowing them, "for who can understand defects?"[15]

In view of Augustine's stress on the will as the cause of evil, the question arises: How does he interpret natural evils, which occur independently of human volition? At first sight, it might seem that his conception of evil as privation cannot apply here, since physical events like earthquakes and volcanic eruptions are not caused by human wills. Actually, however, Augustine understands natural no less than moral evil as privation of the good.

We have already noted that he exemplifies his basic conception by referring to diseases not traceable to human acts. In the *City of God* he goes farther, denying that there is such a thing as natural evil. One chapter carries the heading "Of Those Who Do not Approve of Certain Things Which are a Part of this Good Creation of a Good Creator, and Who Think that there is Some Natural Evil." Here, in vigorous opposition to the Manichaean dualists, he asserts again that the world is the work of the goodness of God and therefore good. There are, he admits, things like fire, frost, and wild beasts that injure our frail mortal flesh, "which is at present under just punishment." Yet these things are excellent in their own places and natures and harmoniously adjusted to the remainder of creation. Even poisons, though harmful when unwisely used, are wholesome and therapeutic when used in accord with their design. If their utility is hidden to us, as it often is, we should accept this concealment as a lesson in humility. "For no nature at all is evil, and this is a name for nothing but the want of good." [16]

Augustine's argument here, like all he has to say on evil, is integral to his attack on the Manichaean "heretics." Their basic error for him is that they suppose that the good God, instead of being the sole Author of a good creation, is forced to struggle for supremacy against a competing evil principle. To grant being or substantial status to any kind of evil would call into question the creative power, effective goodness, unchangeability, and incorrupt-ibility of the sovereign Creator of all that is.

It should be noted that the present discussion concentrates attention on Augustine's conception of evil as privation. A full examination of his theodicy would deal more in detail with his view of misused free will as the origin of evil and also with his exposition of the principle of plenitude (discussed under Thomas Aquinas in this chapter) and his view that from God's standpoint evil is seen to contribute to the perfect whole of creation. These will be further discussed in chapters 9 and 10.

Most elements in Augustine's notion of evil as privation appear again eight centuries later in the theology of Thomas Aquinas, though with modifications traceable mainly to the influence of Aristotle. Especially important is the relation between matter and form in the Aristotelian and Thomistic metaphysics. According to this, every being is constituted by, and is a union of, matter and form, which are distinct but inseparably related. Matter is indeterminate potentiality for receiving form, or what has that potentiality. Form is the intelligible structure attained when potentiality becomes actuality or possibility is fulfilled.[17] Reality is an active process in which all entities are in various stages of development from potency to actuality, with the exception that God, and God alone, is pure actuality or act, and has no matter whatever to be further actualized. He is fully realized perfection.

This conception of reality is quite evident in Thomas's discussion of good and evil. "Every nature," he writes, "is either act or potency or a composite of the two. Whatever is act, is a perfection and is good in its very concept. And what is in potency has a natural appetite for the reception of act; but what all beings desire is good." Hence whatever consists of both act and potency participates in goodness. Whatever participates in act is to that extent good: "The form which makes a thing actual is a perfection and a good." Implicitly, then, potency is also good, for it is "ordained to act." Thus every nature or being is good. Thomas reaches the same conclusion on the basis of the goodness of God. Every being other than God is a creature of God, and therefore good (I Tim. 4:4).[18]

This means that evil can be nothing but the absence of good, the privation of perfect being. Nothing can be evil in itself, "in its very essence." Evil can exist only in something good as its subject; as privation, it requires a substratum or foundation that is a being, hence good. Yet evil is not just absence of being as a negative; it is not evil for a man to lack the strength of a lion or the speed of a deer. Rather, "a thing is called evil if it lacks a perfection it ought to have." This may involve a defect either in the thing itself or in its action. Thus it is evil for a man or an animal (though not for a stone) to lack the sense of sight, and lameness in a man is evil since it is action not rightly related to the end of walking.

All beings that unite potency and form are susceptible to the privation that is evil. They may go on to actualize or "form" their potentialities, but they are also liable to deprivation of their potencies and thus to loss of that fulfillment that is their end. "The subject of privation is a being in potentiality." This evil is opposed to every good that partakes of potentiality, "but not to the highest good, who is pure act." [19]

In this way Thomas, like Augustine, relates his doctrine of evil as privation to his opposition to any kind of dualism. Since there can be no being that is essentially evil, the only way for an evil first principle to exist would be with the highest good as its subject or foundation. But God, who is act or form alone, with no iota of potentiality, is not subject to privation or evil. Since his being includes no potency, he cannot be deprived of his perfection. "So there cannot be a being that is supremely evil, in the way that there is a being that is supremely good because it is essentially good." "The highest good is the cause of every being. . . . Therefore there cannot be any principle opposed to it as the cause of evils." [20]

By a bit of ingenious logic, Thomas uses his interpretation of evil as an argument for the existence of God. It is erroneous, he insists, to conclude from the presence of evil in the world that there is no God, as when a philosopher cited by Boethius asks, "If there be a God, whence comes evil?" On the contrary, writes Thomas, "he should have argued: If there is evil, there is a God. For there would be no evil, if the order of good were removed, the privation of which is evil; and there would be no such order, if there were no God." [21]

If a good God is the sole Creator of the universe, with no opposition from an evil principle, and if everything that exists (created by the good God) is good, the question naturally arises, Whence then comes the privation of being that is evil? Thomas replies that the divine providence that governs the world does not exclude corruption and defects in the created order. Two of the reasons he advances for this condition are particularly significant.

First, though God is the First Cause, he works partly through secondary causes. These secondary agents always depend on and act by the power of God, who remains the ultimate cause of all effects.

However, they are not wholly determined, so that defects may occur in things through defective action by a secondary cause without any defect in the primary agent. Thus a perfect craftsman may produce a defective work because of a defect in his instrument; and a man who has healthy locomotive power may walk with a limp because his leg is crooked. In similar fashion, evil actions may occur in the world ruled by God through the defective functioning of secondary causes. "Therefore it is evident that evil deeds, considered as defective, are not from God, but from their defective proximate causes." [22]

Of course, if God so willed, he could produce all effects by himself without utilizing lesser agents. But in his immense goodness he wills to communicate his likeness to things, not only by giving them being, but also by granting them ability to be causes of other things. In the moral realm this involves the gift of freedom, without which human beings could not really love God. Men and women are free to choose for or against God and the right. This entails the possibility of wrong choices, which are evil. This evil is not willed by God, but its possibility is a corollary of the good that people are created free to serve God. This possibility results in the fact that they sometimes fall from goodness, "because that which can fail, at times does fail." [23] In such cases the course chosen, though that of an essentially good will, lacks its true end.

Second, Thomas makes use of the ancient principle of plenitude. The perfection and beauty of the universe require the presence in it of a full range of beings of every possible variety. These form a hierarchy from the highest to the lowest, a great chain of being in which the different links overlap, with no gaps unaccounted for. This chain extends from immaterial angels to the four physical elements of earth, air, fire, and water. Fullness of being demands that some beings exist that are not subject to evil and that others manifest defects in accord with their natures. The complete elimination of evil would mean that things would not be ruled by providence in keeping with their natures; and this would be more defective than the particular defects thus eliminated. To put the matter differently, perfect goodness requires that all possible degrees of goodness be fulfilled; there must be different levels of likeness to God. Further, absence of inequality in goodness would entail the eradication of multitude, since one thing can be better than another only if they

89

differ from one another. Absolute equality in things would mean the existence of only one created good—a condition derogatory to the goodness of the created order. Therefore the perfection of the world requires the existence of creatures that vary widely in their capacities to attain or fail to attain goodness.[24]

The conception of evil as privation of being or the good has persisted down to the present, with various modifications. The views of Jacques Maritain and Karl Barth provide representative twentieth-century expressions. Maritain's basic principle regarding God's permission of evil is that of the "irreducible dissymmetry" between the line of good and that of evil. *"Ens et bonum convertuntur*. The good is being, and plenitude or completion of being." Hence to reason in the line of the good is to reason in the line of being, or "of that which exercises being or bears being to its accomplishment." On the contrary, evil is "absence of being, privation of being or of good." It is "a vacuum of being," "a nothingness which corrodes being." Thus to reason in the line of evil is to reason in the line of nonbeing. As a result, there is a fundamental difference between our ways of looking at and explaining things in the two perspectives. On the basis of this distinction, Maritain develops his interpretation of evil in thoroughly Thomistic fashion.[25]

Karl Barth's treatment of evil manifests both Augustinian and Thomistic influence, though it bears the stamp of his own originality. He designates evil as *das Nichtige*. This term, translatable only unsatisfactorily as "the negative" or "nonbeing," does not mean simply "nothing" (*Nichts*). But neither would it be correct to say that *das Nichtige* is. Only God and his creation can truly be, and since *das Nichtige* is neither, it cannot be as they are. In relation to God's creation, it is threatening, destructive nonessence (*Unwesen*). It is that which must be repudiated and from which one can only turn away since it cannot be respected. God occupies himself with it, struggles against it, and conquers it; therefore it is not nothing. Nevertheless, it has no duration or permanence. It is overcome in Christ's resurrection and the promise of his return. Barth sharply distinguishes evil from the "shadow-sides" of creation—night, pain, lack, finitude, and the end of life. These have meaning and belong to the good creation without impairing its values. By contrast, he understands *das Nichtige* as evil in the strongest sense possible, that which is utterly hostile to God and his creation.[26]

There are several elements of unimpeachable value in the doctrine that evil has no being of its own but is rather privation of being or the good.

1. The distinction between evil as existentially and as ultimately real is a valuable one, underlining the importance of seeing all experienced evil in its total context. The felt evil of an event is unquestionably actual, but this does not mean that it partakes of the fundamental nature of reality. When we hear Augustine saying that whatever is, is good, our first tendency is to reject what sounds like an indiscriminate blessing of the status quo. But what he means is that what *really* is, is good—that only the good is truly real; it alone accords with the structure and movement of the universe, hence it alone has true being. We noted above that when Pope asserts that whatever is, is right, he refers, not to every particular occurrence, but to reality seen in its wholeness. Hegel defends the same position when he declares that "the real is the rational": the surface appearances of consciousness must be reformulated by critical, coherent thought if we are to approximate ultimate truth; and that "the true is the whole": things must be seen in their relations, and the wider the relationships we are able to consider, the closer we come to true knowledge. On this basis we can fully acknowledge the factuality of evil happenings, yet recognize that they do not have the same claim to reality, or the same ultimate status in reality, as do those that fit the character of the whole. Or, to use Aristotelian and Thomistic language, attitudes and events that are only potentially good are not so fully real as those in which the potential is actualized. Only when we see what happens to us in relation to experience as a whole can we soundly judge whether it is really good or evil.

2. The conception of evil as privation of being recognizes a positive quality in the good that cannot be claimed for evil. The Neoplatonic language used by Augustine and Aquinas is foreign to twentieth-century minds that do not think in terms of substance philosophy. Thus it is easy to dismiss as antiquated speculation the notion that being and goodness coincide, so that the *better* anything is the more it *is*—that it becomes real to the degree that it "real-izes" the good intended by the Creator. However, the basic concern of these theologians is to assert the intrinsic or original nature of the good in contrast to the derivative nature of its opposite. Evil cannot be understood apart from its relation to good, but good has an affirmative meaning that does not depend on comparison with evil. Evil, writes Paul Ricoeur, "is not symmetrical with the good; wickedness is not something that replaces the goodness of man; it is the staining, the darkening, the disfiguring of an innocence, a light, and a beauty that remain. However radical evil may be, it cannot be as primordial as goodness."[27]

Evidence for this judgment is abundant in ordinary life. Physical health is not simply the absence of disease, but is such functioning of the body as promotes life and the welfare of the person; whereas sickness entails faulty action or malfunctioning of some part of the bodily organism. Right conduct is regarded as right because it accords with the norm of the realization of some aspect of value; and it does not need to be contrasted with wrong to be seen as good. Freedom is more primordial than its withdrawal or denial. The confinement of a man judged guilty of a crime—or of dissent in a fascist state—superimposes the derivative evil of lost liberty on the basic, positive good of the freedom the prisoner once knew. This primacy of good over evil disclosed in experience is effectively underlined by the privative view.

3. The doctrine that evil is the absence of good enabled Augustine and Thomas to set up a strong bulwark against Manichaean dualism and to preserve in Christian thought the sole sovereignty of God and the oneness of his creation. They have helped to chart a course that avoids the pitfalls of dualism in our time as well as theirs. Dualism always exerts a strong appeal for persons who regard evil with the seriousness it demands, but it offers no explanation for the manifest unity of reality within which it is possible for evil agencies to operate. Convincing evidence of this oneness is found in the interdependence of existence as we experience it. We find closely intermeshed human relationships, interaction within the physical order, and intimate connections between human life and its total environment. Such interrelated functioning would be impossible if two antagonistic powers or forces were constantly competing for control. We can provide fully for the devastating actuality of evil without positing a cosmic principle of evil and thus substituting a duoverse or multiverse for the universe we experience. The privative view offers positive stimulus in this direction.[28]

4. Aquinas' teaching concerning primary and secondary causes provides a way of maintaining the supreme rule of God while making room for genuine freedom in his creatures. The finite agent draws on power that is derived ultimately from God alone, but he may use it to perform acts supportive of or opposed to the divine will. This account of moral evil accords well with the data of human experience. Furthermore, since Thomas does not restrict secondary causation to the human realm, his theory anticipates by almost eight hundred years the hypothesis advanced by some physicists today— that a kind of freedom may extend to subhuman and even suborganic entities. Such indeterminacy may indeed be operative in some events that exert adverse effects on human life.[29] On the positive side, to assign to human beings the status of secondary causes attributes to them a creative capacity that enables them, in ways appropriate to their finite limitations, to share the creative work of God.

Along with these values, the privative view of evil exhibits a number of difficulties.

1. Whatever may be the ultimate status of evil, as encountered in human life it is not the absence of anything, but an experience that is agonizingly present. Selfishness is as actual as self-forgetful love, and a tornado in Kansas is as much a fact as a bountiful wheat harvest. The relentless pain caused by malignant tissue is no more fictitious than the enjoyment of perfect health.

Actions called dehumanizing, inhuman, and depersonalizing are indeed described with the help of negative prefixes. These serve to clarify their meaning by relating them to ethical norms that they violate. But the conduct designated is excruciatingly actual to those victimized by it, and it becomes no less so when it is said to be only lacking in goodness. As I write this, with the temperature outside at five degrees following a heavy snowstorm, I am reminded that those who freeze to death in blizzards are aware not so much of absence of warmth as of numbing pain signalling an active assault on all their life-supporting resources. Persons now starving in Bangladesh and Ethiopia experience immediately, not the absence of nourishing food, but gnawing pain that demands to be treated as fact.

Evils like these may have no essence of their own, but they hurt as

93

much as any substantial evil could. The torment and distress they occasion remain undiminished by redefinition. They come to consciousness as evil, and they must be dealt with as such.

2. Hence the basic theological question remains. If evil is regarded as privation of good, the factuality of the privation itself becomes the problem. To say that evil has no real being of its own, that it is at heart the spoiling of something essentially good, does not increase understanding of God's permission of its occurrence or of the havoc it wreaks. How account for this corruption of the good? In the simple and earthy language of Austin Farrer, "A good God created good sorts. The problem remains, why he should let them go so rotten."[30] Thus we still face the question of how to reconcile experienced evil with belief in the power, wisdom, and love of God. The privative view of evil does not address this question.

3. Further difficulties appear in Augustine's treatment of natural evil. Applying his privative view to suffering not attributable to human choices, he insists that since the world is the work of a good Creator it is good, hence natural evil is excluded. He is right in suggesting that forces like fire and cold "in their own places" serve important functions, and in emphasizing the bearing of human use and misuse on the effects of poisonous substances. However, his explanations do not fit much of the suffering occasioned by natural forces. In many instances persons who are also "in their own places" have no way to avoid being where typhoons and disastrous fires occur, and much distress results from harmful substances while humanity is in the process of discovering what use of them accords with God's design. Concealment of their usefulness or danger may be a lesson in humility, but it is a costly lesson for those who die before it is learned. Moreover, the implication that suffering connected with natural forces is just punishment for sin overlooks the plain fact that many victims are genuinely devoted to the service of God, while many of the injuries sustained have no discernible relation to either the misuse of otherwise wholesome things or the sinful wills of the sufferers.

Considerations like these lead to the conclusion that the privative view of evil, in spite of important elements of strength—particularly the light it sheds on the relationship of good and evil—is not a satisfactory answer to the theological problem of human suffering.[31]

5 Dualism of Good and Evil

On January 25, 1976, in Boston, in a fire that began before dawn while the family slept, the five-month-old grandson and five of the nine children of Robert and Pauline Senske, trapped in upstairs bedrooms and hallways, were burned to death, and Mrs. Senske broke both legs when she jumped to safety. Two days later Jeremiah V. Murphy, a newspaper columnist, published his reflections on the tragedy, communicating his shock and bewilderment in these words: "Why did all this happen to the Senske family? There is no intention here of being sacrilegious, but sometimes God's will is too terrible to be attributed to God." [1]

Let us suppose that a concerned reader telephones the columnist and asks him to what he would attribute the tragedy. Murphy apparently assumes that some nonhuman will or activity was involved, but he draws back from identifying it with God's will. The event must have been caused, he seems to imply, by some other power evil enough to be capable of so horrible an act. Thus he moves hesitatingly toward a dualistic interpretation. As a dualist, he would have several options. If he feels able to respond to the telephoned query with more than "I don't really know," he might reply that he was thinking of some power or principle of disorder that competes with God for control of the world, sometimes causing fires that upset the divine intention. Or he might suggest that there is a rebellious created spirit who bends every effort to thwart the good purposes of the Creator. Each of these responses might be modified by complex, overlapping alternatives. What are some of them?

The first option just mentioned is metaphysical dualism, which holds that reality consists ultimately of two fundamental, opposed, irreducible principles, substances, or forms of being. These may either conflict with or complement each other. Examples are found in the thinking and extended substances of Descartes, phenomenal and noumenal reality in Kant, God and the world, matter and spirit (or idea), and good and evil. Most religious dualism is also metaphysical, since it involves some theory regarding the nature of reality. However, it centers in belief in two contrary powers or gods, or groups of divine and demonic beings, thought to control the cosmos and human destiny. To them, human beings relate through worship, ethical action, and other ways, particularly action aimed at release from or victory over evil. Indeed, religious dualisms seem to be centrally not objective attempts to explain the world but responses to human anguish and the longing for salvation. Their concern for understanding is closely linked with the search for deliverance from sin and suffering.

It is not easy to gain a clear picture of the various kinds of religious dualism and their interrelations. They exhibit considerable overlapping, and dualistic features may appear in monistic, monotheistic, and polytheistic religions as well as in those that are essentially dualistic. However, some classification must be attempted if understanding is to be advanced.

In a definitive account of religious dualism, Ugo Bianchi of the University of Messina suggests two major distinctions: that between absolute (radical) and mitigated (relative) dualism and that between dialectical and eschatological dualism.[2] Inasmuch as both of the latter appear to be radical, I am adopting a slightly different classification, including them as subforms within absolute or thoroughgoing dualism. I am also including a third type that has recently found new expression—the view that both good and evil are original elements within one God. We shall therefore examine dualistic responses to the problem of evil under the following headings, combining brief exposition of typical examples with critical evaluation:

1. Ultimate, eternal, radical dualism
    a. Dialectical
    b. Eschatological

c. Twentieth-century
2. Relative, qualified dualism
3. Original dualism within one God

Ultimate Dualism

In ultimate or radical dualism two fundamental principles, or powers, are thought to exist from eternity. In dialectical dualism these are arrayed against each other in a continuing tension that produces repetitive or cyclical movement in history. In eschatological dualism the world is seen as a battleground between two forces struggling for supremacy; central attention is focused on a denouement at the end of a history linearly conceived, when the conflict will be finally resolved in the victory of the good and the destruction of evil.

Dialectical Dualism

In Western culture, Orphic mysticism in Greece in the sixth century B.C. offers a typical instance of dialectical dualism. According to Orphism all things in the sensible world come from the One, and seek to overcome their material diversification by return to the One. On the human level, the soul, essentially akin to the gods, is imprisoned or entombed in the body, and seeks through secret cultic beliefs and practices to find release and return to its true status.

In the thought of Plato (428–348/347 B.C.) the real world is a hierarchy of nonmaterial, eternal, unchanging Forms, or Ideas. These are mainly essences or patterns of objects in the visible world or universals like beauty and justice that find expression in particular instances of these qualities in human life. The highest Form is the Idea of the Good. Over against the Forms, which exist independently, is the transitory realm of appearances, the material objects experienced by the senses. These are but poor copies of the eternal Forms. The world of sense perception is not created, but is generated out of what Plato calls the receptacle, "the nurse of all becoming." The agent is the Demiurge, or God, the divine Artisan who organizes and orders a cosmos out of the chaotic spatio-temporal matrix of the receptacle. Evil arises because the Demiurge encounters obstacles as it tries to fashion the universe according to the eternal patterns. Necessity gets in the way—a recalcitrance or imperviousness to the ordering of mind. This results in the absence of order, which is evil.

The duality of the spiritual and material orders appears also in Plato's view of human life. The soul is tripartite, and it attains its goal of the good life when spirit and appetite are controlled by reason according to the eternal norms. Moral evil or vice is occasioned by ignorance or false knowledge: the passions lead the reason to accept apparent rather than real sources of happiness.

Indian religion also exhibits, though differently, both antitheses found in Plato: those between reality and appearance and those between the One and the many. In one of the ancient hymns of the Rig-Veda (10.90), Purusa, "the Immortal that is in heaven," is portrayed as opposed to the physical world. Other early Indian speculation conceived the *atman,* or "self," as identical with Brahman, the cosmos, and regarded this basic unity of ultimate reality and the human mind as opposed to its appearance in the *maya,* or "illusion," of the multifarious world of sense perception.

A more complex form of Indian dualism appears in the worship of the two main gods of Hinduism—Vishnu and Shiva. Here Brahman, the great All, remains as the absolute, ultimate reality, but is manifested in the triad or trinity of gods called the *trimurti* (the One or Whole with three forms). These are Brahma, the Creator; Vishnu, the Preserver; and Shiva, the Destroyer. Brahma, a kind of personification of the impersonal Brahman, remains in the background as a demiurge, and is seldom worshiped. This theology directs attention to the opposition in human existence between life and death, creation and dissolution.

Vishnu is regarded as the special manifestation of the protective, sustaining aspects of the One, including the preservation of moral order (*dharma*). Combining many lesser cult deities, he is approached mainly through his incarnations. These are believed to number a thousand or more, but ten are most commonly recognized, and of these Rama and Krishna are accorded chief status. Vishnu is thought to show himself, or aspects of himself, especially when he is needed in the struggle against evil.

Although Shiva lacks the many incarnations of Vishnu, in some respects he is a more complicated deity. In the Rig-Veda he is reproached, yet appealed to for help in disasters that he may have caused. In the Vedic period (*ca.* 1500–*ca.* 1200 B.C.) he entered the company of honorable gods who preside over various aspects of human life, being related especially to the erratic, dangerous, and fearsome aspects of nature. Though in the main he represents the destructive, negative elements in existence, he is also identified with reproductive or restorative power, since in Hinduism destruction entails restoration as a consequence. In this aspect his symbol is the *linga,* a phallic representation that often appears in Hindu sculpture portraying Shiva. He is also regarded as the great ascetic and as the god of the arts, particularly dancing. However, in this respect he dances the grim dance that destroys the world. On the whole, Shiva emerges less as an active agent of evil bent on overthrowing the good than as a manifestation of the disintegration that is always going on in the world we know. Dissolution as well as creativity is real, and Shiva's function is to enable human beings to face the precariousness of their lives, the ravages of time, the inescapable reality of death.

The opposition-in-complementarity noted in Hinduism appears also in the Yin and Yang principles in Taoism. These terms designate literally the dark and the sunny sides of a hill. In Taoist religious thought the ultimate, transcendent reality, Tao (the Way) is one, eternal, and indivisible. However, it is active in space-time in two opposed but correlative and interdependent principles or phases. According to Taoist mythology, light, ethereal Yang breath formed Heaven, and the heavier, cruder Yin breath produced the earth. The diversifications and interactions of the two resulted in "the Ten Thousand Beings"—the manifold phenomena of the empirical world. For instance, the warm breath of Yang accumulated to form fire, from the essence of which the sun was derived, while the solid breath of Yin resulted in water, the essence of which formed the moon. More broadly, Yin and Yang stand for the harmonious interactions of all pairs of opposites: respectively, lunar and solar, terrestrial and celestial, passive and active, dark and bright, feminine and masculine—the entire range of opposites in the universe.

Eschatological Dualism

In the dualisms sketched so far we have had to do mainly with opposing principles or characteristics of reality, involving not only good and evil but many other sets of contraries that often exist in interaction and complement each other as facets of one ultimate Whole. In eschatological dualism, the opposition is more concentrated in good and evil *per se,* with much greater stress on active struggle for supremacy, with the added belief in the final triumph of the good.

In Zoroastrianism and Parsiism, the Iranian religious movement founded by Zoroaster (*ca.* 628–*ca.* 551 B.C.), the world began as a battlefield. The whole process of creation was initiated by the attack of Ahriman, the power of evil, on Ormazd (Ahura Mazda), the power of good, both of whom have existed from eternity. Medieval Zoroastrianism exhibits this radical opposition in its most extreme form. It has little interest in metaphysical questions, but sees the world process in terms of a moral conflict that involves human beings as well as the two great superhuman antagonists. Ormazd is perfectly good, lofty, and omniscient, and he dwells in the light. Ahriman is wholly evil, debased, ignorant, and aggressive, and he lives in darkness. The combat that rages in the world as a whole occurs in human existence in the opposition between light and darkness, health and sickness, purity and pollution, truth and falsehood, life and death. In nature, too, contention is rife between gentle, life-giving rains and violent storms or droughts, and between edible grains and weeds. Thus our human moral struggle is fought in a cosmic arena. We are called on to ally ourselves with either the God of light or the Prince of darkness. Moreover, the contest is not between spirit and matter or soul and body; so the whole person, physical as well as spiritual, should participate. However, it will not continue forever. The ultimate victory of Ormazd is assured; the forces of evil will be vanquished, and righteousness will be securely enthroned. Therefore, though the dualism characterizes all existence from the beginning, it moves toward its end in the triumph of the power of goodness.

Gnosticism, a complex syncretistic religious movement that reached maximum strength in the second century A.D., often combined dualistic and monistic features, but the former illustrate well the appeal of dualism during the period of the early development of Christianity. Utilizing among other sources the Iranian notion of opposition between light and darkness and the Platonic dichotomy of

Idea and matter, the Gnostics saw reality as divided between the supreme power above, perfect and good, and the universe below, imperfect and evil. The human spirit is related to the transcendent divine realm, ruled by the high God, but it has fallen into the region of change and death created by an inferior and imperfect being, the demiurge, and ruled by the planetary spirits. The soul, now imprisoned in the body, cries out for release from its bondage to the physical world. This deliverance becomes possible through *gnosis,* a mystical enlightenment revealed to initiates through a heaven-sent redeemer who reproduces in his own life the great cosmic drama. Those who respond and follow the magical rites and practices prescribed are restored to their true home.

In passing it should be mentioned that this theosophical movement constituted a grave threat to the early church in its growing pains. Gnosticism severed Christianity from its historical foundations. In its teaching, the Creator-God portrayed in the Old Testament as the Maker of heaven and earth becomes only an inferior source of this evil physical world and is opposed to the righteous Redeemer-God of the New Testament gospel. It ordinarily incorporated Christ in its scheme as the bearer of saving truth from above, but it made him the enemy both of the historical order and of its creator. It was dangers like these that moved the young church to clarify and strengthen its position by determining its canon of Scriptures, defining its beliefs, and adopting an episcopal order.

Though Gnosticism declined in the latter part of the second century, its major features were embodied in Manichaeism, which arose in the third century in Persia as an outgrowth of the teachings of Mani (n. A.D.216). We have already noted how vigorously Augustine fought to overcome the influence of Manichaeism in the fourth and fifth centuries.

The Manichaeans felt the human situation to be radically evil, estranged, and unendurable. Human beings are enslaved by the body and the world of space and time. Entangled in evil, they yearn for deliverance. Conscious of their own alienation, they discover that God himself is an alien in the world. Since God is perfect goodness and truth, he cannot have willed human suffering. It must therefore be attributed to an evil power hostile to God. According to Mani's dramatic mythology, a primordial kingdom of darkness, disorder, and wickedness attacked in remote antiquity the equally primeval kingdom of light, order, peace, and goodness. In the attack the forces of evil succeeded in robbing a portion of the qualities of light and righteousness and cleverly mingling them with their opposites, so that human beings have difficulty in separating them and following the good. The dominion of light, rejecting any use of unjust violence, contrived a more subtle process of gradual purification to restore the separation of good and evil and establish it securely forever. This process could be advanced in the human realm through esoteric knowledge and quietistic ascetic practices, by which the elect could refine from the contaminated mixture of good and evil an unspotted perfection in their own lives, and so attain salvation. Human beings come to know that they are basically related not to the evil world but to the God of light, that they share the nature of God, that they have fallen from this relationship, and that by internal illumination of the *nous,* or intelligence, they can return to their original situation. Specialized gnosis reveals to initiates knowledge of the hidden truth about the whole of reality and within that context their own condition and destiny. The result is purification and deliverance.

Twentieth-Century Dualisms

The ancient oriental dualisms are very much alive today in Hinduism and Taoism. On the contrary, neither the dualistic theories of Orphic religion and the Platonists nor the eschatological dualisms just considered are live options for Westerners in the twentieth century. Among other features, their heavy reliance on mythological motifs excludes them from serious consideration by people immersed in a scientific and technological culture. However, dualism in more sophisticated forms continues to win support among thinkers who are deeply concerned over the problems of natural and moral evil. Some understanding of the older theories is essential for historical perspective, but it must be supplemented by acquaintance with typical twentieth-century hypotheses. Our purposes should be served by brief examination of the thought of the British philosopher C. E. M. Joad and the American theologian Edwin Lewis. The former combines aspects of both dialectical and eschatological dualism; he sees the world as the sphere of a perpetual conflict between two powerful antagonists, but he seems not to envisage the triumph of the good. Lewis clearly represents dualism of the eschatological type, since he does anticipate the subjection of the Adversary.

Joad testifies that his acceptance of dualism freed him from a longstanding commitment to atheism. Logically, he asserts, the extent of evil is not compatible with the creation of the world by a being who is both all-powerful and all-good. It is contradictory to ascribe to God the creation of evil; likewise, much evil cannot be attributed to the misuse of free will by human beings. We are therefore led to surrender belief in the omnipotence of God and acceptance of the existence of a principle of evil that exists independently of God and in spite of him.

Both good and evil are to be found in the world. If some ultimate principle is invoked to explain the one, an equivalent source must be called on to explain the other. If God exists, the devil must also exist, or else some principle of inertia that obstructs the divine activity. The notion of two gods respectively good and bad is revolting; the alternative is belief in a good God and a thwarting, hampering principle through which and in spite of which God must work. Joad concludes that sound religious belief is possible only on the basis of dualism.

> This consists in accepting good and evil as two equal and independent principles, the expression of two equally real and conceivably equally powerful antagonists, God who is good but limited, and God's adversary who is evil, between whom a perpetual battle is fought in the hearts of men for the governance of the world.[3]

Though a conception that assigns independent reality to evil has often been regarded by orthodox Christians as heretical, Joad contends that it is more harmonious with the data of human experience than any other hypothesis that refers the phenomena of the natural order to some supernatural principle.

The proposals of Edwin Lewis rather closely parallel those of Joad, but they are worked out in more systematic detail. He offers them quite undogmatically as "a speculative venture," but also in all seriousness as "an evangelical interpretation of the Christian faith in terms of conflict."[4] So impressed is Lewis by the glaring reality of the struggle between good and evil in the biblical revelation and in human experience that he rejects traditional absolutistic theism in favor of an unabashedly dualistic view. Finding it incredible that a good God could will many of the tragic aspects of life, he concludes that the perfectly good will of God is conditioned by an ultimate, uncreated adversary standing over against God in absolute otherness.

Strictly speaking, existence for Lewis consists of three primal existents: the Creator, the Adversary, and the residue. Opposed to the creative divine is the discreative demonic. That which makes their conflict possible is the uncreative residual constant, "the permanent possibility of empiric actualities." Creation inevitably involves strife with discreativity; it is "a song which is also a cry." The Adversary cannot initiate anything, but its obstructive activity always stands in the way of creation. The Creator must reckon not only with human freedom but with "a dark insensate, irrational power, the enemy of the good." Though this demonic power is more than a principle, it is not truly personal, since it lacks rational and moral qualities. The best way to conceive it is to imagine a completely bad man, degenerate, disorganized, decentralized— "discreative corruptibility become absolute."[5]

Since the Creator always confronts the frustrating activity of the Adversary, the cross is inherent in the creative process; it is also, however, the demonstration and promise of divine victory through tribulation. God is greater than the Adversary. He can outsuffer, outendure, and outplan him; for he can love even unto death and beyond, and this his opponent cannot do.

With this interpretation, Lewis believes we can understand the power of temptation and sin even in lives that seek to fulfill the divine will. With it we can also face the awful reality of cancerous tissue, pain-racked bodies, demented minds, and famine-stricken peoples, yet say convincingly that these are not what God wants, but that all of his resources are pitted against them.[6]

Evaluation

With various types of ultimate dualism now before us, what should be said by way of evaluation? Leaving aside the mythological concepts that led ancient dualisms to populate the world with all manner of strange and sinister beings, there are in basic dualistic theory several elements of genuine strength.

1. It takes evil with utter seriousness. There is in it nothing of the tendency, noted in some monistic views, to dismiss suffering as illusory; nor is there the tendency to regard belief in suffering as the result of a partial view, the correction of which by a wholistic interpretation discloses suffering to be a necessary part of a perfect whole, hence not really evil. Dualism accords to evil the full recognition that the facts of experience seem to demand. The many forms of evil make on human lives an impact so powerful and inescapable that it cannot be soundly denied or evaded.

2. This concern for the data of experience enables dualism to avoid the kind of *a priori* commitment to divine omnipotence that weakens traditional absolutistic approaches to the problem of evil. It is usually not guilty of assuming in advance of all investigation what God *must* be, regardless of the evidence. It is adventurous enough, for example, to be willing to consider alternatives to classical Christian theism if the harsh aspects of human existence raise questions difficult to answer within that framework.

3. Dualism offers a fairly simple solution of the theological problem of evil. Since it locates the source of suffering outside God, the difficulty of harmonizing God's perfect goodness with his unlimited power disappears. If the righteous God is the cause of only the good in human existence, he is relieved of all responsibility for evil. Human experiences like disease, pain, temptation to sin, and the disruptions occasioned by natural disasters raise no questions regarding the love of God if they are attributable to a competing agency with which God no less than men and women must reckon.

Over against these features of positive value must be placed four serious difficulties.

1. If the world is a battleground between two hostile powers, or even a mixture of good and evil energies, the problem arises as to how to account for its manifest unity. If the opposition is really cosmic, as absolute dualisms ordinarily assume, it is present in physical nature as well as the moral life of human beings. But the whole enterprise of scientific investigation of the natural order presupposes and provides overwhelming evidence for the regularity and uniformity that the sciences formulate in what are called natural

laws. Phenomena such as volcanic eruptions and earthquakes, sometimes cited as indications of disorder, actually illustrate order and interconnectedness. All large earthquakes and many small ones are caused principally by the fracturing of rocks near the surface of the earth in consequence of the gradual accumulation of strain during well-understood geological processes. Sudden fractures occur when the strain exceeds the strength of the rocks. Ruptures follow lines and surfaces of weakness called faults. Volcanic eruptions likewise involve relatively predictable phenomena and events. At temperatures between eight hundred and fifteen hundred degrees centigrade, accumulated pressure produces the ejection of magma (molten rock) and gases from fractures in the earth's crust. Hot springs and geysers are also manifestations of volcanic activity.

Such events are evil only when they occur in inhabited areas. They argue strongly for a universe rather than a duoverse or multiverse, and offer no support whatever for the objective existence of a demonic power that contends with God for mastery. Moreover, if two opposing forces did exist, they would need a third as the ground or basis of their operations—a kind of cosmic environment. Hindu monism provides for this in its notion of the All, or Brahman, but it still gives no account of the fact that the opposition does not destroy the oneness everywhere evident.

2. It is by no means clear that, as Edwin Lewis maintains, the concept of the demonic is "as indispensable as the concept of the divine." On the contrary, in our experience, good seems to have a positive, ultimate quality that its opposite does not have. Value stands in its own right, not depending on disvalue for its meaning; whereas evil is derivative, meaningless apart from its contrast with good. Full awareness of the evil of a flat automobile tire seems possible only when we know the "goodness" of a properly inflated tire. This does not in any sense deny or underestimate the distress and havoc that the flat tire can cause, but only recognizes that evil depends on good for its content to a degree greater than the dependence of good on evil. One does not have to accept Augustine's view of evil as privation to perceive the truth in these words of his: "As, then, there may be life without pain, while there cannot be pain without some kind of life, so there may be peace without war, but there cannot be war without some kind of peace." [7]

There is in the good or valuable a creative, productive, affirmative quality without which the discreative, obstructive activities would lose much of their meaning.

3. If both good and evil are ultimate, there seems to be no reason for regarding the former as any more authoritative or normative than the latter. Both principles would claim objective validity, and both would demand allegiance and commitment from human beings facing moral choices. Under the pressures exerted by both, the ethical *ought* would disappear, or else there would be two competing *oughts,* comparable to the urgent appeals of opposing candidates in a hard-fought political campaign. In such a situation there would be no basis for either praise or blame—or there would be an awareness of approval from one side and disapproval from the other. But in human moral experience as we know it, pangs of conscience are not felt when conduct thought to be evil is rejected; whereas guilt is experienced when the agent is false to his understanding of the good. "Well done, good and faithful servant" is an appropriate accolade when persons struggle courageously for the welfare of others. But such language would be obviously contradictory if addressed by an evil spirit to his followers; nor would it help if the appraisal were changed to "Poorly done, bad and faithless servant." The supporter of evil could be expected to give himself with consistency and ardor to his cause, that is, to be a *good* devotee of evil. Such reflections may serve to point up the incongruities involved in any effort to interpret human moral experience on dualistic premises.

4. Dualism as an explanation of moral evil projects outward tendencies and drives that are better understood if located in human nature itself. We sin when we trust ourselves rather than God, placing ourselves in the center instead of him, who alone is our true Center, and substituting our own limited ends for the inclusive purposes of God. We need not look outside our human situation, individual and social, to find abundant occasions for such self-centeredness. Its origin is not clarified by one iota if we trace it to some transhuman evil power. Pertinent in this connection is the suggestion of Thomas Aquinas that since human beings are empowered by God to act as "secondary causes," evil deeds spring, "not from God, but from their defective proximate causes."[8] Sin originates in the alienated human will; basically, "original" sin means that every person is his or her own Adam. Even if an objective source of the pressure toward sin is assumed, the capitulation is still the sinner's. Temptation and moral struggle are intense, but the responsibility for succumbing remains our own. The supposition of a ground of evil beyond ourselves tends to diminish our responsibility, while adding nothing whatever to our understanding.

Relative, Qualified Dualism

A form of dualism distinctly different from those examined thus far is that which posits an evil power derived from and subordinate to the good God who is the sole Ruler of the universe. Emerging in late Judaism, early Christianity, and Islam is the belief in Satan or the devil, an angel created by God who in jealousy and pride rebelled and continually tries to usurp God's place. He is therefore not ultimate or independently real, but an inferior malevolent spirit who does his utmost to undermine the divine will, especially by tempting human beings to sin and disrupting the harmonious relationship between God and his earthly children.

Satan as the antagonist of God does not appear in the Hebrew Bible. In fact, the name Satan is completely missing from Hebrew literature produced before the Exile in Babylon (586–538 B.C.). The term appears at only three points in postexilic writings: in the prologue to Job (chaps. 1–2), I Chronicles 21:1, and Zechariah 3:1-2. In these passages Satan is a member of the heavenly court, one of the Lord's vice-regents. As an accuser or public prosecutor, his function is to test human beings and determine the quality of their faith in God. It seems likely that the Hebrews first became acquainted with the idea of a powerful superhuman adversary to the God they worshiped during the Captivity, when they came under the influence of Iranian dualism. Slowly the idea took hold, gaining considerable acceptance in postbiblical Judaism. Thus the devil or Satan appears frequently in the Apocrypha and the Pseudepigrapha.[9] But so strongly rooted was the monotheism of Hebrew faith that the Jews never embraced any absolute dualism, but only the modified form that restricted the hostile agency to the role of a demonic power who, fallen from his original status as one of God's angelic creatures, is able to wreak havoc in human life but is doomed to final defeat. Also cast from heaven in punishment are other angels whom he enticed to join his revolt. As ruler of the fallen angels, he carries on with them his struggle against the divine kingdom and God's saving activity.[10]

In the New Testament, Satan and his demonic followers play an active role. The name Satan (the adversary) appears thirty-five times, while the word "devil" (*diabolos*) appears in thirty-seven passages. Many other terms are used to designate satanic activity: Beelzebul or Beelzebub ("the god of flies"), Belial, the evil one, the tempter, the prince of the power of the air, the ruler of this world, the old snake, the great dragon, and others. Satan figures prominently in the temptations of Jesus recorded in the Synoptic Gospels. He is often portrayed as the real antagonist of the Christ, the Messiah who has come to release human beings from Satan's power. Satan's activity and that of lesser demons are seen as the cause of much of the suffering in human life, especially that occasioned by sin, physical disease, and mental and emotional disorders, as evidenced in the accounts of the work of Jesus and the apostles in healing and casting out demons. Such descriptions of demonic activity are not offered as theoretical explanations of human anguish, but are integral to the good news of deliverance and life fulfillment through Christ. Some references to Satan are no doubt metaphorical. In the narratives of the temptations of Jesus, for example, since there is literally no place where the devil could have shown him all the kingdoms of the world, we probably have to do with objective projections of what must have been profoundly inner experiences of Jesus as he struggled with the competing appeals of alternative forms of ministry. But there can be little doubt that the New Testament writings reflect widespread belief among the earliest Christians in the personal activity of Satan and his supporters.

This belief continues in the writings of some of the early church fathers, who apply the name Satan to the fallen angel of Isaiah 14:12-15, called Lucifer in the King James translation, the Day Star in the Revised Standard Version, and the bright morning star in the New English Bible.[11] During this period the devil and his cohorts are portrayed as tempting and seeking constantly to destroy the faithful, and as causing various kinds of calamities, natural and accidental. Their activity results in earthquakes, famines, physical and mental disease, and wars. In the view of the atonement represented by Irenaeus, Origen, Athanasius, Gregory of Nyssa, and to some extent by Augustine, much was made of the death of Christ as a ransom paid to Satan. In one interpretation Christ was the bait in the mousetrap that deceived and caught the devil. Centrally, however, this conception held that the incarnate Logos, uniting God's immortal with man's mortal nature, delivered humanity from corruption and mortality. His death on the cross—which was a crowning act of obedience, a recapitulation in reverse of Adam's fall, and a ransom paid the devil for man's release—was followed by his resurrection, which demonstrated his supremacy over death and sin and destroyed their power.

The medieval belief in hierarchies of both good angels and demonic spirits is amply attested in the *Summa Theologica* of Thomas Aquinas and elsewhere. Through the centuries in literature and art, the power of evil has frequently been depicted as operating in the form of Satan and his minions. Examples include the "archangel ruin'd" in Milton's *Paradise Lost,* Mephistopheles in Goethe's *Faust,* and Lucifer in Byron's drama *Cain.*[12]

Since the Enlightenment, many theologians have sought to demythologize the devil, rejecting his personal existence and viewing him rather as a symbol of the ever-present power of evil in human life. Nevertheless, large numbers of conservative evangelical Christians continue to assert literal belief in Satan. Whether or not the atonement theories of the Swedish theologians Gustav Aulén and Gustaf Wingren mean by Satan a personal spirit of evil, they clearly find in him a true portrayal of the awesome menace of evil in human existence. Aulén, in his *Christus Victor,* presents the ransom view of Irenaeus as in essence the "classic" theory of the atonement.[13] Like Aulén, Wingren sees humanity as the battleground of a cosmic duel in which a life-and-death struggle is being fought between God and Satan. The gospel presupposes that the hearer is enslaved by "an active, evil power" that must be killed if deliverance is to occur. Caught in a grim conflict between God's goodness and the destroyer's evil, humanity cries out for release. This occurs through the cross and resurrection of Christ, who thereby wins a decisive victory over Satan. In routing the forces of evil, he conquers our enemies as well as his.[14]

Recent popular acceptance of exorcism suggests that belief in the personal existence of the devil or demons may be increasing in the West. The volume of suffering and senseless violence makes it easy to think of life as beset by malevolent forces beyond human control. Theologians as astute as Vladimir S. Solovyov (1853–1900) and C. S. Lewis have suggested that Satan's most cunning strategem— and the most certain proof of his existence!—is to convince human beings that he does not exist.

Evaluation of belief in the devil or demonic activity will in some respects inevitably overlap with our earlier assessment of strengths and weaknesses in absolute dualisms. Where this occurs, a brief reference to the previous discussion may suffice. Two elements of strength previously noted apply here. First, belief in Satan recognizes realistically the presence and power of evil in human experience, especially the reality of temptation and struggle in the moral life. Second, by ascribing evil to a rebellious power hostile to God, it decreases the force of questions regarding the goodness of God and makes somewhat easier the reconciliation of divine goodness and power. However, it still leaves unanswered the question as to why God allows so much leeway to an inferior being that he himself created. As an American Indian reportedly asked Samuel Eliot, "Why does not God kill the devil?" Along with these features of positive worth, there is also abiding truth in theories of God's redemptive activity that use Satanic imagery to stress the victory of God over evil—action that frees human beings from the power of sin and the fear of death.

On the negative side, the crudity of the traditional ransom conception of the atonement, involving the deception of Satan and the ascription to him of a claim on the human race that even God must respect, renders it quite untenable today. It implies estimates of the character and the sovereignty of God that are out of accord with both the gospel and Christian experience. Further, the conception of the devil as a fallen angel offers no explanation as to why he rebelled against God or was even tempted to rebel. The limitations of finite human existence, requiring for example the control of emotions and bodily appetites by intelligence and will in complex social situations, help to account for sin in men and women. But the theory of an extramundane fall of Satan offers no clue as to why a spiritual being enjoying a high degree of perfection, and sharing the bliss of an angelic order in fellowship with God, should in jealous pride attempt to usurp the divine authority.

This reference to pride recalls our earlier objection to absolute dualism on the ground that it projects outside human beings a responsibility that is actually theirs. A proud rebellion by Satan in heaven simply refers to an extrahuman source the trust in self instead of God that characterizes sin on the human level. But the reference is quite unnecessary, and it adds nothing to our understanding to be told that we put ourselves in the center because one who has already done so urges us to follow him. It is just as hard to explain the wrong preference in one case as in the other. The famous dictum of William of Ockham called Ockham's razor is applicable here: "Entities should not be multiplied above necessity." Long before Ockham, Augustine related the principle directly to the question of temptation and sin: "The devil . . . would not have ensnared man in the open and manifest sin of doing what God had forbidden, had man not already begun to live for himself. . . . This secret desire . . . already secretly existed in him, and the open sin was the consequence."[15] This insight apparently did not prevent Augustine from believing in the devil, but it should help others to avoid his mistake.

A fourth consideration applicable here is the unity of creation noted in connection with our evaluation of absolute dualisms. This is not so great a difficulty as it is when two eternal, ultimate powers are presupposed. However, in view of the vast capacity to obstruct the divine will that Satan is usually assumed to possess, it is still hard to understand why, in spite of his worst efforts, the world continues to function as a unitary system. There is no evidence that any of the uniform patterns discernible in nature are disturbed by his activity.

None of these objections exclude the activity in human existence of forces so detrimental to human welfare and so unmanageable by finite persons that they are fittingly designated demonic. In the thought of Arthur McGill and others, the demonic refers to those qualities and structures of transhuman powerfulness that are experienced as destructive to human life and values but cannot be ascribed to self-conscious human decisions. For our age, writes McGill:

The demonic does not—and cannot—wear the old forms (satyrs, dragons, malicious will of Satan), but rather appears as a formless and impersonal dynamism that seizes upon us unexpectedly in the cancer cell, in the auto accident, in the cascade of napalm bombs, or more subtly in the impersonality of bureaucratic systems on which we depend.[16]

Encounter with such dynamisms is part of the existential content of our creaturely humanness. But the considerations adduced render unwarranted any attribution to them of objective, superhuman, personal reality.

Dualism Within God

Quite different from the foregoing types of dualistic thought is a third variety that relates evil to an original dualism within God himself. This appears vividly in the "tragic myth," one of the five classic myths of evil illuminatingly explored by Paul Ricoeur. It contrasts sharply with the "Adamic myth"—Ricoeur's name for the view that grounds the fall of man in the supramundane fall of Satan. In the tragic myth, typified by both Babylonian cosmogonies and ancient Greek drama, evil is not an accident or rebellion that upsets a previously existing order. It is instead a category of being *per se,* "coextensive with the origin of things." It is primordially involved in the very coming-to-be of the gods, part of the primeval chaos that precedes the establishment of order. There is in the origin of things a tragic negativity as inescapable as it is real. Because of it the distinction between the divine and the demonic disappears. The tragic myth tends to concentrate both good and evil at the summit of the divine, as in Zeus, who originates both. The "wicked God" of tragedy is a logical moment in the dialectic of being. Thus evil in human existence roots in the tragedy in being itself, and the problem of evil as usually conceived is resolved at or before the beginning of the world. The clue to the overcoming of evil lies in the creative process itself, through which primordial chaos yields to order.[17]

An early modern expression of this view is found in the mystical theosophy of Jakob Boehme (1575–1624). According to Boehme's obscure doctrine, there is a play of contraries at the heart of creation. Out of the innermost being of God, which can be characterized only as the Nothing (*das Nichts*) or the No-ground (*der Ungrund*), development moves in great stages downward to nature. God reveals himself in nature in two wills: the fiery will to love and the dark will to wrath. This opposition lies at the core of all life, and it alone makes life possible. In this dualism, which is oriented especially toward the problem of evil, evil is seen as rooted in God. If we think of God as love alone, evil is that in him which is not God. But it is a divine constituent, having broken away from God to become "God against God." [18]

A much clearer statement of a dualism within God appears in two recent books by Frederick Sontag, *The God of Evil* and *God, Why Did You Do That?* Believing that people today are naturally more atheistic than religious, Sontag seeks a concept of God based on the factors that lead to his rejection. This means beginning with "the lowly and the negative," hence providing for violence and undeserved suffering in our thought of God. It requires encountering the full force of the activity of the devil, understood as the coalescence of the powers of destruction. God must be viewed as including within himself the forces of evil. He "combines and balances a number of forces, both good and malignant." [19]

The question in the book title, "God, why did you do that?" is equivalent to asking, "Why did you select these circumstances for creation?" Sontag believes that both the amount and types of the evil we experience have been freely and deliberately chosen by God. The only necessity attributable to him is that of selecting out of the infinite potentialities of nonbeing the kinds of being that comprise creation. The result is not the best possible world, but the one willed by God "as capable of being a vehicle for his purpose." He appears to have included in his elected universe more wastefulness, difficulty, violence, and suffering than were necessary. For example, hereditary insanity could have been "programmed out of the biological mechanism from the beginning," and God could have eliminated mental deficiency, but "evidently chose not to." His selection of so destructive a world as ours suggests an element of violence in his nature. [20]

In himself God is not evil; however, in the created world, his potential for evil is actualized. Since he controls evil within himself, he is good; but to the extent that he allows needless havoc in human existence, he is not good. In one aspect of his nature he is love, but he is also responsible for unleashing on us indiscriminately the wild powers of destruction. The various facets of God are not assimilated with one another, but "held together in a flexible federation." As a result, some meaning and value are realized. Ours is a self-sustaining universe in which life is possible and human beings are able to resist the complete subversion of life by evil. Hence atheism too faces problems.[21]

The tragic myth as represented in the thought of the ancient Greeks and Babylonians and the theosophy of Boehme is not a live option for most people today, whereas the conception of the good-and-evil God advanced by Sontag is without question a viable proposal. It therefore seems wise to restrict our evaluation to Sontag's views. Some aspects of the earlier critiques are equally pertinent here and need not be repeated. In particular, Sontag's theory faces much the same difficulties in accounting for the unity of creation and the normative quality of the good as those noted in absolute and relative dualisms. But there are strengths and weaknesses that are to a considerable degree peculiar to his position.

On the positive side, three features deserve attention.

1. Sontag's concern to work out his conception of God in the light of the reality and power of evil guarantees a healthy respect for the data of experience. Theistic thought often emphasizes the values that support faith, while dealing only tangentially with the difficulties. Sontag finds, and I believe rightly, that the two main grounds for the rise of atheism in our time are the power of evil and the human search for freedom from divine dominance. Hence he begins to rethink the meaning of God by examining the argument against his existence that centers in the pervasiveness of evil. He insists that God "must account for more than order, design, or purpose." This leads to a resolute willingness to be guided by the evidence, however the path may diverge from traditional directions. His inquiry is speculative in the best sense, but it proceeds in close contact with empirical data. The one question to be raised in this connection is whether it maintains wholeness by an adequate recognition of the elements of positive worth that are also a part of experience.

2. Every theist must face directly Sontag's query regarding the amount of evil allowed by a presumably all-powerful God. Through scientific research in medicine, weather forecasting, and the like, human beings have made considerable progress in alleviating suffering. Why then did not God do more to lighten the burden of physical and mental pain in his original design for the world? Why did God choose to actualize a world that is less than the best he might have created, and so much in need of alteration? Traditional theists may regard such questions as impudent, and many critics will reject Sontag's answer, but the queries are pertinent, and understanding should be advanced by a forthright attempt to deal with them.

3. Sontag sheds some needed light on the problem of sin by pointing out the obstacles confronted by human beings because of the very conditions of their existence. Thus the question of responsibility inevitably arises: How much of it is God's, and how much the sinner's? Since the conditions we face are grounded ultimately in our creation, Sontag understandably believes that a considerable share of responsibility is God's. The ambiguities of the situation in which we must act, the confusing multiplicity of standards, the insufficiency of human knowledge and power—for these God assumed responsibility in creating us as he did. Presumably he could have lightened the burden of sin by giving us more favorable conditions, but apparently he chose not to. The critic may find good reasons for asserting a large measure of human responsibility and for rejecting the supposition of an evil factor in God, but he has no right to evade the issue. By posing it Sontag has rendered an important service.

Along with such strengths as those mentioned, there are serious difficulties in Sontag's method and conclusions. In addition to the two already listed, the following should be stated.

1. Throughout his investigation, Sontag assumes the reality of a God of unlimited power and sovereignty, one who could have chosen not to conceal himself and not to permit evil. The situation we find is "exactly as he intended it." However, examination of the writings of atheists discloses that their objection to God because of evil ordinarily presupposes a traditional view of God as absolute sovereign. This is frequently linked with rejection of God because his existence would exclude human freedom. Sontag recognizes this when he points out that in most theological traditions God has been identified with necessity, foreknowledge, and a fixed future, and that this denial of freedom is a major source of unbelief. Since Sontag is so concerned to take account of atheistic arguments, it seems strange that he does not consider alternative conceptions that modify or repudiate traditional notions of omnipotence and omniscience, no less than that which abandons the unsullied goodness of God to make way for a divine will to evil.[22] His failure to do so makes him almost as vulnerable as traditional theism to atheistic objections.

2. Sontag repeatedly declares that God deliberately chose the world we know, with its horrors as well as its values, when better choices were open to him. Such evils as cancer, mental deficiency, insanity, and famine were selected for inclusion in creation by the same God who must deliver us. All the imperfections that we are slowly overcoming by scientific endeavor could have been eliminated at the beginning. "With only a little calculation" all the goods we experience could have been achieved with less suffering. The fact that God did not provide for a world that would have eliminated or greatly diminished pain shows that he did not wish to do so.[23] Unfortunately, for these sweeping allegations, Sontag offers no evidence whatever. One wonders whence he derived the inside information needed to justify such self-assurance. How does he know so much about the inner workings of the divine mind and will? A further ground for skepticism regarding these extreme statements is his failure to consider other alternatives to the arbitrary decisions he attributes to God. The seriousness of the problem would seem to make desirable, for example, examination of the possible effect of human and subhuman freedom and of alternative conceptions of divine power and knowledge. Some admission of the limitations of human wisdom would also be desirable. But Sontag puts all his eggs in the one basket of a free divine choice of avoidable evil.

3. The meaning of God for religious experience is seriously qualified, if not undermined, by his complicity in evil. Sontag holds that God in himself is good, since his infinite power enables him to control evil in his own nature, whereas his limited human creatures are unable to hold in check the forces that wreak such havoc. Such a deity may be feared, but it is difficult to see how he can be an object of faith, worship, and commitment, or with what assurance human beings might turn to him for salvation. Sontag seems to have given little attention to the evidence of concrete religious experience, yet that would seem to be essential to any sound effort to reconceive what or who God is. As things stand, he offers an account of ultimate reality, but the appropriateness of the term *God* for the good-and-evil he finds at the heart of things is highly dubious. This is not to suggest that we should tailor-make divinity to fit our religious needs, but only that some other term might more accurately describe the reality Sontag affirms. The proposal of a God who unites evil with good in his creative work is a mind-stretching hypothesis, but it does not advance us very far on the road to a solution of the problem of suffering.

This chapter opened with a reference to a disastrous fire. A newspaper columnist, hesitating to ascribe it to God's will, apparently attributed it to some other nonhuman power. We have explored several forms of the dualism implied in his comment. In them we have found elements of decided strength. On balance, however, serious difficulties in the dualistic proposals prevent them from offering a convincing answer to the reporter's question, "Why did all this happen to the Senske family?" For such an answer to this and similar questions we must look further.

6 Suffering as Judgment

"I prayed in the dark, eyes open, that God would stop this awful punishment." In these words Juan Rumpich Chay, thirty-seven, described his first response to the earthquake in Guatemala at 3:00 A.M., February 4, 1976, as he and his wife and children huddled together in their adobe hut in the village of Chimaltenango. More than twenty-two thousand people died; seventy-four thousand were reported injured; two hundred thousand homes were irreparably damaged; and one million persons were left homeless.[1]

Juan's agonizing prayer is a moving contemporary version of a very old interpretation of evil: suffering represents the judgment of God on human sin. At least initially, Juan does not question the justice of the divine punishment, but accepts it and cries out for deliverance. This understanding of suffering, which appears again and again in literature and in oral responses to personal affliction and mass disaster, will occupy us in this chapter.

Suffering and Sin in the Biblical Writings

The conception of suffering as a penalty for wrongdoing appears frequently in the Hebrew Bible. The intense pain of childbearing and the necessity for hard manual labor to produce food are seen as consequences of the disobedience of the woman and the man in Eden (Gen. 3:16-19).[2] The First Letter to Timothy assigns a subservient status to women on the ground that Eve was deceived and became a sinner before Adam (2:13-15). In Genesis 6–9 the Lord sends the

119

flood and destroys all life because human wickedness has frustrated his purpose in creation, exempting only the righteous family of Noah and the animals needed to replenish the earth. When Joseph's brothers journey to Egypt to buy grain, they interpret the famine in Canaan as punishment for their treatment of Joseph: "No doubt we deserve to be punished because of our brother. . . . That is why these sufferings have come upon us." Reuben declares: "Did I not tell you not to do the boy a wrong? But you would not listen, and his blood is on our heads, and we must pay" (Gen. 42:21-22). The possibility of natural causation of the famine does not occur to the brothers, and their sense of guilt rules out for them any problem of reconciling the distress with God's goodness and power. The narrator reports the worldwide extent of the famine (Gen. 41:54, 57), but he is silent regarding the possible sin of other sufferers. If we question whether Egypt's escape implies superior righteousness, we need to remember that the account attributes her bountiful food supply to Joseph's wise planning, and probably implies that the Egyptians who elevated him to leadership benefit vicariously from his enjoyment of the divine favor.

When we turn to the writings of the great prophets of the eighth to the sixth centuries B.C., we find a similar interpretation of national catastrophes, actual or believed impending, in the histories of Israel and Judah. "If disaster falls on a city," asks Amos, "has not the Lord been at work?" (3:6*b*), attributing the evil to the sins of the people, especially the wealthy and powerful. Israel can expect punishment all the greater because of her special covenant relationship with the Lord:

> For you only have I cared
> among all the nations of the world;
> therefore will I punish you
> for all your iniquities. (Amos 3:2)

The iniquities of the nation include injustice to the poor in lawcourts, exorbitant taxation of the poor, bribery, lust for profit, dishonesty in business, arrogance, self-righteousness, luxurious living, indifference to the needs of the lowly, and cruelty in war. Amos warns that these and other forms of wickedness will inevitably bring retribution in the form of drought, blight, mildew, destruction of foliage by locusts, famine, and pestilence, as well as war, devastation of the land by invasion, and exile. In listing the instruments of divine judgment Amos makes no distinction between destructive occurrences in nature and historical events involving human agency. God is the righteous ruler of both nature and history, and violation of his will justly provokes his indignation, with human suffering as the result.[3]

Isaiah interprets the downfall of Israel in 722/21 B.C. and the coming fall of Judah as the righteous judgment of God on the faithlessness and injustice of the people. The invasion of Israel by Assyria and the resultant capture of Samaria are retribution for the pride and arrogance of the people, the oppression of the poor and needy, and the rejection of the Lord and his law from which these iniquities spring. In consequence, Israel became an Assyrian province, and twenty-seven thousand of her citizens were deported and replaced by people from other parts of the empire. Isaiah warns of a similar doom ahead for Judah, with earthquake or pestilence to be expected as well as invasion. Judah's alliance with Egypt for protection against Sennacherib involves in Isaiah's eyes substituting a covenant with the Egyptians for the holy covenant with God. Her haughtiness, oppression of the weak, idol worship, and reliance on military might instead of trust in the Lord will call down the fury of God and the dissolution of the nation. Assyria is the rod of God's anger, but after she has accomplished the divine purpose respecting Judah, she, too, will feel the judgment of the Lord of history.[4] A fitting epitome of Isaiah's prophecy on God's condemnation of disloyalty and injustice is found in his song of the vineyard (5:1-7; cf. Matt. 21:33-46 par.). The passage pictures the loving intention of God for his people, Judah's proud rejection of the divine will, the destruction to which her unrighteousness leads, and the sadness and pathos with which the Lord abandons his venture.

When Jeremiah's prophetic ministry began about 609 B.C., control of Palestine had passed from Assyria to Egypt. Both powers fell before Babylonian might in the battle of Carchemish (609 B.C.). In 599, when Judah withheld the tribute demanded by Nebuchadnezzar of Babylon (605–562), he invaded the land and in 598 deported 3,023 of its inhabitants (Jer. 52:28). About 589 B.C., a pro-Egyptian faction counseling revolt against Babylonia gained the upper hand in Jerusalem, and tribute was again withheld. The Babylonian army once more invaded Palestine, and in 587 captured Jerusalem, destroyed the city, and deported 832 persons (Jer. 52:29). During these power struggles, Jeremiah opposed revolt and called for submission to Babylon, mainly on the ground that foreign occupation was Yahweh's punishment of his wicked people, who would only compound their sins by trying to escape his judgment. Though he was arrested, imprisoned, and narrowly escaped death, he persisted in proclaiming his unpopular message.

In his catalogue of the sins of the people, Jeremiah includes failure to practice justice, oppression of aliens, widows, and orphans, and indifference to the plight of the needy (Jer. 5:28, 29; 9:24). However, all such instances of injustice grow out of the basic sin of infidelity to Yahweh and rejection of his ordinances. They have forsaken the Lord and his covenant, preferring their own counsels and worship of other gods like the Egyptian queen of heaven and idols of wood and stone, even to the point of practicing child sacrifice.

> Two sins have my people committed:
>> they have forsaken me,
>> a spring of living water,
> and they have hewn out for themselves cisterns,
> cracked cisterns that can hold no water.[5]   (Jer. 2:13)

In spite of their iniquities, the people have refused to repent (6:15; 8:6, 7, 12). But unless they do, warns Jeremiah, the Babylonian hosts will invade Judah and its neighbors and "utterly destroy them," making them "a horror, a hissing, and an everlasting reproach. . . . This whole land shall become a ruin and a waste" (Jer. 25:9-11 RSV). In spite of their burnt offerings, the unrepentant worshipers will be consumed "by the sword, by famine, and by pestilence" (Jer. 14:12; 32:36; 38:2 RSV). Looking back later on the fall of Jerusalem, Jeremiah uses the same words to describe the desolation that had been wrought (Jer. 44:13).

Like Isaiah, Jeremiah recognizes the sinfulness of the nation used by Yahweh to discipline his people, and predicts its destruction. The land of the Chaldeans will also become a waste (Jer. 25:12). In fact, the God of Israel is the Lord of all history. He can be counted on to punish Babylon and Egypt for their iniquity just as he has chastised Judah and Assyria (Jer. 50:17-18; 44:13).

A good summary of Jeremiah's understanding of the causal connection between suffering and wrongdoing is found in his message to the Hebrews who fled to Egypt when Jerusalem fell, taking Jeremiah with them. He declares that the Lord could no longer tolerate their wicked deeds. Therefore,

> your land became a desolate waste, an object of horror and ridicule, with no inhabitants, as it still is. This calamity has come upon you because you burnt these sacrifices and sinned against the Lord and did not obey the Lord or conform to his laws, statutes, and teachings.
>
> (Jer. 44:22*b*-23; cf. 25:9; 27:6; 43:10)

Most expressions of the penal view of suffering in the Hebrew Bible have to do with nations or smaller groups rather than individuals. Nevertheless, the application of this explanation to individuals is by no means missing. The drama of Job is of course a classic example. The three so-called comforters no doubt exemplify a widely held view when they insist that Job would not have been so grievously afflicted had he not sinned against God, even though he will not admit his iniquity:

> What a train of disaster he has
> brought on himself!
> The root of the trouble lies in him.
> (Job 19:28; cf. 4:8; Lam. 3:38; Ecclus. 39:29)

Ironically, Job himself seems to accept the punitive conception in part when he denies his guilt, implying that had he been guilty, he should have suffered.[6]

Something of the same attitude appears in some of the psalms that register perplexity in the presence of evil. In Psalm 10, for example, the prosperity and boastfulness of the wicked who renounce God and take advantage of the poor prompts the writer to cry out,

> Why stand so far off, Lord,
> hiding thyself in time of need? (10:1)

Obviously his complaint implies the belief that the wicked should encounter hardship while the righteous should prosper. The same inference regarding the nation may be drawn from Psalm 44. The author describes the defeat inflicted on Israel by her enemies, attributing this and her scattering among the nations to the action of the Lord himself, then laments:

> All this has befallen us, but we do not forget thee
>   and have not betrayed thy covenant;
> we have not gone back on our purpose,
> nor have our feet strayed from thy path.
> Yet thou hast crushed us as the sea-serpent was crushed
> and covered us with the darkness of death.
>
> (Ps. 44:17-19)

However, in these psalms, as in many others, the writer goes on to pray with assurance for deliverance or to rejoice in the conviction that the Lord will overthrow the wicked and vindicate the righteous:

> Thou has heard the lament of the humble, O Lord,
> and art attentive to their heart's desire,
> bringing justice to the orphan and the downtrodden
> that fear may never drive men from their homes again.
>
> (Ps. 10:17-18; cf. Ps. 44:22-26)

In effect, the response of faith is that evildoing will be punished, righteousness will be requited in the future, and the mystery of the temporary inequity can be accepted in trust. Yet psalms like these reject the notion that suffering is always sent by God as a consequence of the wrongdoing of the sufferer.

This is likewise the negative conclusion supported by the drama of Job. Job steadfastly refuses to accept the charge that his sufferings are due to his sin. He is quite "ready to argue with God" (13:3), and adds more emphatically,

> If he would slay me, I should not hesitate;
> I should still argue my cause to his face.   (13:15)

However, the book offers no solution of the problem as to why Job or other righteous people must suffer. The purpose of God in sending or

124

allowing misfortune remains shrouded in mystery. The law of retribution is rejected as inapplicable in cases like that of Job. Instead, suffering as well as joy is to be accepted as coming from God, though its meaning is as mysterious to finite minds as the marvels of God's creation. The conception that all suffering is chastisement for sin is renounced in favor of trust in the hidden God. Job is confident that he will ultimately be justified:

> In my heart I know that my vindicator lives
> and that he will rise last to speak in court;
> and I shall discern my witness standing at my side
> and see my defending counsel, even God himself.
> (Job 19:25-26)

On the whole, the central teaching of the Psalms and Job may be summarized in three affirmations: (1) the law of God provides that sooner or later the wicked suffer for their wrongdoing, while the righteous live in the divine favor; (2) while freedom from distress always indicates righteousness, this principle cannot be logically converted to assert that all cases of suffering are punishment for known or hidden sin—even the righteous sometimes suffer; (3) though the anguish of the righteous often cannot be comprehended, it is to be accepted as falling within the providence of God, who will not desert his people, and whose good purposes will ultimately prevail.

> The strong arm of the wicked shall be broken,
> but the Lord upholds the righteous. (Ps. 37:17)

The New Testament writings affirm consistently that righteousness promotes well-being, while iniquity leads to unhappiness, distress, and suffering. The narrative of Jesus' forgiveness and healing of the paralytic in Capernaum (Mark 2:1-12) does not make a causal connection between the man's illness and his sin, but it makes clear that he was troubled by a sense of guilt as well as by paralysis, and therefore needed forgiveness as well as physical healing. The fact that forgiveness came first suggests that he suffered even more from his awareness of sin than from his physical sickness.

The teachings of Jesus make unmistakably clear his conviction that wrong attitudes and actions bring painful consequences.

Violence begets violence and destruction: ''All who take the sword die by the sword'' (Matt. 26:52). Fig trees that yield no fruit after being properly fertilized and cared for are to be dug up and removed (Luke 13:6-9). Grapes cannot be picked from briars, nor figs from thistles. ''A good tree always yields good fruit, and a poor tree bad fruit. . . . And when a tree does not yield good fruit it is cut down and burnt. That is why I say you will recognize them [false prophets] by their fruits'' (Matt. 7:16-20). It is those who do the will of God who enter the kingdom, whereas those who render only lip service are cast out (Matt. 7:21). Those who hear the words of Jesus and act on them build their houses on firm foundations that survive the worst storms, while those who fail to follow words with actions build houses that crash when winds blow and rains and floods come, because they are erected on sand (Matt. 7:24-27). A similar contrast appears in the separation of the sheep and the goats, a parable of the last judgment. Those who feed the hungry, give water to the thirsty and shelter to the stranger, clothe the naked, help the sick, and visit the prisoners receive God's blessing and enter the kingdom. Those who fail to demonstrate concern for the needy in such concrete ways are decisively rejected (Matt. 25:31-46).

Comparable verdicts are pronounced on the nation as a whole, and especially on its political and religious leaders. If they misuse the Lord's vineyard, they will lose it. If they are disloyal to their covenant with God, the kingdom will be taken away from them (Matt. 21:23-43; cf. Isa. 5:1-7). Stern judgment is pronounced on those who repudiate God's righteous purpose for his people—the hypocrites and blind guides who observe the outer forms of correct worship but neglect ''the weightier demands of the Law, justice, mercy, and good faith'' (Matt. 23:23). The capital city of such a nation can expect only ruin:

O Jerusalem, Jerusalem, the city that murders the prophets and stones the messengers sent to her! How often have I longed to gather your children, as a hen gathers her brood under her wings; but you would not let me. Look, look! there is your temple, forsaken by God. (Matt. 23:37)

The agricultural motif noted in Jesus' teachings emerges also in Paul. ''Remember,'' he writes, ''sparse sowing, sparse reaping; sow bountifully, and you will reap bountifully'' (II Cor. 9:6). Again he declares:

> Make no mistake about this: God is not to be fooled; a man reaps what
> he sows. If he sows seed in the field of his lower nature, he will reap
> from it a harvest of corruption, but if he sows in the field of the Spirit,
> the Spirit will bring him a harvest of eternal life. (Gal. 6:7-8; cf.
> Rom. 6:23)

The disastrous results of evildoing are dramatically set forth in the Apocalypse, where the author seeks to strengthen the faith of persecuted Christians by prophesying the destruction of Rome, the unscrupulous persecutor: "Fallen, fallen is Babylon the great! She has become a dwelling for demons, a haunt for every unclean spirit, for every vile and loathsome bird" (Rev. 18:2).[7]

However, what was noted in the teaching of Job and the Psalms is also true of the passages in the New Testament where the question of sin and punishment is specifically addressed. The judgment that sin produces suffering cannot be logically converted, interchanging subject and predicate, without qualifying the new subject. It can be soundly asserted that some suffering is caused by sin, but not that all suffering is so caused. The latter was of course the erroneous conclusion of Job's "friends" and many of their contemporaries, but it is clearly rejected by Jesus.

In one incident recorded in the Fourth Gospel, he and his disciples saw a man blind from birth. The disciples asked, "Who sinned, this man or his parents? Why was he born blind?" Jesus answered, "It is not that this man or his parents sinned; he was born blind that God's power might be displayed in curing him." He then gave the man his sight (John 9:1-7). Whether the positive part of the reply is to be taken literally as Jesus' own opinion, or whether it reflects the view of the author, who in the light of the later healing read back into the initial conversation his own interpretation of the total event, we cannot know. In any case, the narrative as we have it explicitly excludes any punitive explanation of the blindness.

Jesus takes a similar position in his comment on two other events involving suffering on a much wider scale. The occasion is reported by the Gospel of Luke:

At that very time there were some people present who told him about the Galileans whose blood Pilate had mixed with their sacrifices. He answered them: "Do you imagine that, because these Galileans suffered this fate, they must have been greater sinners than anyone else in Galilee? I tell you they were not; but unless you repent, you will all of you come to the same end. Or the eighteen people who were killed when the tower fell on them at Siloam—do you imagine they were more guilty than all the other people living in Jerusalem? I tell you they were not; but unless you repent, you will all of you come to the same end. (Luke 13:1-5)

Here Jesus considers two quite different events, one involving human violence, the other a natural disaster. In both cases he makes plain that the victims did not suffer because of their sins, since they were not more sinful than other people who escaped. He offers no explanation, but admonishes his hearers to repent lest they also perish. This juxtaposition of a call to repentance with repudiation of a punitive explanation seems incongruous, since a need to repent implies sinfulness. However, Jesus' admonition may be comparable to the prophetic warning to Israel and Judah that injustice and idolatry would bring destruction. He utilizes the discussion of sudden death to sensitize the consciences of his hearers. We need to remember that he is here not concerned with a theoretical discussion of the problem of evil. He is rather, as always, alert to an opportunity to urge men and women to enter a life-transforming relationship with God. The only parallel involved is that between the end of the victims in the illustrations and the destiny of those who flout the divine invitation. This redemptive concern of Jesus is quite consistent with his clear declaration that the fate of those killed by Pilate's men and those who died at Siloam was not the result of their guilt.

Suffering and Sin in Postbiblical Thought

In postbiblical Christian thought, both sophisticated and popular, the understanding of suffering as punishment appears repeatedly, from ancient times down to the present. In fact, it is probable that this conception and the view that evil is an instrument of God in building character—the position to be examined in chapter 7—are the two major theoretical responses to suffering that have emerged in traditional Christian theology. Here we shall examine some typical expressions of the explanation of suffering as punishment.

Augustine combines a penal view of evil with his notion of evil as privation of being, already examined in chapter 4. Though evil is basically lack of the good, this lack is brought about by sin, original or actual. Evil springs from the misuse by human beings of their God-given freedom. In his *Confessions,* Augustine asserts that free will is "the cause of our doing evil, and Thy righteous judgment of our suffering it. . . . What I did against my will I saw that I suffered rather than did, and that I judged not to be my fault, but my punishment." This dual conception of evil appears more explicitly in another treatise, where he writes:

> Evil is of two sorts, one which a man doth, the other which he suffers.
> What he doth, is sin; what he suffers, punishment. The Providence of
> God governing and controlling all things, man doth ill which he wills,
> so as to suffer ill which he wills not.[8]

God is not unrighteous in inflicting penal justice on those who have earned it, and all human beings have earned it.[9] Even natural evils are indirectly caused by human sin. Such things as "fire, frost, wild beasts, and so forth," which sometimes injure our frail bodies, do so because we are "under just punishment." Moreover, punishment continues eternally: "In the world to come the pain continues that it may torment, and the nature endures that it may be sensible of it, and neither ceases to exist, lest punishment also should cease."[10]

However, this is not the outlook for the whole human race. God's providential power mysteriously overrules human sin, brings an infinite good out of finite evil, and eventually makes the city of God a reality. All human beings deserve everlasting punishment, but God's sovereign grace elects some for eternal felicity, the perpetual sabbath in which they are no longer able to sin.[11]

On this issue the evidence in the writings of John Calvin is somewhat mixed. In his treatise *Forms of Prayer for the Church,* he agrees completely with Augustine. Citing the teachings of the Scriptures, he regards calamities like war and pestilence (see Jer. 24:10; 28:8; 29:17-18; 34:17) as chastisements of God called forth by sin. Stricken nations and individuals who are in prison or afflicted with poverty or disease experience these sufferings because of their sins. Therefore the devout worshiper prays: "Seeing that thou art a just Judge, thou afflictest not thy people when not offending. . . . Even now we see thy hand stretched forth for our punishment." But no matter how severe the disasters visited on us, "we confess that we are worthy of them, and have merited them by our crimes." [12] Similarly, in Calvin's systematic discussion of divine providence he insists that all particular events, whether good or evil in their effect on human life, proceed from God's "determinate counsel." Good crops are his "singular benediction," while penury, famine, and destruction of crops by hail or storm are the work of his "malediction and vengeance." "Not a drop of rain falls but at the express command of God." [13]

However, when Calvin applies his doctrine of providence "to render it useful to us" he omits a punitive interpretation of human ills. Though God does order all events according to his righteous will, he does not amuse himself by tossing people around "like tennis-balls." His counsels are directed by "the best of reasons." He designs to teach his people patience, to correct or subdue their corrupt desires, to lead them to practice self-denial, or to arouse them from indolence. On the other hand, he aims "to abase the proud, to disappoint the cunning of the wicked, and to confound their machinations." These aims correspond closely to Calvin's statement of the three uses of the moral law: to convict people of their failure to fulfill God's will and elicit their repentance; to restrain, through knowledge of its terrible sanctions and fear of its penalties, those who otherwise would lack concern for righteousness; and to provide guidance for the conduct of believers and prompt them to obedience. In these passages Calvin makes plain his conviction that sin brings punishment, hence suffering, but he does not advance a penal conception of all suffering. [14]

Indeed, in his discussion of providence, in upholding the divine sovereignty, he gives more weight to the hiddenness of God's purposes than to the demand that sin be justly punished. Referring to Jesus' refusal to ascribe to sin the plight of the man born blind (John 9:3), he declares:

Though our miseries ought always to remind us of our sins, that the punishment itself may urge us to repentance, yet we see that Christ ascribes more sovereignty to the secret purpose of the Father in afflicting men, than to require him to punish every individual according to his demerits.[15]

Here Calvin is loyal enough to Jesus' teaching in the New Testament text to allow that in the hidden counsels of God there is no necessary equivalence between sin and its painful consequences.

An important eighteenth-century work on the problem of evil is *De Origine Mali* (1702) by William King (1650–1729), Archbishop of Dublin.[16] King finds divine punishment operative in some natural disasters, but not in all. Maintaining that earthquakes, storms, deluges, and inundations are not arguments against the goodness and wisdom of God, he states that "they are sometimes sent by a just and gracious God for the punishment of mankind." However, he points out that they often depend on the orderly functioning of nature, and could be eliminated only with greater damage to the whole.

An outstanding example of the penal conception of suffering is the response to the Lisbon earthquake of 1755. The horror it aroused in the ordinary people of Europe in the mid-eighteenth century was due in considerable measure to their belief that any earthquake is the work of a wrathful God. This belief was shared and encouraged by large numbers of the clergy in Portugal and other lands, who saw in the awful event the chastisement by God of a sinful people. Gabriel Malagrida, a Jesuit in Lisbon, proclaimed to the citizens of the stricken city that the earthquake was caused not by "comets, stars, vapours and exhalations, and similar natural phenomena," but by their "abominable sins." In the wake of the disaster, therefore, the highest priority should be repentance, not the construction of "huts and new buildings." God wants to exercise his mercy, said Malagrida, but "be sure that wherever we are, He is watching us, scourge in hand." So effective was this appeal that Pombal, minister of King José I and dictator of Portugal at the time of the earthquake, was seriously hindered in his work of reconstruction by the tendency of many people to attend first to acts of penitence, prayers for the avoidance of further punishment, and preparation for a future life. Malagrida was banished from Lisbon for his refusal to cooperate.[17]

In England, John Wesley's widely circulated pamphlet, *Serious*

Thoughts Occasioned by the Late Earthquake at Lisbon (1755), interpreted the disaster as a clear sign of God's anger. To attribute it to natural causes, he declared, would rule God out of his world and leave human beings defenseless before the unfeeling power of the elements. Better to see in any earthquake the work of God, to whom we can pray for forgiveness, amendment of our lives, and salvation.

By royal proclamation, a general Fast Day was held in England on February 6, 1756. The principal collect recommended for use in this observance expresses well the theological significance of the Lisbon earthquake as it was widely construed in the eighteenth century:

> We, vile dust and miserable sinners, in a most awful sense of thy amazing power . . . beseech thee, O Lord, to awaken our consciences yet farther, that we may see and duly consider thy hand, which, in the most astonishing manner, has been lifted up so near us. Pardon those crying sins, which produced these tokens of thy heavy displeasure, and grant us all such a measure of thy grace, that we may no more disobey thy laws, abuse thy forbearance, or despise thy chastisements, lest a worse thing come upon us.[18]

The basic message of the English pastors on the Fast Day was, "Except ye repent, ye shall all likewise perish" (Luke 13:3).

Specifically, what were the sins that were so widely regarded as the occasion of the earthquake? Four main forms of iniquity are cited in the literature of the period: (1) the fabulous wealth of Lisbon, with the treasures of its palaces and churches, its vast stores of bullion, jewels, and merchandise in its wharves and business establishments, and its great commercial importance; (2) the severity of the Portuguese Inquisition, of which Lisbon was the major center; (3) superstition and the worship of images; and (4) a lax, indulgent, casuistical moral code.[19]

It should be mentioned that some theological interpretations muted the note of punishment and saw the earthquake more as a warning. António do Sacramento, preaching in a Franciscan church in 1757, said that the shocks were not simply a chastisement, but an act of love aimed to bring a sinful people back to God. The fact that the punishment was relatively light compared to the Flood in Noah's day indicated that God wanted primarily to change the hearts of his people and guard them from further wrongdoing and suffering. Pastor Élie Bertrand of the French church in Berne regarded the event as a signal to draw nearer to him who is holy, immutable, and loving, by faith, charity, humility, and penitence.[20]

The Archbishop of Canterbury, Thomas Herring (1693–1757), took a dim view of Wesley's fervent appeal. In a letter to his friend William Duncombe, he expressed what might be termed an Enlightenment theology:

> I think the rising and setting of the sun is a more durable argument for religion than all the extraordinary convulsions of nature put together. . . . I have no constitution for these frights and fervors; if I can but keep up to the regular practice of a Christian life, upon Christian reasons, I shall be in no pain for futurity.

The Bishop of Exeter decried the presumptuous pronouncements of "raving designing monks, Methodists, and ignorant enthusiasts." However, in a Fast Day sermon he said that since Londoners had not suffered as had Lisbon, the British should take the disaster as a warning to become better and more genuinely Christian people, without accusing others of special wickedness.[21]

Very different from the Lisbon earthquake in its causation was the American Civil War, brought about not by natural forces but by clashing human choices and inertia in a complex social situation. It wrought incalculable physical and mental suffering and resulted in a total of about 617,528 dead and more than a half million wounded. The economic cost for both sides was stupendous, with the impoverishment of the South particularly bitter. Some of the emotional and spiritual damage left by the conflict has not yet been repaired. The pain and hardship caused by the struggle have often been interpreted in terms of divine judgment. Samples of this view are found in both the unsophisticated theology of a young soldier and the sober, mature thought of Abraham Lincoln.

On June 12, 1864, my grandfather Edward Schilling, then aged twenty, wrote one of at least ninety letters addressed to his parents, brothers, and sister during his three years of service in the Union Army, Maryland Infantry. On one occasion he states that he would like to come home for a week of rest, which would prepare him to take part with more vigor in the siege of Richmond. Then he continues:

> But this cannot be. We must first end the war, then what a happy reunion there will be of parents and brothers and sisters. But ah, there will be many a sad and aching heart, a long-looked-for loved one that will never come. But in all this we must meekly bow to the will of God, thank him for blessing us, and say he is right in punishing us and making us suffer.

There is something forbidding about these last words, suggesting as they do that God sent the war in a spirit of retributive punishment. However, as I read and reread them I hear a young soldier in the field expressing a view closely akin to that voiced by Abraham Lincoln in his Second Inaugural Address on March 4, 1865. Lincoln quotes from Matthew 18:7: "Woe unto the world because of offenses! for it must needs be that offenses come; but woe to that man by whom the offense cometh." He then supposes that American slavery is one of those offenses that God in his providence now wills to remove, and that "He gives to both North and South this terrible war, as the woe to those by whom the offense came." This, he believes, would not involve any departure from the attributes that believers have always ascribed to the living God.

> Fondly do we hope—fervently do we pray—that this mighty scourge of war may speedily pass away. Yet, if it be God's will that it continue until all the wealth piled up by the bondsman's two hundred and fifty years of unrequited toil shall be sunk, and until every drop of blood drawn with the lash shall be paid by another drawn with the sword, . . . so still it must be said, "The judgments of the Lord are true and righteous altogether."

In a basic article written at the beginning of the twentieth century, T. B. Kilpatrick affirms that suffering in both nature and human life is due to human sin. In his view God does not intend that any of his sentient creatures should suffer; rather, human beings cause suffering by their disobedience to the divine will. Presenting what he regards as the position of Jesus and the apostle Paul, Kilpatrick emphasizes the intimate relation between the natural order and human life. Since the two are so closely correlated, evil on the human level produces pain in nature. "Nature stands so close to spirit that it thrills responsive to the breach that sin has wrought between the human spirit and the divine." Thus suffering of whatever kind is traceable basically to human obstruction to the purpose of God: ''There is suffering in nature; and there is suffering in man as part of nature. And all suffering, in nature or in little children, is the exposition and illustration of that which, in self-conscious and self-determining man, is sin.''[22]

An eloquent contemporary expression of the conflict between the acceptance of human agony as deserved punishment and the vehement rejection of this view is found in Archibald MacLeish's drama *J.B.* When J.B. insists that God, who has allowed such suffering in his family, is just, his wife Sarah retorts hysterically:

> God is just!
> If God is just our slaughtered children
> Stank with sin, were rotten with it!

Then with greater self-control she adds:

> Oh, my dear! my dear! my dear!
> Does God demand deception of us?—
> Purchase His innocence by ours?
> Must we be guilty for Him?—bear
> The burden of the world's malevolence
> For Him who made the world?

When J.B., unlike Job in the biblical drama, reiterates that God must know he is guilty, since he has been punished, Sarah continues:

> They are
> Dead and they were innocent: I will not
> Let you sacrifice their death
> To make injustice justice and God good.

Yet J.B. persists in defending the justice of God, and though deeply perplexed confesses his guilt:

> God is God or we are nothing. . . .
> We have no choice but to be guilty.
> God is unthinkable if we are innocent.

But a few moments later J.B. wavers; maybe God is thinkable if our suffering has not been sent by him in judgment on our sins. In his next words J. B. cries out in anguished prayer: *"Show me my guilt, O God!"* [23]

Suffering and Wrongdoing in Hinduism, Buddhism, and Greek Thought

If we turn from the Hebrew-Christian tradition to Hinduism, we find a degree of overlapping between the penal understanding of suffering and the Hindu doctrines of *karma* and *samsara,* though the latter are concerned only with the lives of individuals. Subject to the operation of universal moral law, the self is formed by its karma, the precise accumulations of its actions, good and bad, in a tight causal sequence. Samsara is the series of rebirths of the self into other existences, each of which depends on the quality of its preceding existences. Sarvepalli Radhakrishnan offers a clarifying summary of these intimately related teachings as set forth in the Upanishads:

> Until we negate the ego and get fixed in the Divine Ground we are bound to the endless procession of events called *samsara.* The principle which governs this world of becoming is called *karma.* There are moral and spiritual laws as well as physical laws. If we neglect the laws of health, we injure our health; if we neglect the laws of morality, we wreck our higher life. . . . The law of *karma* is not external to the individual. The judge is not without but within. The law by which virtue brings its triumph and ill-doing its retribution is the unfolding of the law of our being.[24]

Obviously there are similarities here to the Pauline principle that we reap as we sow, though in Paul there is no rebirth into other forms of existence, and in karma/samsara the individual works out his own salvation (or fails to) with no help from divine grace.

In Hindu teaching, suffering results directly from the working out of karma. Each self reaps the fruits of its own thoughts and acts in either its present or its future existences, and these fruits depend in part on its previous actions. Suffering becomes a problem only when we forget the ultimate oneness of reality and ascribe to the opposition between pleasure and pain a reality that it does not have. We need to recognize that the *atman,* the seemingly differentiated self, is nothing independent or separate, but a manifestation of *Brahman:* "That is the true. That is the self. That art thou." When we realize

136

this, we can rise above the vicissitudes of life. Seen in relation to the whole, suffering is found to be not final truth but, like physical objects, transient and illusory. It may manifest Brahman, but it is not Brahman, who alone is ultimately real.[25]

In Buddhism, also, karma and samsara combine to produce suffering. Behind each effect is a long chain of causation that links events in one's present and previous existences. The operation of cause and effect is precise and unavoidable. Once an evil deed has been committed, nothing can enable the doer to escape from its results.

> Nowhere
> can there be found on this wide
> earth a corner
> Where karma does not catch up with
> the culprit. . . .
> Whatever deeds a man may do, be they
> delightful, be they bad,
> They make a heritage for him; deeds
> do not vanish without trace. . . .
> The evil-doer by his own deeds
> Is led to a life full of suffering.[26]

Also functioning in suffering according to Buddhist thought is *dukkha,* impermanence or change. Though a person may be happy, he knows that his joy will not endure forever. This awareness brings sorrow. Realism requires that we recognize the facts of life as they are, and dukkha is a given fact; indeed it ranks as the First Truth.[27]

It is clear that in Hinduism and Buddhism, suffering is not punishment in the sense in which a fine or a prison sentence meted out by a judge is punishment for a crime. However, in principle, the explanation they offer of experienced evil is of the same kind as that found in Western theories that perceive suffering as resulting from sin. It should also be noted that interpretations within the Judaeo-Christian tradition often regard the connection between wrongdoing and its consequences as internally as do the Eastern teachings. In both traditions, moreover, other considerations contribute to the total understanding of evil; e.g., transcending illusion by relation to the whole of reality, control of desire, the value of suffering in the growth of character, and the like.

Some of the ancient Greeks also express views of suffering comparable to those of the Hebrew prophets. Solon (*ca. 630–ca. 560* B.C.) advocates an internal or immanent conception of the character of justice and punishment in society. Hesiod, one of the earliest Greek epic poets (eighth century B.C.), regards both natural and moral evil as retribution for human wrong. Because Prometheus stole fire from heaven, "Zeus planned sorrow and mischief against men." He created Pandora, who opened the jar containing all human ills, thereby scattering abroad hard toil, sicknesses, famine, strife, and other miseries. Stated nonmythologically, this means that "neither famine nor disaster ever haunt men who do true justice," but "for them who practise violence and cruel deeds far-seeing Zeus . . . ordains a punishment."[28]

Evaluation

It is clear that the penal interpretation of suffering, in various forms, has been widely and persistently held through the centuries. How true is it? Is there wheat as well as chaff in this harvest of several millennia of religious thought? If so, how can the two be separated? Four observations seem especially pertinent.

1. It is important to distinguish between suffering wrought by natural calamities and that in which wrong human choices play a substantial part. There is no warrant whatever for regarding natural evil as punishment for or consequential to moral evil. At least three considerations support this conclusion.

a. It is impossible to discover any connection between many life-destroying events in nature and immoral attitudes and actions of human beings. In the Lucan narrative the collapse of the tower of Siloam was not occasioned by the sinfulness of the eighteen persons who died; it was probably due to slow deterioration, weakened foundations, high winds, or other natural causes. Similarly nonmoral origins are evident in seismic disturbances, hurricanes, and volcanic eruptions.

John Wesley's theological argument that natural causation of earthquakes would leave us at the mercy of uncaring elements is irrelevant in the face of empirically validated knowledge of the geological processes that produce earth tremors. Though some earthquakes have been produced by human disturbance of subsurface conditions,[29] most are caused by geological processes that are unaffected by human choices. The location of San Francisco on the San Andreas Fault provides an explanation of the disastrous quake of 1906 on which the moral character of its citizens sheds no light whatever. Famine and starvation are sometimes caused partly by faulty agricultural practices, but many such tragedies are traceable chiefly to prolonged absence of rainfall, plant diseases, and attacks by insects—circumstances independent of the righteousness or sinfulness of the people affected. The damage wrought in much of the world by the epidemic of Spanish influenza in 1918 was doubtless increased by the conditions obtaining in World War I, but the existence of the myxovirus that caused the infection was not attributable to the evil choices of human beings.

b. There is little discernible correlation between the suffering experienced by human beings through events in nature and the ethical quality of their lives. It is true that some people undermine their health by loose living, but serious accidents happen to all kinds of persons, and the distribution of pain does not seem to be proportional to merit. The eighteen crushed by the Tower of Siloam were not sinners more than other citizens of Jerusalem, and it can be assumed that those who escaped were not more righteous. Thomas Alcock, preaching after the Lisbon earthquake on Luke 13:2-5, asked, "If Popish superstition and the cruelty of the Inquisition made Lisbon fall, how came Rome to stand?"[30] He was typical of many British preachers who even in denouncing the wickedness of Lisbon maintained that the sins of their own nation were still more shocking.

As a youth, I worked one summer in a mountaintop peach orchard in West Virginia. Also in the labor force were a boy and his father respected by all. One afternoon during a violent storm the boy was killed by lightning, while others of less sturdy character were unscathed. Two years later a good friend who was a skilled athlete died suddenly of pneumonia at the age of nineteen. A mutual friend observed, "It might have been expected. After all, he didn't believe in God." But I remembered that one of the many deaths in my home town during the flu epidemic of 1918 was that of a church-school classmate who did believe in God. Even as the sun shines and rain falls on just and unjust alike, so train wrecks and plane crashes do not discriminate according to moral fitness. Among my acquaintances who have died in air accidents were a bishop and a theologian. I do not imply that their professional status guaranteed moral superiority, but both were in fact persons of integrity and concern for their fellows. Amid all the dangers to which human beings are exposed, the just and the unjust seem to suffer and escape in about the same proportion.

c. Closely related to the indiscriminate nature of supposed punishment is the question raised by the penal theory regarding the character of God. Both New Testament teaching and sensitive religious experience and thought argue against a God who in wrath uses events in nature to scourge his wayward children. Voltaire, in his *Poème sur le désastre de Lisbonne,* finds it impossible to reconcile the 100,000 victims with the providence of a benevolent God: Are the corpses those of sinners justly punished for their crimes? Did ruined Lisbon have more vices than Paris or London, which remain unscathed? Could not an omnipotent and omniscient God attain his purposes in some other way? If earthquakes are necessary, why could they not occur in desert regions? "Je respecte mon Dieu," writes Voltaire, "mais j'aime l'univers." [31] Similar questions may be raised regarding Wesley's view that to ascribe earth tremors to natural causes would leave us at the mercy of wild and indifferent forces. Perceptive minds might well wonder whether our plight would be better if it were in the hands of a God who in vindictive anger sent punishment that engulfed innocent and guilty alike.

2. In large measure, experience confirms the judgment of the Hebrew prophets that injustice produces adversity, and that of the New Testament and the Upanishads that we reap as we sow. This does not mean that a divine monarch externally decrees punishment for those who transgress his code but that God has built into his creation a moral structure within which evil is ultimately self-defeating. Just as there are physical and biological laws that we dare not ignore, so there are in the very being of individuals and societies norms of value that we disregard at our peril. There seems to be a pattern or framework in reality that determines the conditions on which human well-being is possible. Individuals, groups, and programs that flout it invite trouble, and sooner or later they compass their own downfall.

This tendency of evil to overreach itself may be properly regarded by the theist as a form of the judgment of God. It appears in the confirmation of the prophetic message by the actual course of events in the ancient Middle East; in the decline and fall of Rome; in the agony and the aftermath of the American Civil War; in the collapse of a once mighty but morally bankrupt Nazi Germany, after only twelve years of Hitler's promised thousand-year *Reich;* in the disintegration of Western colonial imperialism; in the debacle resulting from American intervention in the Vietnamese war; and in its bitter harvest of national division, alienation of youth, runaway inflation, economic recession, and decline in moral sensitivity.

In spite of the strong objection lodged above to the interpretation of natural evils as punishment for moral evil, even some evils that are primarily natural in causation may nevertheless manifest divine judgment. A good example is Jeremiah's linkage of famine and pestilence with war as consequences of sin (Jer. 14:12; 32:36; 38:2; 44:13). We know enough about the national arrogance, the power struggles, the militarism, and the pressure for markets, raw materials, and profits that cause international conflicts to recognize that war is hell in the deepest sense. It is the outcome of our substitution of selfish idolatries and competing partial interests for the universal values of the God of all humanity. Its woes are thus the judgment of God that men and women bring on themselves. But hunger and disease are its inevitable concomitants, as press dispatches and telecasts from Bangladesh, the villages of Vietnam, and strife-ridden Beirut have made gruesomely plain. These, too, caused as they are by human inhumanity, become part of the judgment.

The same may be said of the by-products of some inventions originating in war, such as poison gases and nuclear weapons. Quantities of gases manufactured in the United States and later banned have been buried deep in the Atlantic Ocean, but the containers will not last forever, and eventually pollution of the ocean will result. Radioactive fallout from nuclear explosions and the threat of suicidal atomic warfare are not the only perils of nuclear energy. Even the production of nuclear power for peaceful uses generates wastes that threaten to contaminate the environment for untold centuries. We can imagine a victim a thousand years hence asking,

"Why did this happen to me?" His suffering could be seen in part as a consequence of Einstein's famous letter to President Franklin D. Roosevelt in 1939 urging "watchfulness and, if necessary, quick action"—a recommendation that led to the Manhattan Project in atomic-bomb research and later to the "irreversible decision."

3. Though in broad terms we may affirm that individuals and societies reap as they sow, the principle is subject to serious qualifications. Experience exhibits no neat one-to-one correlation between righteousness and well-being, wrongdoing and painful consequences. Indeed, as Immanual Kant points out, though we assume that virtue ought to produce happiness, experience shows that there is no necessary connection between the two. This fact (and the consequent need for unlimited time for pursuit of the supreme good in its fullness) leads Kant to postulate immortality as a demand of the moral reason.[32]

Any easy presumption that the moral harvest always corresponds with the seed sown is undermined by abundant exceptions. These seem to be due chiefly to the fact that other causative factors besides right and wrong attitudes and actions are at work: the effects of the decisions of others, our own past decisions, external factors that circumscribe our options, or historical circumstances. "In my empty existence," writes the Preacher, "I have seen it all, from a righteous man perishing in his righteousness to a wicked man growing old in his wickedness" (Eccles. 7:15). Even those whose existence is not empty but full would have to concur in this observation.

Though we can agree with Lincoln in regarding the agonies of the Civil War as the judgment of God on both North and South, we must recognize that large numbers of ordinary people who contributed little or nothing to the onset of the war—including many of the freed slaves themselves—suffered more than many who bore chief responsibility. This is true in every war—from the German boys needlessly sacrificed to Hitler's megolomania at Stalingrad to the helpless Vietnamese peasants massacred at My Lai or robbed of their source of food by bombing of their rice paddies. In automobile crashes, innocent pedestrians or helpless passengers often suffer more than drivers whose carelessness, excessive speed, or intoxication caused the accidents. In MacLeish's *J.B.,* when Sarah receives the shattering news that her children, Mary and Jonathan, have been killed in a car accident, she cries,

> Why did He do it to them?
> What had they done to Him—those children . . .
> What had they done to Him . . .
>   and we—
> What had we done? . . .
>   What had *we* done?[33]

Leaving aside Sarah's assumption that God did it, highlighted here is the inequitable distribution of suffering and the impossibility of ascribing it uncritically to the previous deeds of those who suffer. If further evidence for the falsity of this explanation is desired, it may be found in the passion and crucifixion of Jesus. No event in history provides a more decisive rebuttal of the penal view.

Clearly the principle that we reap as we sow is constantly modified by another—that our lives are interlocked with others and affected for good or ill by their choices and actions. Hence the innocent suffer with the guilty, and sometimes more so, even as we all benefit from the positive contributions of others. The consequences of human acts are not strictly proportionate to the merits or demerits of the persons most closely involved.

4. With the important qualifications noted, we may still affirm in general that sin produces evil results. But this statement may not soundly be converted—as is frequently done both in popular thought and supposedly sophisticated theology—into the assertion that all suffering is the consequence of sin. In logic a proposition is converted when its subject and predicate are transposed so that each stands in the place previously occupied by the other. Thus a negative statement like "No birds growl" can be converted into "No growling creatures are birds." But when this occurs, no term must be distributed—used in its fullest extent—in the new proposition that was undistributed in the original. In the statement "All whales are mammals," the subject as a universal term is employed in its fullest extent, or distributed, whereas the predicate term *mammals* is undistributed, used in a limited extent: the class of mammals includes other creatures besides whales. The proposition is equivalent to saying "All whales are some mammals"; it does not

143

assert anything of the whole class of mammals. Thus it would be fallacious to convert the statement into one asserting "All mammals are whales," though it would be sound to declare that some mammals are whales.

Precisely this kind of illogical conversion occurs when the statement "All sin produces suffering" is converted to assert "All suffering is produced by sin." It overlooks the plain fact that some suffering may spring from other causes. This erroneous transposition of subject and predicate can easily occur in the heat of argument or when critical faculties are dulled by the impact of pain or tragedy. Thus Job's "comforters" can ascribe his sufferings to his unrecognized guilt, Juan Chay can assume that the Guatemalan earthquake is divine punishment, and even an Augustine can argue that our suffering is God's just chastisement which we have earned by our disobedience.

This fallacy seems to be operative in Richard L. Rubenstein's interpretation of the murder of six million Jews by the Nazis during World War II. Traditional Jewish theology, he maintains, interprets historical catastrophes as instruments of God in the punishment or discipline of his chosen but sinful people. But to be consistent in this view it is necessary to regard the holocaust, "the most demonic, antihuman explosion in all history," as "a meaningful expression of God's purposes."[34] Unwilling to do this, Rubenstein decisively rejects historic Jewish theism.

It is true, as we have seen, that the great Hebrew prophets did declare that faithlessness and injustice would bring disaster, and some disasters they interpreted as divine judgment. But it is open to serious question whether they inferred from these convictions that all national anguish must be seen as divine punishment. As was noted above, the Psalms and Job make clear provision for suffering that is unjustly undergone, which God does not send but in which his strengthening presence may be experienced.

In sharp contrast to Rubenstein's response to the holocaust is that of Emil L. Fackenheim. He, too, refuses to regard Auschwitz as punishment of his people, but he does not therefore reject the God of Israel. Rather he repudiates a false doctrine concerning the way in which God works. To him the penal view is irreconcilable with the deaths in the Nazi holocaust of more than a million innocent children, whose only crime was that their great-grandparents kept their covenant faith and raised their children as Jews. It also overlooks that "it was not our Western, agnostic, faithless, and rich but rather the poorest, most pious, and most faithful Jewish communities which were most grievously stricken."[35] It is religiously absurd and even sacrilegious to charge God with willing such suffering, but the rejection of this slanderous doctrine does not carry with it denial of the God of history.

5. A special problem arises in Augustine's view of evil as punishment, a question rooted in his doctrine of original sin. Basically, according to him, human beings are sinful because they have inherited the sin of Adam. As his descendants, they share the corruption that his disobedience introduced into the human race. Therefore, all deserve damnation and the lesser evils it entails. However, through divine grace the elect are saved from this inheritance and given eternal blessedness. Thus the inequitable distribution of suffering and the lack of correlation between sin and pain noted above become interminable features of the universe, and an ultimate dichotomy is established. God's action in deriving good from evil benefits only a small minority, while the vast majority are consigned to everlasting torment. In addition to the questions these provisions raise regarding the divine goodness, they intensify rather than help solve the problem of evil, and thus assure the permanence of the utmost evil—hell. For, as John Hick observes, "a combination of sin and suffering that is endless is, by definition, an evil that is never turned to good but remains forever a blot upon God's creation."[36]

These comments provide a fitting summary of the conclusions reached in this chapter. Some suffering may be soundly regarded as the judgment of a righteous God, but to extend this verdict to the totality of human agony is to ignore the witness of religious experience as a whole and to adopt an indefensible understanding of God.

7   The World as Vale of Soul-making

On the path leading from the parking area to the Visitor Center in Acadia National Park the tourist's attention is attracted to a rustic placard with this message:

> Mt. Desert Island is a rock fortress surrounded by its outpost islets at the edge of a hostile sea. Allied with other natural forces of land destruction the ocean forever seeks to level these heights down to a plain. This endless struggle has . . . resulted in all the beauty that surrounds you. For nature it is simply the course of things. To man it means not merely physical recreation, but an uplifting of the human spirit and increased understanding of all life—including his own.

In these words someone in the National Park Service interprets even the destructive forces of nature as contributing to the enrichment of human life.

One of the letters of John Keats, written to his sister and brother in April, 1819, applies this interpretation in general to the hardships, anxieties, troubles, and annoyances to which human life is subject. The world is not a "vale of tears" from which God eventually releases us and takes us to heaven. It is rather a "vale of Soul-making" in which human beings acquire personal identity—genuine individuality. Our pains and difficulties are necessary to enable us to develop the differences and peculiarities that make up truly individual existence, and to make possible the attainment of real happiness.[1] Keats's letter is a classic formulation of the teleological type of theodicy. According to this view, life, in the purpose of God, is a school of character formation, a training ground for the growth of moral personality. The sufferings encountered are valuable instruments for the fashioning of mature men and women. The conditions that give rise to adversity do not spring from a hostile or indifferent universe; they are provided instead by a loving God who aims to create persons fitted for fellowship with one another and with him.

Suffering as Instrumental to Personal Growth

Biblical and Irenaean Interpretations

Recurrent in the biblical writings are two interrerlated themes: (1) our sufferings serve sometimes to test our faith; (2) our trials are disciplines designed to purify character. The former appears in the narrative of the Lord's command to Abraham to sacrifice his son Isaac (Gen. 22:1-19) and in the prologue to the book of Job (1:6-12). The two motifs are united in the words of the psalmist:

> For thou, O God, hast put us to the proof
> and refined us like silver.   (Ps. 66:10)

But believers are assured that when they are called on to endure hardship, they will be strengthened by the divine presence:

> Walk through fire and you will not be scorched,
> through flames and they will not burn you. . . .
> Have no fear; for I am with you.   (Isa. 43:2c-5)

Writing no doubt to people who were themselves facing suffering, the author of the Letter to Hebrews reminds them of the passage in Proverbs (3:11) that declares,

> for the Lord disciplines those whom he loves;
> he lays the rod on every son whom he acknowledges.

He emphasizes, however, that God is treating them as sons. He disciplines us "for our true welfare," so that we may "attain life"

147

and "share his holiness" (Heb. 12:5-11). The Letter of James opens with a similar message: "My brothers, whenever you have to face trials of many kinds, count yourselves supremely happy, in the knowledge that such testing of your faith breeds fortitude, and if you give fortitude full play you will go on to complete a balanced character that will fall short in nothing" (1:2-5). A little later he adds that the person who remains steadfast in trials "will receive for his prize the gift of life" (1:12).

In the letters of Paul, the expectation of fullness of life attained partly through suffering is specifically related to the suffering and victory of Jesus Christ. God makes us sons and heirs and fellow heirs of Christ—"if we share his sufferings now in order to share his splendour hereafter" (Rom. 8:14-17). Our troubles are relatively light and short-lived, and they lead to an eternal glory that far outweighs them (II Cor. 4:17). However, the fulfillment comes not only in eternity; indeed, in everything the Spirit "co-operates for good with those who love God" (Rom. 8:28-29). Followers of Christ are therefore admonished ever to be glad in the midst of trials: "Let us even exult in our present sufferings, because we know that suffering trains us to endure, and endurance brings proof that we have stood the test, and this proof is the ground of hope" (Rom. 5:3-4).

It is a misconception to treat Hebrews 2:10 as equivalent to a generalized formula concerning the purifying effects of suffering. The author states simply that it was "clearly fitting" for God, "for whom and through whom all things exist," to make the deliverer of his children perfect through sufferings.[2] However, he goes on to relate Jesus' sufferings to ours: "For since he himself has passed through the test of suffering, he is able to help those who are meeting their test now" (Heb. 2:18). The grace of God is available to all who face adversity on their way toward maturity.

Implicit in such passages as these is an understanding of suffering that has been vigorously espoused throughout nineteen centuries of Christian thought. It was systematically formulated first by Irenaeus (*ca.* 120/140–200/203), a native of Asia Minor who as a missionary in Gaul became Bishop of Lugdunum (Lyons) in 177. For this reason John Hick names it the Irenaean type of theodicy in contrast to the Augustinian type, which we have examined in chapters 4 and 6.

Along with other similarities, both types regard God as ultimately responsible for the existence of evil. However, the nature of the divine responsibility and the resultant role of human beings are quite differently conceived. In the Augustinian-Calvinistic tradition, man was created perfect, but fell because of free and culpable disobedience to the divine will; his rebellion disrupted the divine plan and introduced evil into the world, though this event itself falls within the predestination of the sovereign God. All human beings inherit Adam's guilt, and their tribulations are divine punishment for sin. According to Irenaeus, God created human beings imperfect, with the intention of bringing them finally, through a process of moral development, to the perfection that will fulfill his purpose for them. In this view the fall of Adam was an occurrence in the childhood of the human species, a lapse attributable to its early incompetence and immaturity. The good and evil that we find mixed in our world provide the environment needed for the growth toward maturity that God intends.[3]

Irenaeus believes that only by experiencing the opposition of good and evil can we learn to cherish the one and avoid the other. How could we understand the meaning of the good if we had no knowledge of its contrary?

> For just as the tongue receives experience of sweet and bitter by means of tasting, and the eye discriminates between black and white by means of vision, and the ear recognizes the distractions of sound by hearing; so also does the mind, receiving through the experience of both the knowledge of what is good, become more tenacious of its preservation, by acting in obedience to God. . . . But if anyone do shun the knowledge of both kinds of things, . . . he unawares divests himself of the character of a human being.[4]

Realizing therefore that we are God's workmanship, we are called on to accept the events of our lives in a teachable spirit, as means whereby his creative purpose for us is fulfilled. "By preserving the framework thou shalt ascend to that which is perfect."[5]

This teleological understanding of human life in relation to good and evil was shared by Clement of Alexandria and, to some extent, by Methodius and Gregory of Nazianzus. It has characterized Eastern Orthodox theology from the second century to the twentieth.

Appearing repeatedly in this tradition is the Irenaean view of man as created originally in the divine "image" and being brought through his exercise of responsible freedom to the "likeness" of God—a development interrupted by the fall but renewed by the incarnation of God in Christ and carried forward by the activity of God's Holy Spirit.

With reference to sin, the theme of evil as a means to good is strikingly formulated in the words sung by the deacon in the ancient vigil for Easter Eve: "O felix culpa quae talem ac tantum meruit habere redemptorem"—"O fortunate fault which merited such and so great a redeemer." Approval of this paradox is expressed by theologians representing both the Augustinian and Irenaean traditions. Augustine himself declares that God "judged it better to bring good out of evil, than not to permit any evil to exist." [6] But this motif is not integral to Augustine's theodicy as it is in theodicies of the Irenaean variety. It clearly fits well into the teleological view of man and his sin.

Apart from its use in the Eastern liturgy, the paradox has become most widely known through Milton's use of it in *Paradise Lost*. [7] However, the idea of the fortunate fall appears in many other authors, times, and places, from Ambrose (340–397), to Wyclif's sermons in the late fourteenth century, to Francis de Sales in the early seventeenth century. To most formulations of it are applicable the words of Arthur O. Lovejoy: "The more intense the feeling of the sublimity of the redemptive act and the magnitude of the good both inherent in it and resultant from it, the more apparent the impossibility of regarding as merely evil the sin which had evoked it." [8] Indeed, in Milton and some other interpreters the fall is seen as the indispensable means of winning for man, and possibly even for God, a far greater good than could have been attained without it.

John Hick, who places himself firmly in the Irenaean tradition, is in basic agreement with Milton. To him it is inconceivable that God would allow the terrible evil of sin unless he already intended a greater value to follow than would otherwise have been possible. "Sin plus redemption is of more value in the sight of God than an innocence that permits neither sin nor redemption." Hick believes that the significance of the doctrine is largely vitiated if, as in Augustine, the benefits gained are restricted to the elect. But if this restriction is removed the insight of "O felix culpa" is "one of the cornerstones of Christian theology," "the heart of Christian theodicy," and one of our "few authentic flashes of light" on the mystery of evil.[9]

Modern Interpretations

The first major theologian in modern times to adopt a broadly Irenaean interpretation of evil was Friedrich Schleiermacher (1768– 1834). In the light of scientific knowledge of human beginnings, he regarded as untenable the notion of an original human perfection and a primordial fall. Rather, the imperfections apparent in human beings are involved in their nature as created by God and also in the circumstances of human life. The universe is good, since it provides an environment within which God's purpose for humanity may be fulfilled; and human beings by their response may help to realize that purpose. Both the imperfection that leads to sin and the redemption that overcomes it fall within the divine plan, and the former is the precondition of the latter. Whereas in Augustine grace intervenes to undo the havoc wrought by sin, in Schleiermacher sin is preparation for grace. God has created men and women lacking in perfect righteousness in order that, moved by his grace, they may freely turn to him and grow in his likeness. Hence a universe in which God permits sin and other forms of evil is better than one in which evils are not allowed. "The early gradual and imperfect unfolding of the power of the God-consciousness is one of the necessary conditions of the human stage of existence." [10]

The conception of evil and suffering as instrumental, and possibly even necessary, to the making of persons appears frequently in twentieth-century theologians and philosophers of religion. Understanding of the contemporary status and significance of this position should be furthered by examination of the thought of several typical representatives. We begin with Nicolas Berdyaev, whose views provide a valuable bridge between ancient Eastern theologians and present-day Eastern Orthodoxy.

The ultimate context of Berdyaev's interpretation of evil is the mystery of freedom. He repudiates the "official rational systems" of Christian theology, for which God must be ultimately the sole cause of everything, with only secondary and derivative causes operative in the external world. In this theory, evil must be seen as determined by God. Instead, Berdyaev postulates freedom as the spontaneous origin of evil, together with everything new in the world—a freedom that is independent of divine creation and determination. This postulate does not imply an ontological dualism or any metaphysical doctrine; it exposes the limitations of every rationalized doctrine of the origin of evil. Freedom appears as "irrational, abysmal, without foundations, inexplicable, non-objectifiable." We simply find it disclosed in existence, in spiritual experience. Like Boehme's *Ungrund,* it cannot be formulated conceptionally, but only symbolically and mythologically. The best we can say is that "evil and suffering exist because freedom exists; but freedom has no foundation in existence, it is a frontier." [11]

In such a view there is clearly no basis for regarding evil as sent by God or divinely ordered in order to achieve certain results. However, we can observe what happens in the paradoxical interplay of good and evil in human experience. Here we discover that the struggle for good presupposes the existence and resistance of evil, and that good is enriched by our experience of evil. Contradiction and struggle call forth creative effort; the division and polarization that occur when we undergo trials result in increased knowledge. [12]

The teleological value of suffering becomes evident especially when we consider the development of spirituality. This involves passage from the "unhappy" or disrupted consciousness toward superconsciousness, in which the individual escapes the domination of necessity and cause-and-effect and enters the sphere of freedom and love. Evil, which causes suffering, continues to be the most serious problem of our existence. However, as spirituality grows, it liberates the soul from the power of evil and enlightens consciousness.

> If there were no suffering in this wicked world, then very likely there would be no acuity of consciousness or growth of spirituality. Inability to suffer sometimes becomes the greatest evil of all. Dostoievsky maintained that suffering was the unique *raison d'être* of the consciousness. [13]

Thus sensitivity to evils and capacity for suffering are attributes of "spiritual man." If suffering contributes to the development of interior strength and the life enrichment that opens the way to a larger good, it cannot be regarded merely as evil.[14]

Further light is shed when we see the suffering of Jesus as the epitome of the suffering of the world. The one crucified was not only the most righteous of men, but the Son of God. The agony which he unjustly endured was God's as well, and this unjust divine suffering expiated all human suffering. The evil of the world crucified him, and with him God himself. But in the mystery of the love with which he endured the cross, his suffering became expiation. Berdyaev does not elaborate this in a closely knit theory of atonement. For him it suffices that in the paradox of suffering and the cross is the mystery of divine pity and love through which the burden of guilt is removed and our lives are illumined and spiritualized. Suffering thus illumined leads to salvation.[15]

Moreover, salvation for Berdyaev includes deliverance from the most terrible of all evils, death. This constitutes probably the most dramatic instance of the teleological value of evil, since death opens "the way to eternal life, or at least one of the ways." The consummation of the divine purpose for the cosmos links personal eschatology with the historical eschatology of the world as a whole. On the one hand, for the individual to be absorbed exclusively in his own immortality or his personal salvation is "transcendent egoism"; it is also a contradiction of the love that is our major spiritual weapon against the power of death. It was because Christ incarnated the universal divine love that he conquered death. Likewise, when we genuinely love others, we conquer death. However, the immortality of all implies the immortality of each one. The goal of spiritualization is not the immortality of the race, of ideas, of created works, or in the memory of one's descendants; it is rather personal immortality, the ongoing, enlarging life of the subject, not simply of the objects that concern him. Love calls for universal resurrection.

> Were there to be but one creature possessing an existential centre, which was not resuscitated to eternal life, the world would have been a failure and a theodicy would be impossible. . . . I depend upon the destiny of the world and of those who are near to me, and the destiny of those who are near to me and of the world depends upon me.[16]

This close connection between the individual and his fellows applies also to life in the present order. The spiritual growth wrought through suffering, especially when it is seen in the light of the cross, inevitably and responsibly relates the individual to other human beings who suffer. Expiation has a profoundly social reference; it is

> the peculiar virtue of the suffering of love and willing sacrifice, of a Cross willingly borne. Everything turns on this. It is not only essential to be aware of one's burden, but also to bear the Cross of one's fellow-men, to abstain from condemning them that are no more sinful than I am. . . . Christian spirituality . . . should acknowledge the absolute validity of each personality and it should be more sensitive to the painful destiny of each man. The paradox of suffering and evil is resolved in the experience of compassion and love.[17]

Berdyaev emphasizes that to recognize the purposive role of suffering does not imply negation of the reality of evil and injustice or of the human struggle for "a less torturing and more joyful life."[18] My experience of pain may be for me a way of spiritualization and illumination, but I must not make this a general rational justification of suffering. To do so could easily lead to a hypocritical extenuation of the suffering of the unfortunate. Insofar as suffering really deepens my spirituality, it sensitizes me to the sufferings of other people and increases my concern for the alleviation of injustice and hardship.

Very different from Berdyaev's orientation is that of Bernard Bosanquet, the British absolute idealist who utilizes explicitly Keats's soul-making motif. Bosanquet disclaims any attempt at a theodicy, since he does not regard the world as "ruled by an omnipotent moral person." However, for him reality is ultimately one Mind or Idea, a whole of which all finite entities are parts. The universe in its various aspects forms a mental or spiritual system. Through the interconnections involved in natural selection and the complex life of society, particular centers of consciousness are not only molded into a deepening harmony with their environment but adapted as members of an individuality that transcends their own. Through the reinforcement of some of their qualities by others, the supplying of their deficiencies, and the removal of their internal contradictions, they come increasingly to resemble the character of the absolute. In the processes of this vale of soul-making there is an ongoing reiteration of both demand and the response of either adaptation or failure. This is the way in which particular centers of experience attain form and content. The goal is the perfection of the whole, "the harmony of all being."[19]

Bosanquet suggests that souls have their value precisely in and through the process of their formation. A drama would have little interest if its characters ceased to develop. However, soul-making is necessarily severe, since there is much to be remade as well as made. "Finiteness resting on infinity" entails a "hazardous and adventurous character" shared by both good and evil.[20]

Most of us would ask to be spared suffering, especially its more cruel forms. Yet our finite judgment would almost always be wrong. If our choice of pains were granted, we should miss our greatest opportunities for the achievement of value, in both the individual and the age or nation. The possibility for the finite spirit to become more than finite depends on the infinite depths of the universe. To attempt to set those depths within the limited judgment of the finite spirit is inherently contradictory, undermining the whole notion that the finite partakes of and reaches into infinity. "The whole point of the connection is that the finite spirit is more than it knows. If we let it, taking itself as infinite, lay down its own ultimate limits, why then, of course, all that it dreads is gone, and with it all that made life worth living." As finite beings, we lack the basis on which we could make a confident estimate of the universe. Since we do not possess perfection we cannot "grasp in detail the nature of the satisfaction" it would offer.[21]

However, we can see all our experiences, including those which bring anguish and frustration, as contributory to the harmony and perfection of the whole. If we can desire and approve that totality, we can accept the fragments that constitute it. In all the risks and terrors of life "there is, after all, nothing but what flows from the source of its strength and value, the continued passing of the finite beyond itself in the venture of achieving a fuller world."[22]

Another philosopher who relates evil to its function in the making of persons is the American Radoslav A. Tsanoff. However, the central motifs in his understanding of reality are not the absolute, infinity, system, and totality, but dynamic activity, upward reach, and various levels of attainment. The self gains fulfillment less by removal of contradictions and harmonization with the perfect whole than by surmounting obstacles in the struggle for higher values. "Perfection is perfectibility."

The cosmic process is gradational, exhibiting a hierarchy of activities. These range from mechanism to life to consciousness, from nonrational to rational action, from processes conforming to law to actions guided by principle in pursuit of ideal goals. Values, likewise, whether logical, aesthetic, ethical, or religious, are also gradational. Some experiences are higher, better, preferable, or more worthy than others. The meaning of terms like *higher* and *lower* is itself constantly expanding as the range, complexity, and realization of values are enhanced. Permeating the entire process, and working at all levels for the maximum actualization of experiences of worth, is the activity we call God. "Just this upward-urging, ever more perfectly active character of the cosmos is what we can intelligently mean by God." He is "the Apogee of Value." Thus faith in God is a conviction of "the ultimate reality, conservation, and enhancement of value."[23]

In this scheme of things evil is quite literally *degradation,* the obstruction of the higher by the lower, the downward-pulling action that results in the realization of lower grades of value than those that are sought, or that ought to be sought. It is the frustration or perversion of the higher possibilities.

There is therefore no coming to terms with evil. It must be resisted, combated, and, to the greatest possible degree, overcome. But precisely because of this circumstance it can become the means to good. It exists, and it must be accepted realistically. However, to accept it is in no sense to condone it, but rather to oppose it with all strenuousness. Tsanoff mentions the frequent observation that the articles of the ancient Christian creeds can be best understood in light of the heresies they were meant to combat; similarly, he holds that truth is best pursued through removal of error, virtue through opposition to vice, and beauty through repudiation of ugliness. To see such evils for what they are, and as conditions of good, does not make them any less evil. It means simply acknowledging that "they *are—to be resisted.*" The perception of evil is a requisite for the courageous struggle for good. It is thus always relative to good; but if we make our peace with it and fail to recognize and resist it, we absolutize it and accomplish our own damnation, losing our God-given capacity for the actualization of ever higher levels of value.[24]

Tsanoff's gradational view of value and evil does not offer, strictly speaking, a theodicy. He does not maintain that God has ordained evil as a stimulus to good, but only that in our world negative realities do become, to the degree that we resist them, instruments to the attainment of higher and richer ranges of value. The worthier features of existence gain reality through effort to eliminate or reduce evil. "This contest is at the heart of things; it has neither beginning nor end, and it makes our world significant and stirring."[25]

The theism of F. R. Tennant, like that of Tsanoff, interprets evil in the context of an evolutionary order. For him the purpose of the universe is the fullest possible realization of values, especially moral values, by finite, developing persons. "The best thing in the world . . . is moral character; the best possible world is the world which affords opportunity for moral growth."[26] If such fulfillment is taken to be the goal of creation, then the process necessary to its attainment is good in spite of the evil that may be incidental to it. The creation of persons of sturdy character committed to the actualization and enhancement of values is worth what it costs, provided the cost is unavoidable and the evil involved is not superfluous or supreme. For Tenant this is true of physical and mental as well as moral evil.

Tennant is acutely critical of simplistic, pious forms of the soul-making theory that regard every instance of suffering as fulfilling the special purpose of an all-wise and perfectly good God. To say that a particular instance of pain advances some good fails to get to the root of the problem. It may be pointed out, for example, that some distress serves as a warning that prevents greater misery. The toothache makes us aware of decay that requires removal; severe abdominal discomfort informs us of a dangerous ulcer. The painful warning may be valuable, and necessary, for the avoidance of grave danger. But why the greater danger? How shall we explain the remoter evil that makes the more immediate evil salutary? We are forced farther back to deal with the total situation of which the particular remedial event is only a part. Indeed, says Tennant, it must be shown that pain in such cases is not only a physical but a logical necessity—that its absence would somehow contradict the nature and purpose of God. It must be made clear that no suffering experienced by human beings exceeds what is necessary "to the cosmos as a coherent system."[27] This condition is not met. Though sometimes the endurance of pain does help to strengthen virtues like patience, courage, and sympathy, the extent and severity of evil in the world are far greater than required for these ends.

Three further considerations render untenable the belief that particular ills are willed by a good God for the moral perfecting of the individuals afflicted. First, some babies are so tragically malformed or handicapped at birth that they are incapable of learning from what they endure. Second, the distribution of suffering among normal individuals cannot be reconciled with any supposed divine plan to adapt particular ills to the particular needs, circumstances, and stages of moral development of the persons concerned. Third, the apportionment of evils seems utterly chaotic. "The wind is not always tempered to the shorn lamb." The most excruciating trials may overtake those who do not need the discipline they impose or who lack the faith or experience that would enable them to benefit from their hardships or endure them for the glory of God. On the other hand, many persons who seem to be in glaring need of correction, repentance, and moral transformation do not receive the chastening that presumably might accomplish these ends, but pass their lives in relative comfort.[28]

These difficulties lead Tennant to reject the notion that afflictions arising from our relation to the physical world are specifically willed by God in order to strengthen character. Instead, he offers a "wider theodicy" that sees such ills as "inevitable, if incidental, accompaniments of the order of Nature; they are logical consequences of the World-plan." God does will the existence of a moral order in a finite world, and many cases of suffering are bound to happen if such an order is to be realized. On the whole, the ordered cosmos ministers beneficently to human well-being, and it is a *sine qua non* of a world aimed at the development of persons capable of realizing high values. Thus physical ills are not as such antecedently willed by God. They occur, rather, as unavoidable by-products; they are "logical consequences of the cosmos or moral order which *is* willed absolutely by God, and the willing of which is due to the fact that God is Love.'' In this context, it may well be that no evil is really superfluous—that not even the pain of cancer, the pathetic limitations enforced by physical malformation and mental retardation, or the devastating effects of earthquakes are logically unnecessary elements of the kind of universe required by a moral order.[29]

Tennant recognizes, however, that another question must be satisfactorily answered if suffering is to be reconciled with belief in a loving God. Though physical evil may be necessary to a moral order, can human beings themselves deem it a justifiable price to pay for the dignity and worth of their moral perfecting? Are persons who as individuals are ends in themselves treated in such as way that they do not become merely means? Are *their* lives enriched, or do all the advantages accrue to humanity or to God? With regard to both physical ills and the temptations and struggles involved in moral evil, Tennant replies that the goods attainable are worth the cost. However grievous the individual person's burden of suffering, he can endure it willingly ''for the joy that is set before him in rational and moral life.'' Human life is desirable because it brings fulfillment to and for finite persons as well as to and for God and his universal goals.

Yet, complete fulfillment is impossible within the limitations of earthly existence. The problem of evil cannot be adequately dealt with apart from belief in the continuation of individual life beyond physical death. Human beings are intrinsically valuable. In a rational order grounded in the divine goodness we can rightly believe that they are not treated as pawns, but as children of God. They themselves must be able to realize the values made possible partly through their suffering. A total balance of good over evil in the world is not enough. There must be ultimately such a balance in individual life, or else the individual is not treated as an end in himself. The wisdom, power, and goodness of God could not be reconciled with ''a world which produced free beings, with Godward aspirations and illimitable ideals, only to cut them off in everlasting death, mocking their hopes and frustrating their purposes.''[30]

However, the future life should not be regarded as compensation or reward for human toleration of present ills. It is rather an extension and enlargement of the value realization which in the loving purpose of God is begun here. The difficulties of our present life are part of the probation that prepares us for an eternal destiny.

Austin Farrer, working on the basis of the revelation found in the Christian gospel, seeks to address the paradox of a God who acts to save sinful human beings, but who also is Creator of the universe that contains the evil from which they need to be saved. His theodicy is mainly Irenaean, stressing the function of evil as instrumental to good; but his use of Augustine and Aquinas provides one of many indications that the Augustinian and Irenaean traditions are by no means mutually exclusive.

Farrer definitely affirms the free respónsibility of human beings for sin and the evils that result from it. However, in regard to particular evils that have no clear relation to sin, we cannot speak with assurance about the divine purpose. Here, speculation is necessary, but its value is limited. We need, and may be upheld by, the faith that Providence is at work in particular events, but often we cannot detect such Providence. As we quietly fulfill our duties we may be sustained by the belief that ''God will make suffered evils fruitful for good.'' Trusting in his mercy, we may discern that he is leading us ''through and out of evil and into a promised good.''[31]

In this context, faith in the omnipotence and the perfect goodness of God becomes for Farrer less a problem than an answer, since it enables us to face the worst evils with the assurance that God is in control. He quotes with approval the words of Augustine cited also by Aquinas: ''The Almighty God, who, as even the heathen acknowledge, has supreme power over all things, being Himself supremely good, would never permit the existence of anything evil among His works.''[32] Later Farrer modifies this assurance in the direction of the specificity that he usually hesitates to affirm. God, he declares, ''would never have allowed evils to subsist in his creation, were it not that he might find in them the occasion to produce good things unique in kind, and dependent for their unique character on the character of the evils in question.''[33]

. Thus pain, along with the remedial action it arouses, plays a vital role within the purpose of God. Without it no animal species above the elementary level would have the slightest chance of survival. On the human level, God does not send pains so that we may passively endure them; he gives them rather to awaken our detestation of their cause and to stimulate us to eradicate this cause. A good example is compassion: "If we say that God, from the motive of compassion, should have spared his creatures all suffering, we are surely talking nonsense. It is only because God allots pain that there is any object for his compassion, or any sense in speaking of it."[34]

With emphases like these Farrer defends his view that suffering contributes to the formation of human character and the advancement of God's goals for his creation. However, this is not his only response to the problem of evil. He develops with some care the notion that evil often arises from the "mutual interference of systems" in the physical world, pointing out that the elimination of such interdependence and the accidentality that accompanies it would make impossible the universe as we know it.[35] Also pertinent to his approach to suffering are his Gifford Lectures of 1957, where he explores in depth the place and implications of freedom in the physical order and in human life.[36]

The ablest and most convincing contemporary statement of the teleological type of theodicy is that of John Hick. Against the background of a painstaking historical and critical examination of the Augustinian and Irenaean traditions, he offers his own closely knit response to the problem of evil. Writing as both a philosopher and a Christian theologian, he addresses not only Christian believers, but also the skeptics, agnostics, and humanists whom he finds more representative of today's intellectual world. However, the starting point for his understanding of evil is his conviction that our knowledge of God's character and purpose is derived mainly from his incarnation in Jesus Christ. The actions through which Jesus made his impact on the world—teaching, healing, challenging, forgiving—"were the actions of an agape which was continuous with, and directly revelatory of, the eternal agape of God." But these activities all concern personal relationships. Hence we must attempt to interpret evil primarily from the standpoint of God's purpose for the finite persons whom he has created for fellowship with himself. This leads to a theodicy which centers in the development of moral personality, and which sees the world primarily as a "vale of soul-making."[37]

With Irenaeus, Hick sees human beings as still in the process of creation. He recognizes the exegetical dubiousness of Irenaeus' distinction between the "image" and the "likeness" of God in

Genesis 1:26, but regards it nevertheless as suggesting an important truth: Human beings are created personal, in the divine image, but their potentialities must be developed by further creative action so that they mature in those qualities of personal existence which comprise the finite likeness of God. Hick utilizes modern anthropological knowledge and his belief in the essential freedom of persons to suggest a two-stage view of the creation of human beings. God seeks to lead man from the level of biological life (*bios*) to that of fully personal life realizing eternal values (*zoe*). In the first stage, by a long process of evolutionary development, God creates the physical universe, brings forth organic life, and then produces persons capable of conscious fellowship with himself. All this can be accomplished by his creative power without the self-direction of his creatures. The second stage involves the spiritualization or perfecting of persons as children of God. This movement cannot occur by divine fiat, but only through the free and unforced cooperation of human individuals as they respond to God's leading in the environment where he has placed them.

This conception of the world as a place where God is fashioning souls, "bringing many sons to glory" (Heb. 2:10), offers in Hick's opinion our best clue to the meaning of evil. If suffering were excluded, could the world effectively further the making of souls? Hick relates this question to both moral evil and the suffering that is traceable at least partially to natural causes. In both cases his answer is negative.

Light is shed on moral evil if we recognize that persons become truly good by their responsible decisions in concrete situations, by facing and surmounting temptations, by various challenges and disciplines, by learning to choose high values even in the midst of difficulties. The world is not intended to be a paradise of ease and comfort, like the pen that a child might build for a pet animal with maximum regard for health, safety, and pleasure. It is rather a place where human personalities may grow and mature according to the pattern of Christ. The product of such a process is so valuable to God and to the finite individuals engaged in it as to justify all the travail involved. Persons can move toward becoming the perfected creatures God wants only by participating in "a hazardous adventure in individual freedom."[38]

This adventure is indeed so hazardous that human beings are exposed to suffering brought about by their own self-centeredness, lovelessness, and cruelty. If they are to be related to their Creator in uncompelled faith, they must be set initially "at an epistemic 'distance' from him." This requires that they see their environment as apparently autonomous, "as if there were no God." In such circumstances it becomes virtually inevitable that they will center their lives on themselves rather than on God. This kind of fallenness is the price that must be paid for the freedom of individuals capable of turning voluntarily to the personal Infinite. But it opens the way for them as prodigal children to return from the far country to their true home, moved by their own need and the love of their Father. Thus even human sinfulness and the suffering it occasions fall within the scope of the divine providence. They have no intrinsic value, but they contribute paradoxically to the redemptive activity that overcomes them and the resultant service that forgiven sinners render to each other amid suffering.[39]

Physical pain and other forms of suffering not clearly caused by sin are also best understood if the world that contains them is seen as a vale of soul-making. If our environment were radically altered into a soft, easy, unchallenging order, it would produce "a soft, unchallenged race of men." A painless world would exclude physical and mental toil, hunger and thirst, and extremes of heat and cold. But it would also render needless the activities by which people meet these painful exigencies—hunting, agriculture, construction of shelter, and social organization. It would likewise exclude the painful effort needed for the advancement of knowledge and pursuit of the arts, drastically altering the nature of human life and thus eliminating the creative enterprises that make life most valuable. Presumably God might have made a world without pain, but in so doing he would have destroyed the possibility of creating souls capable of realizing high values in fellowship with him and each other.[40]

However, we still face the reality of suffering so intense and crushing that it exceeds what is needed for soul-making. Indeed, some obstacles and calamities have the opposite effect, producing resentment, rebellion, and disintegration of character. How does Christian theodicy deal with evils that seem to be completely dysteleological? Hick speaks of this as "the really insoluble problem." Excessive, undeserved, and debilitating suffering constitutes a mystery so baffling that our best rationalizing efforts cannot penetrate it. Yet even this mystery, itself an occasion of anguish, can be comprehended within the soul-making interpretation of life if we recognize that human beings have in the divine purpose an eternal destiny. Our theodicy must be eschatological. Apart from faith in life beyond the grave there is no answer. But in terms of the kingdom of God portrayed by Jesus, we can anticipate beyond earthly history a final blessedness, an ultimate good that will make worth while all the wretchedness and agony endured on the way to it. The struggles, sufferings, and defeated hopes of earthly existence will find justification in their outcome in God's completed creation. In faith we can affirm that all our suffering will ultimately contribute to the perfecting of persons that fulfills God's loving purpose. In the perspective of that fulfillment, it will be seen that nothing was utterly and irredeemably evil. The reality of evil is interim, not final.[41]

The various strands composing Hick's theodicy are woven together in his own summary:

> God has ordained a world which contains evil—real evil—as a means to the creation of the infinite good of a Kingdom of Heaven within which His creatures will have come as perfected persons to love and serve Him, through a process in which their own free insight and response have been an essential element.[42]

With this survey we have before us a fair sampling of biblical writers and later thinkers who in various ways see evil and suffering as means to the maturation and fulfillment of finite persons.[43]

Evaluation

It seems to me that the basic premise on which the teleological type of theodicy is erected is sound. The world is a setting in which God is seeking to create moral persons for maturing fellowship with one another and himself. There are three aspects to this postulate: (1) the world is a place of character formation; (2) human potentialities can be perfected only through the exercise of responsible freedom;

(3) the creative process is still going on, and the fulfillment it aims toward is open-ended.

This interpretation is supported by much evidence concerning the nature of human life derived from our experience as a whole. It is also consistent with the biblical understanding of the relation between God and his human creatures. In a variety of historical situations he is disclosed as the Creator, Redeemer, and Life-giver. For Christians the New Testament witness is particularly revealing. "When anyone is united to Christ," writes the apostle Paul, "there is a new world; the old order has gone, and a new order has already begun" (II Cor. 5:17). Neither circumcision nor uncircumcision matters; "the only thing that counts is new creation!" (Gal. 6:15). Paul reports that he himself has not yet reached perfection, but is pressing on, and he invites the Philippians to join him in striving toward the goal (Phil. 3:12-15). Jesus declares, "There must be no limit to your goodness, as your heavenly Father's goodness knows no bounds" (Matt. 5:48). The Revelation of John envisions "a new Jerusalem" and "a new heaven and a new earth," and proclaims with joy the God who is "making all things new" (Rev. 3:12; 21:1, 5).

We can therefore affirm, in basic agreement with the Irenaeans, that our world is a sphere for the production of worthy persons who are created for fellowship with God and one another in the realization of values. However, it is not clear that this conception of the divine purpose requires for its fulfillment the nature, volume, and intensity of evil as we confront it. The foundation is solid, but a different or a modified superstructure may be more in keeping with it than the one erected by those who stress the instrumentality of evil in the growth of character.

Positively, it must be recognized that some intrinsically evil experiences are instrumental to the attainment of goods that might not otherwise be possible. Some of these benefits accrue primarily in the lives of the sufferers themselves, while others occur mainly in other persons affected by those who suffer.

1. Participation in suffering and the struggle it often entails does in many instances aid the moral growth of the sufferer. As the dying Faust observes, regarding the insecurity and danger of life:

> He only earns his freedom and existence,
> Who daily conquers them anew.[44]

The conquest of difficulties, and even the very act of enduring them, sometimes serves to strengthen, purify, deepen, and enrich character.

William E. Hulme has written in anguish of the almost incredible human blunders that led quite unnecessarily to the death of his daughter in 1974. For him the event was definitely not willed by God. But in a paragraph on the place of God in the event he testifies that the "disturbed faith" of the family "has given us the ability to accept the fallenness of this world, its people and its institutions. It has also given us a clearer vision of the eternal dimensions of life in Christ. The Spirit, in truth, does bear witness with our spirits."[45]

On December 20, 1975, the *Aquarius,* an old lobster boat without a radio, left Gloucester, Massachusetts, on a training trip in preparation for a winter cruise to the Bahamas. Struck by a raging gale, the boat was wrecked a half mile from shore after a night-long attempt by the crew to ride out the storm. Three persons perished, and three survived. Each of the survivors has pondered the question, "Why did I escape death?" and found no answer. But they report gaining a greater sensitivity to life around them. Said one: "I notice things a lot more than I did before—smells, sounds, tastes, the ground under my feet. You think about living. . . . Life is a serious matter, and I appreciate it."[46] These words do not include a conscious reference to God like that found in Hulme's interpretation, but they do reflect a new awareness of a dimension of depth in existence that could hardly have come to this young college student without his direct experience with tragedy.

Characteristic of all human life is what Paul Ricoeur calls "the evil infinite of desire" and Ernst Bloch terms the *not,* the painful experience of lack or of hunger for something which is *not-yet.* To be human is to be dissatisfied with present attainment, to be lured by the desire for something more or something else—things, happiness, knowledge, skill, power, virtue, liberation from bondage. Such restlessness, writes Ricoeur, "seems to be our true nature, or rather the absence of nature that makes us free." It can plunge us into misery, and it can become the serpent's voice goading us into sinful rebellion against God (Gen. 3:5). But it can also motivate the pursuit of all the values that characterize human culture at its best. Through struggle the not-yet can become real. Hence human beings are always on the way toward some new goal, taking part in a dangerous pilgrimage, drawn by the promise of a future that transcends every present.[47] Thus the suffering of their discontent brings enrichment to individuals and societies alike.

2. The positive value of some forms of suffering consists primarily in the constructive contributions they make to other persons or movements influenced by the sufferer. These may occur through the deepened insight of the one who suffers, through time made available to him or her because of circumscribed activities, through unconscious influence, through the opening up of unexpected forms of service, or through the power of suffering to redeem and transform.

George Pickering traces with care the effects of psychoneuroses on the creative work of Charles Darwin and Florence Nightingale. Darwin became ill in 1837 after his return from the voyage of the *Beagle*. According to Pickering the illness resulted from the conflict between Darwin's desire to develop and provide solid evidence for his theories on natural selection and the transmutation of species and the large amount of time required for social intercourse with friends and fellow scientists. The illness solved his problem by protecting him from social relationships and providing time for the writing of the *Origin of Species*. Darwin himself wrote, "Even ill health, though it has annihilated several years of my life, has saved me from the distractions of society and amusement."[48] Once the book was published he recovered.

Through Florence Nightingale's experiences in the Crimean War, she became convinced that saving the lives of countless soldiers demanded correction of the inept administration of the British War Office and dissemination of basic knowledge of sanitation. The attainment of these goals would require a vast expenditure of time and energy for the preparation of informed, lucid, and logically convincing reports, articles, books, memoranda, and recommendations. But the irritating trivialities forced on her by her family stood in the way. In Pickering's view, the persistent demands of her sister and mother forced her to become an invalid and a recluse, thus freeing her from seeing them or other undesired visitors. As a result of twelve years of concentrated work sixteen hours a day, augmented by similarly dedicated labors of colleagues and helpers, under the constant threat of death, she succeeded in transforming "the War Office, the British Army, the Indian Army, sanitation, hospitals, nursing [and] the Poor Law," and founded the scientific discipline of epidemiology. All this she accomplished mostly from her bed. She did not return to ordinary contacts with the world until she was sixty, and she lived to the age of ninety. "She had less need for her illness, *and so it improved.*" Pickering concludes that the world is indebted to the maladies of persons like these for "the great contributions they have made to their own times and to posterity."[49]

I referred earlier to a child who because of cerebral palsy and degeneration of the central nervous system is incapable of any genuinely human existence. Yet the suffering that her condition has occasioned for her family has enriched their lives and given them compassion. It cannot be claimed that her sad affliction has had value for her; but the suffering it has brought to her parents, two sisters, and a brother has unquestionably deepened their sensitivity. All of them have grown in responsiveness, capacity for love, and spiritual awareness. Through wise parental guidance, the three normal children, instead of resenting the special attention demanded by their helpless sister, have become caring persons who manifest unselfish concern not only for her but for others within and outside the family circle.

Similar results follow on a broader scale when sensitive persons share inwardly the sufferings of the victims of social injustice, as did Eugene Debs (1855–1926). "While there is a lower class," he wrote, "I am in it; while there is a criminal element I am of it; while there is a soul in prison I am not free."[50] Those who care as deeply as Debs are not content to bewail oppression; they act to remove it. Many persons, aroused by the plight of those who through no fault of their own are condemned to poverty and ignorance and denied basic human rights, are moved to act selflessly and courageously to change unjust social structures.

Redemptive as well as creative influences flowed from the life of a close friend of mine who died of cancer in Baltimore in 1953. A pastor, he lay for six months in the parsonage next door to the church he served, except for several occasions when he somehow summoned strength to preach to his congregation. He spoke of feeling his world close in on him as he relinquished one responsibility after another. Yet during his illness a new world opened. From his bed of pain he ministered to numerous parishioners even as they visited to minister to him, for they observed unmistakably the sustaining power of the faith he had proclaimed. Through the way in which he faced disease, infirmity, and the certainty of death, he may have reached more lives at deeper levels than he could have in a ministry of fifty years. He drew those he touched into a fellowship of victorious suffering in which all were enriched, a convincing embodiment of what Whitehead has called "the notion of redemption through suffering, which haunts the world." [51]

For Christians, the supreme instance of the power of evil to become instrumental in the accomplishment of good is the death of Jesus. Something in the depths of reality enabled the crucifixion, in spite of its flagrant miscarriage of justice and its agonizing tragedy, to become for many millions their highest disclosure of the forgiving, reconciling love of God and the way to personal and social transformation. Those who sought by violence to secure their own position and power unintentionally advanced the movement they hoped to destroy.

The evidence just cited makes plain that various forms of evil often do serve to build character and enrich human life. However, some proponents of the soul-making hypothesis go beyond this to maintain that God, who is perfect in power, love, and wisdom, sends, ordains, wills, or plans evil and suffering as means to the holy ends he seeks. This claim involves grave difficulties, which must now be critically examined.

1. We have already noted Tennant's incisive criticism of the view that some evils serve the useful purpose of warning us of greater dangers. To justify a lesser evil by reference to a worse one only compounds the problem, leaving unexplained the threatening circumstances that require the warning. As Ducasse has made clear, even if it can be shown that all evils work for good great enough to outweigh the evil, this would mean only "that the world is less evil than it would be if evil never bred goods but only further evils." [52] Even the enlarged ministry to others made possible by my Baltimore friend's courageous battle with cancer leaves unanswered the question, Why do people face so much suffering in their own lives that they need such examples?

2. Many critics point to the inequitable distribution of suffering and its disproportionateness to the needs of sufferers or their capacity to benefit from it. For millions the way to a fully human existence is effectively barred, while others no more worthy enjoy almost unlimited opportunities. Why must some be physically and spiritually impoverished while others apparently want for nothing? W. R. Jones observes that "collapsing suffering into a form of spiritual pedagogy misses the impact of the maldistribution of ethnic suffering."[53] This sound observation needs only to be extended to a recognition that the pedagogical interpretation overlooks the maldistribution of *all* suffering. Human anguish is not apportioned according to disciplinary need. The characters of some individuals and peoples might be genuinely enhanced if they faced more obstacles than they do, while others confront far greater hardships than they can bear, and are crushed by them.

3. A related problem is that of superfluous or gratuitous suffering. The view that evil is a kind of schoolmaster in moral education seems to imply that no suffering is purposeless. But it would be hard to maintain that this condition is met. There are evils that cannot reasonably be interpreted as contributory to the formation of character or to any other larger good. Even Tennant's "wider theodicy" is in this respect inadequate. To regard physical ills as unavoidable though incidental by-products of a natural order that is willed by God for our good is far more cogent than to treat them as specifically purposed in particular situations. It *may* be, as Tennant suggests, that even cancer is not superfluous to "a determinate cosmos" intended to be an arena for moral growth. But the opposite may also be true, and this possibility renders suspect an argument that hinges on the requirements of "a moral order in general."

Supportive of this suspicion is the fact that the proponents of the soul-making theory, like most other people, recognize that evil is really evil and do their utmost to remove or minimize it. If distress actually breeds good, should we not welcome it instead of opposing it? Should not the obligation to increase the total good in the universe lead to the cessation of efforts to eradicate disease, lest decreased pain mean weaker character? Obviously, no one would seriously answer this question affirmatively. The explanation can be only that much suffering is excessive, going far beyond the total needed for character formation.

4. Ironically, the interpretation of suffering that focuses attention on the growth of persons is ambiguous regarding the status of the individual. On the one hand, writers like Tennant emphasize the role played even by excessive pain in the general moral order, or in "the cosmos as a coherent system." Are not individuals and their value-realizing potentialities then sacrificed to the system? Persons suffer as individuals, and many must endure so much evil that the benefits of the cosmic plan are lost for them. Then they are not the ends in themselves that the world order is presumably designed to serve.

On the other hand, some formulations of the soul-making view seem too individualistic. John Hick, for example, finds that human life today moves on about the same moral plane as four thousand years ago, but that during this time, millions of souls have experienced earthly existence, with God's purpose moving toward fulfillment in each of them—not within a human aggregate.[54] In this kind of personal growth we should rejoice, but overemphasis on it can blur the social dimension. The biblical concerns for a covenant people and the kingdom of God make plain that souls in process of fulfillment contribute to, and grow best in, a community of justice and love. Failure to recognize this also makes it easy to justify or accept without the radical action demanded the human anguish attributable to unjust social structures.

5. Evil is instrumental in unmaking souls as well as making them. The blows of adversity fall so heavily on some persons that they become incapable of coping with them and deteriorate under their impact. In 1934, in the depths of the economic depression, a young unemployed father in Baltimore was unable to pay his fuel bill, and the company turned off the gas. Desperate, he found a way to tap the gas main, and was arrested and jailed. A few days before Christmas he hanged himself in his cell, leaving his wife and little girl to face a hostile world alone. The biblical writings bear witness to the fact that suffering, instead of ennobling character, can produce bitter imprecations and prayers for vengeance (see Pss. 17:13-14; 149:6-9;

Jer. 20:12). Those who pass through fiery trials may be assured by the hymn writer that the Lord is saying:

> I only design
> Thy dross to consume and thy gold to refine;

but often it is they themselves who are consumed. Some no doubt grow as they endure poverty, disease, oppression, or natural disaster, but others are hardened, debased, and incapacitated.

6. Two difficulties arise in connection with the eschatological theodicy of Berdyaev, Tennant, Hick, and others, which finds suffering ultimately justified by its outcome beyond earthly death. Undoubtedly, the soul-making interpretation makes more sense when the learning, value-realizing process is understood as extending beyond our present existence. Yet we must remember that in this recognition we are not dealing with empirical evidence, such as the testimony of survivors on what they learned from shipwreck, or historical records of the accomplishments of sufferers from illness. We have to do rather with what a good God might reasonably be expected to provide for those denied fulfillment in this life. But the crucial question of the divine goodness remains. Faith in life beyond the grave is, I believe, a reasonable faith, but we who hold it must acknowledge that though it offers a logical completion for the character-building process, it is not in itself evidence for that process as a solution of the problem of evil.

The related question is whether even larger opportunities beyond death can justify the terrible agonies that some people are compelled to endure in their present existence. Would a beneficent, all-powerful God prepare a helpless boy for life eternal by subjecting him to the terrors of bubonic plague so heartrendingly recounted by Camus, or allow for the sake of later benefits the cruel torture by her parents of the five-year-old girl described by Dostoyevsky, who through her unresentful tears pleaded with "dear kind God" to protect her?[55] The same insistent questions arise out of historical events: the hopeless sufferings of black slaves in the American South, the crass denial of basic rights to ethnic minorities in the American North, the slow starvation of thousands in persistent drought, the crippling tortures of Vietnamese tiger cages, the utter poverty of Calcutta, the barrenness of existence in urban and rural ghettos in the United States. Can any opportunities in eternity derive sufficient worth from torments like these to justify their duration or severity? "Suffering passes away," writes Lèon Bloy, "but the fact of having suffered never disappears."[56] Berdyaev takes this to mean that one can never forget that one has suffered, and this experience when overcome brings enrichment. This may well be what Bloy has in mind. But another meaning seems at least equally valid: the experienced reality of suffering is unerasable; its debilitating effects endure. And we might add that no future can provide sufficient warrant for its terrors.

What conclusions can be drawn from this examination of values and difficulties? On the positive side, it is clear that evil and suffering often contribute significantly to the growth of persons as realizers of value. However, the problems encountered, particularly the reality of excessive pain and the role of suffering in frustrating, undermining, and debasing persons, make it unsound to hold that an all-powerful, all-wise, and perfectly good God purposes or permits evil *in order to* produce worthy persons. Such a God would presumably have open to him means of achieving his creative ends that would not require so vast a burden of anguish. The soul-making conception needs drastic modification and supplementation. Some statements of it already cited make use of such considerations as the regularity of the natural order and the part played by human freedom. Others imply some kind of limitation of divine power. The importance and value of these and related considerations must now be explored.

8 Evil and an Evolutionary Natural Order

For thinkers like Tennant and Hick, to whom the world is purposed by God as a place where persons can grow as realizers of value, evil is an unavoidable by-product of the orderly functioning of nature. To many other interpreters, also, the regularities of the physical order offer important clues to the understanding of suffering. The present chapter will explore some of the implications of this connection.

Implications of Regularity in Nature

The very possibility of life itself depends on the regularity and constancy of nature. Even minor variations in the uniform operations of physical things—formulated by human observers in generalizations called laws—could bring to an end the existence of most species of life on earth. Erratic changes in such stable characteristics of our world as the tilt of the earth's axis, the rate of the earth's rotation, the distance of the earth from the sun, or the time required for its orbit around the sun would drastically affect conditions like the relative length of night and day and the rotation of the seasons, hence make impossible the dependable knowledge of climatic changes and the predictability essential to agriculture and the production of food. As Jesus perceived in a prescientific age, grapes cannot ''be picked from briars, or figs from thistles'' (Matt. 7:16); if we want to sustain life, we need the assurance that the seeds we plant will produce the same kind of harvest. The successive abrogation and reinstatement of the laws of combustion, for the convenience of individuals in danger from fire, would make it impossible for us to heat our homes or produce the energy so urgently needed by society today. The occasional suspension of the laws of gravitation, because someone might fall off a rooftop or a cliff, would disrupt all forms of movement on sea or land or in the air, and render organized social life impossible.

Tennant's illustration of the need for constancy in nature states the case with clarity and effectiveness:

> If water is to have the various properties in virtue of which it plays its beneficial part in the economy of the physical world and the life of mankind, it cannot at the same time lack its obnoxious capacity to drown us. The specific gravity of water is as much a necessary outcome of its ultimate constitution as its freezing point, or its thirst-quenching and cleansing functions. There cannot be assigned to any substance an arbitrarily selected group of qualities, from which all that might ever prove unfortunate to any sentient organism may be eliminated, especially if one organism's meat is to be another's poison, and yet the world, of which that substance forms a part, be a calculable cosmos.[1]

The alternative to the constancy of a determinate cosmos would be a topsy-turvy chaos in which life itself and the evolutionary development that has brought it forth would be impossible.

A physical world marked by law and regularity is equally necessary for the realization by human beings of all the values that comprise life in its fullness. Friendship and love are possible only within a common environment in which people can meet and associate, an orderly and dependable field with fixed characteristics not subject to the whims of those who inhabit it. Recreation involving games in which one or more persons participate requires rules that all accept. "The chess player's freedom to play chess," writes C. S. Lewis, "depends on the rigidity of the squares and the moves."[2] Children sometimes want to change or suspend the rules of a game when such action seems to their immediate advantage, but mature persons know that more fun for all results when rules are clearly specified and adhered to by all.

Pursuit of intellectual values like knowledge, understanding, and wisdom also presupposes a world of orderly, dependable relationships in life and thought. The acquisition of knowledge in the sciences, for example, involves four main stages: the gathering of data, the formulation of hypotheses suggested by the data, the testing and possible modification of the hypotheses, and the drawing of conclusions in accord with the evidence. At every point this method of knowing, which has yielded such amazing results in both pure science and technology, depends on regularities in the operation of the objects investigated. Without such uniformity, no scientific knowledge would be possible. Nor can reason more broadly conceived carry on its work without assuming some orderly structure in the world it seeks to understand.

Likewise, the moral life of men and women, broadly conceived as the sphere of voluntary choice in pursuit of desired ends, presupposes a reliable regularly functioning physical world. True freedom can be exercised only within a relatively stable order in which causes can be traced and consequences of decisions and acts can be to a considerable degree foreseen. "A predictable regularity in nature," writes Austin Farrer, "is the condition of our imposing effective decisions; and so it is not alien from the picture of a free man's world, but intrinsic to it."[3] Without such regularity we could not be guided by probabilities or accumulated experience, nor could we plan to realize aims, form habits, or build character.

Unfortunately, though a determinate natural order is essential to life and the realization of values, it involves disadvantages as well as advantages. Its very invariability and dependability mean that hardship and suffering occur when living creatures fail to observe its provisions, whether intentionally, carelessly, or ignorantly. The stable properties of things and their interconnections in a world of law expose animals and people to circumstances that often entail pain and death. The operation of meteorological forces causes storms that can destroy harvests and wreck ships and airplanes. Geological processes produce earthquakes and volcanic eruptions that can be devastating to frail human beings and their finest architectural achievements. The water that is indispensable to human existence can also bring life to an abrupt end. The laws of cell growth make possible not only healthy bodily life but the malignant cancers that kill it. The laws of friction and muscular tension and coordination that enable people to walk also contribute to falls and broken bones.

Knives may be used to cut bread and perform life-saving surgery, but equally to stab and murder. Human sex drives may find expression in relationships of profound beauty and enduring love; perverted or unwisely guided, they may arouse hatred and cause extreme anguish.

It seems obvious that in the world we inhabit ills like those just mentioned could be eliminated only by such a drastic alteration of its structure as would destroy its positive potentialities as well. As we have seen, that structure provides the foundation for the immeasurable benefits that enrich human life, and that on balance probably outweigh its evils. Ronald W. Hepburn, in discussing the ambiguities of nature, suggests that some evils may be unavoidable if good is to be attained. If the tubercular bacillus or the polio virus is cited as evidence of the callousness or indifference of nature to all values, the reply can be made: "But without these natural conditions, without just those evolutionary mechanisms, no intelligent life or purpose or awareness of beauty would ever have been possible."[4]

From the standpoint of theistic faith, the harm that can befall human beings because of the fixities of nature could readily suggest that God is indifferent to, or at least neutral toward, human welfare. On the contrary, it might be sounder to regard these uniformities of nature as expressions of God's concern for human life—and possibly of his interest in other ends that may be unknown to us. The evidence suggests that we might speak more appropriately of divine impartiality than of indifference. According to Jesus, it is because of God's good will for all his children that he "makes his sun rise on good and bad alike, and sends the rain on the honest and the dishonest" (Matt. 5:45). The uniform operations of the natural order do not take into account the deserts of those affected by them. The benefits and the difficulties they entail touch the lives of all.

This characteristic of the natural order sheds some light on the problem of the inequitable distribution of suffering noted in chapter 7. Paul F. Andrus has wisely suggested that undeserved suffering seems to be distributed at random, according to the laws of chance and probability, which have no reference to the merits or demerits of the persons involved.[5] Inevitably, therefore, some are called on to endure more than others, but this does not mean that they are being punished for their sins or have been singled out for special discipline.

177

It means rather that they are experiencing the results of impartial provisions through which a good God seeks to safeguard the well-being of his creatures. The evils they undergo are not specifically willed by God for them as particular individuals in particular situations. Rather they are incidental by-products of an order that may therefore in the broad sense be regarded as purposed by God.

Ian Ramsey reaches somewhat similar conclusions, though on a more limited scale. He doubts the capacity of finite minds to make objective statements about reality as a whole or without temporal restrictions. However, we can utilize "super-models" to bring together "good" and "evil," *here and now,* "in terms of a consistent story." We can then use this supermodel, suitably qualified, to speak intelligibly of God. One such model is that which utilizes our need of a constant background, a dependable order, if we are to carry out any effective moral education. We cannot train children to be punctual in school attendance if we never know when classes begin. Likewise, we can see the importance of a general feature of the universe according to which the outside of a sphere cools more quickly than the inside, with resultant strains producing cracks and tremors. Without this feature the outside of our food would be cool enough to eat only when the inside was so cool as to be inedible. Hence a supermodel concerned about moral education always joins features that on the one hand are morally commendable and on the other disastrous. "Good and evil are brought together within a supermodel which has our moral approbation." However, it is logically necessary that such a model be used with "a total commitment to the Universe" that enables us to respond with "soul, life, and all." The problem of evil is resolved only when our manner of speaking carries with it the wholehearted acceptance of a stable, dependable order enabling us "to struggle with and overcome the evil from which the problem began." In short, if we take the model seriously enough to act on it, we both deal effectively with the evil and justify our model in theory.[6]

Insistence on the need for a determinate natural order with its vast potential for harm to sentient creatures—whether it is taken objectively or as part of a consistent supermodel in Ramsey's sense—arouses in some skeptical minds a fundamental question:

Why should God create, or be construed as creating, a world in which so many evils are unavoidable? David Hume, after listing "the conducting of the world by general laws" as one of four circumstances that produce most ills, declares: "This seems nowise necessary to a very perfect being. . . . Might not the Deity exterminate all ill, wherever it were to be found; and produce all good, without any preparation or long progress of causes and effects?" [7] Other skeptics since Hume have raised similar questions. Granted that our susceptibility to pain contributes to successful living in a material environment, and that the stable order in which we are vulnerable to suffering enables us to realize the higher values of human culture, why should it be necessary to attain goods only in the arduous and often agonizing ways required? Could not an infinitely wise and powerful God have created a world with an entirely different structure, one in which achievement would not be so costly? What has been said about constancy is true of the world as given, but could not God have contrived a kind of world in which life would not confront such pervasive threats of tragedy—one possessing only positive potentialities?

From the perspective of faith in God, four main answers to this question may be given.

1. It may be held that we face here an inexplicable mystery. We may wish that reality could be remolded nearer to our hearts' desire but admit that we cannot conceive how that might be done. We know that no one human mind is wise, strong, and good enough to accomplish such a feat, and our experience with committees of experts offers scant hope that group planning could achieve it. Therefore, the path of wisdom is to accept the world that God has given us, rejoicing in the opportunities it presents for creative growth and using our God-given capacities to reduce and overcome the evils that occur.

2. In the spirit of the Irenaean tradition, we may reply that the question whether a better world might not have been created prompts another question: Better for what? If God's purpose in creation is the fashioning of souls, it may well be that the world we have is better adapted to that intention than any other. Thus John Hick suggests that "the kind of goodness which, according to Christian faith, God desires in His creatures, could not in fact be created except through a long process of creaturely experience in response to challenges and disciplines of various kinds." A world designed for this end would have to resemble our present world in operating on general laws and hence involving some suffering for sentient creatures.[8]

3. It can be maintained that the demand for a different world-structure is obviated if we rethink the meaning of divine omnipotence. We should bear in mind, of course, that mainstream Christian theology does not maintain that an all-powerful God can do the nondoable or the irrational, or that he can act in ways contrary to his own character, but rather that he can accomplish whatever he wills. However, some thinkers today defend a more moderate conception of omnipotence, meaning by the term simply that God has all the power there is and all the power he needs ultimately to fulfill his purposes in creation.

At the very least, such power is consistent with divine self-limitation. As George F. Thomas asserts, for God "to create natural beings with definite properties and to give them the power to act constantly in accordance with these properties in order to carry out His purpose is to limit His exercise of His power but only in order to give effect to His will."[9] Alfred Noyes goes farther to suggest that "it may be impossible, even for Omnipotence, without some fundamental self-contradiction, to evolve a race which, ignorant of suffering and unacquainted with grief, should also achieve the heights and sound the depths of intellectual and spiritual life."[10] Philosophers like Edgar S. Brightman and Peter A. Bertocci go still farther to postulate an impediment or recalcitrant factor within the eternal nature of God that sometimes interferes with the complete fulfillment of his perfectly good will.[11] If one interprets omnipotence in such ways as these, then one may consistently maintain that a world much like the determinate order we know may be unavoidable.

4. To demand a different kind of world in order that human beings may have a less dangerous environment may involve an unjustifiably anthropocentric view of reality. Though the realization of high values by human beings may have an important place in God's creative intention, to view the natural world solely as a means to that end involves too narrow a conception. "There is no reason to suppose," writes Thomas, "that God has no other purpose for the natural order than to provide a suitable environment for the realization of moral personality by man.'' It seems more likely that other kinds of creatures, especially living organisms, have their own worth and their place in the divine purpose, rather than existing only as means to human ends.[12] Furthermore, the vastness of the physical universe indicates the probability of the existence of forms of life and consciousness unknown to us earthlings, hence the need of seeing our human concerns in the broadest possible perspective. This does not require us to surrender the validity of the only values we can know, but it should deter us from sweeping judgments based on our too limited knowledge.

As a response to Hume's question, recognition of the element of mystery is both necessary and insufficient—for the same reasons as those pointed out in the broader context of chapter 3. The positive values of the other three suggestions will be developed in the remainder of this chapter.

The World in God

Further light may be shed on the significance of regularity in nature for the problem of evil if we examine more closely the relation of God to the physical order. Hume's criticisms of belief in God because of the pervasiveness of suffering presuppose in the main a deistic conception. According to this view, the deity is external to and detached from the world; he creates it and sets it in motion but governs its operations from the outside. Likewise, the God rejected by many atheists has been conceived as a being above or beyond the region of natural and human existence, yet ruling it by his arbitrary will. Much popular understanding of God's relation to evil seems to imply a similarly exaggerated conception of the divine transcendence and a correspondingly mistaken conception of human beings as aliens in an indifferent cosmos, squatters on territory where they don't belong.

The position espoused in the foregoing discussion affirms instead a profoundly intimate interrelationship between God and his world. The Creator is not a sculptor fashioning a statue or a cobbler making a shoe; he is rather the Spirit who informs and interpenetrates his creation from within, so that it depends at every moment on his energizing activity. He is the ground of all being and becoming, the matrix of all cosmic reality. So closely is he identified with nature and human life that Charles Hartshorne can declare that ultimately there is only one sphere of action, "this-world-in-God." He is "the Life in and for which all things live."[13]

This emphasis on the closeness of God and the world in creation is at least as old as the New Testament. The prologue of the Fourth Gospel declares that *through* the Word all things came to be (John 1:3); and the apostle Paul, recognizing that creation is a continuing process, reminds the Athenians that God is not far from any one of us, "for in him we live and move, in him we exist" (Acts 17:28). The Statement of Faith of the United Church of Christ (U.S.A.) makes creation contemporary as well as past by using the present tense:

> He calls the worlds into being,
>   creates man in his own image,
>   and sets before him the ways of life and death.

Such self-conscious acknowledgment of the fact that creation is constantly going on could do much to dispel false notions of an external relation between God and his world. God, says Whitehead, "is not *before* all creation, but with all creation."[14] Actually, both prepositions are appropriate—whether or not we conceive of creation as beginning in time. God is before the world: he is that on which it continuously depends and without which it could not be. His priority need not be chronological if it is seen as constitutively causal. But this is also to say that his creative activity is with the world, dynamically interfusing it in all its aspects. More important than regarding God as literally the originator of the world in time is recognizing him as its ultimate ground, its indispensable enduring source.

Paradoxically, to regard God as interpenetrating the world is one way of asserting that he transcends it. We may still affirm more traditional notions of transcendence, conceiving God as other than and distinct from the world rather than identical with it. We can also hold that he immeasurably surpasses his creatures in power, wisdom, and goodness, eliciting experiences of ineffability, awe, and reverence as well as of finite limitation. Beyond these meanings, however, divine transcendence implies the very relationship we have been affirming—that God underlies and activates all finite reality, which owes its fundamental structure and motivating power to him. His creative love sustains it and gives it its meaning. In this context, it may also signify that God is the ground of our hope and the promise of our future, going before us to open up possibilities exceeding anything so far attained. As the source of the prospective character of human existence, he is encountered in the goals he places before us and the support he provides on our journey. In ways like these God both permeates and transcends the world.

Now, what bearing does this understanding of the God-world relation have on the propensity of a natural order operating according to constant patterns to occasion suffering in sentient creatures, and on the allied question of whether God might have created a different kind of universe with less likelihood of pain? Both questions seem to imply an external relation between the Creator and his creation, as though God from the outside decided what kind of world he would bring to reality. In this clouded area finite minds dare not speak with dogmatic assurance, but in the search for greater understanding a reflective venture may be in order. Perhaps we stand here in the presence of something ultimate, beyond which we cannot probe. The nature of the world reflects the character of him who is the ground of its being and becoming. The cosmos is what it is because God is what he is. Its laws are his ways of acting. To ask why he "planned" the world as he did or why he doesn't organize it differently is to raise a question that is inappropriate to the given situation. It is somewhat like inquiring why God is wise or why he acts in love rather than indifference or hate. The phenomenal order provides some clues to the Logos that informs and permeates it; they are indistinct and often enigmatic to be sure, but they are what we have to work with in our quest for truth, and they do tell us something about the ultimate nature of reality. It is to this reality, not to another that we might imagine more favorable, that we are related.

For Christian faith, the normative formulation of the self-expression of God in his creation is the doctrine of incarnation, although it has not always carried the broad connotations here suggested. According to Whitehead, "the world lives by its incarnation of God in itself."[15] The term as used here obviously includes all the manifestations of God in the universe, not only that in the life of Jesus Christ. However, there is no reason to suppose that the embodiment of the divine in a particular historical life must exclude other disclosures, or that God's supreme manifestation in Christ must negate other expressions of his creative and redemptive activity. The incarnation in Jesus Christ, writes Origen, was "not a sudden intervention of a God hitherto negligent. . . . For nothing good has happened to men except by the indwelling of the Divine Logos." [16]

Biblical support for the truth of Origen's statement is not lacking. The psalmist declares:

> The earth is the Lord's and all that is in it,
> the world and those who dwell therein.   (Ps. 24:1)

In the Fourth Gospel the Word who became flesh and "came to dwell among us, . . . full of grace and truth," is the same Word through whom "all things came to be" (John 1:3, 14). Likewise, the apostle Paul proclaims that the God who is revealed in Christ as our deliverer from sin is he through whom and for whom "the whole universe" has been created. "And he exists before everything, and all things are held together in him" (Col. 1:14-17).

Among the marvelous mosaics of Ravenna is the great mosaic in the apse of St. Apollinaris in Classe, consecrated about 550 A.D. In the upper center the Christ is represented by a large cross, above which is the hand of God. The three disciples who witnessed the Transfiguration (Matt. 17:2; Mark 9:2) are portrayed as lambs grazing beneath the cross. Below, filling the remaining wall area, is a glade, with St. Apollinaris lifting hands in prayer, while around him are many examples of plant and animal life: grass, lilies, roses, daisies, rocks, shrubs, trees, birds, and sheep. The symbols of the presence of God are one with the representations of nature that surround them. The scene is idyllic, with noteworthy omissions: there are no tigers, grizzly bears, poisonous reptiles, or insect pests. But the artist seems to be saying that the same God who is incarnated in the cross of Christ is manifest in the rest of his creation.

To conceive that the eternal Spirit whose redemptive love acted incomparably in a particular person also works creatively throughout the natural and historical orders both heightens and lightens the problem of evil. It does the former because if the whole world is

God's deed, its occasions of suffering no less than of joy somehow fall within his responsibility. Yet it also lessens the problem, because it portrays him as directly and intimately involved in the anguish of his creatures. For Christian faith, God is indeed incarnate in a world that contains agonizing evils, but he is supremely manifested in one whose suffering love opens the way to victory over evil.

The Travail of Evolution

On the surface, the emphasis we have laid on constancy, stability, and regularity in the natural order might support the inference that our world is one of changeless fixity. On the contrary, the frequent use of terms like becoming, process, energizing activity, and the realization of values, as well as explicit references to development and an evolving race, clearly imply that human life is an outgrowth of and a participant in a dynamic evolutionary movement. Evidence is overwhelming that our complex world is the result of an inconceivably long process of cosmic, planetary, and biological evolution.

The opening chapter of Genesis and the results of scientific investigation alike picture a universe that has moved from primeval formlessness or chaos to orderliness and diversified life—from simplicity to differentiation. Evidences are all around us today. The child grows into the adult. The higher habitually develops out of the lower, fuller existence out of emptier. Amazingly complicated inventions emerge from humble beginnings and reach fulfillment only through increasingly difficult experimental procedures involving painstaking trials and often baffling errors.

We live in an unfinished world, one that is still in the making. It looks more like a vast experiment than a journey following a rigidly prearranged schedule. It is a universe constantly coming to birth, a process always under way, again and again bringing forth new emergents.[17]

The evolutionary character of life serves to reinforce what has been said about the need for regularity and constancy in the world, and the detrimental as well as beneficial results of this circumstance. A stable order is necessary if genuine evolution is to take place; otherwise change would be haphazard and directionless. The occurrence of sudden interventions or special providences, necessarily entailing unpredictable variations in the properties of elements and compounds, would make orderly evolutionary development impossible. This seems to be especially true on the higher levels; the growth of persons as realizers of value depends in part on cause-and-effect relations and other interconnections that can be counted on.

For the present, however, our concern is to emphasize the reality of dynamic movement and its implications for the problem of evil. Stability there is in our world, but it is not the equivalent of dead-level fixity; it is the necessary *context of* rather than a *barrier to* change. The change is ceaseless, but it is also evolutionary; that is, it is not completely fortuitous, but in its broad sweep registers advances from relatively undifferentiated simplicity to richer and more varied complexity. Now, in two respects, this kind of process would lead us to expect difficulties. First, if evolution involves movement from relative disorganization to higher levels of differentiation, it should not be surprising if any stage manifests forms of incompleteness and deficiency that sentient beings would regard as frustrating and therefore evil. In the process of becoming, some kind of lack or imperfection must be removed before a more advanced level can be attained; an existing form must be broken and a new one created. Any level short of the highest—and any "highest" may be itself superseded by a new possibility—entails features needing to be overcome. On the human level, for example, the evolution of moral life requires the adoption of new modes of action; to become better means to break an earlier form of good. Secondly, if the process is not simply the unfolding of previously determined potentialities, it may involve unanticipated exigencies that bring pain to the sentient creatures affected. If it is genuinely experimental, it may lead into blind alleys, producing species permanently locked into the stage they have reached and other species incapable of survival, hence requiring the retracing of steps. It may involve its participants in precarious struggle. There will be no automatic progress and no escalator carrying passengers safely to the heights.

Such expectations are amply justified by the empirical evidence. On all sides are indications of the prodigality and wastefulness of nature, ever jealous of the species and careless of the individual. Writing this in mid-spring, I am aware that most of the peepers and the tadpoles in the nearby marsh cannot possibly survive, that the vast majority and the innumerable minnows soon to be hatched in Lake Wequaquet will quickly fall prey to larger fish, that many of the ducklings shortly to hatch in seemingly secure inlets will be killed by turtles and other predators, and that the dandelions that are temporarily beautiful will soon scatter millions of seeds—to the despair of gardeners who will not readily believe that more are eaten by birds than germinate in their lawns.

In these days of heightened environmental concern, we hear much of aquatic and terrestrial ecosystems, of food chains, of the food webs or cycles in which local food chains are intertwined, and of species endangered by human manipulation or other factors. The *Encyclopaedia Britannica* defines a food chain somewhat euphemistically as "the sequence of energy transfer from organism to organism in the form of food." [18] What this means, of course, is that organisms live on each other, from plankton all the way up to human beings. In a predator chain, plant-eating animals are eaten by larger animals, and they in turn are eaten by larger, stronger, or more cunning animals. Predation operates to balance rather than unbalance populations, the dynamics of which are geared to a high loss-rate among the very young and the sick and aged. Without these interlocking relationships, which bring death to untold millions of unfortunate individuals, life could not continue on this planet. After all is said that can be said about a lower sensitivity to pain among the less developed forms of life, it cannot be denied that a huge amount of suffering is involved, as anyone can attest who has had opportunity to observe terror-stricken animals trying to flee from attackers or threatening forest fires. Widespread pain in the animal world seems to be an inevitable condition of organic evolution.

Another cost of evolution results from the occurrence of chance mutations in the process of natural selection. These are changes that have no relation to the needs of the organism at the time. Chemically, mutation of the gene occurs when, very rarely and apparently accidentally, the DNA molecule that constitutes the gene is not exactly reproduced. Such mutations demonstrate that evolution does not proceed deterministically, and they are the source of all useful advances, including the emergence of human beings with their remarkable capacity for individual and cultural achievement. But they also produce many injurious results. Genetically harmful genes, like favorable ones, are preserved in the genetic constitution of the organism. Through this accumulation, each individual is born with a genetic heritage that, on the human level, accounts for both genius and imbecility. Gene mutations are responsible for hemophilia and many other diseases, congenital idiocy, and premature death.[19]

Further potentiality for both good and evil appears in cultural evolution. Societies as well as individuals and species are involved in a long ongoing process—or, more accurately, many processes in different regions and times—of change. *Homo sapiens* emerged probably during the late middle Pleistocene epoch, approximately two hundred fifty to one hundred thousand years ago. The ability of human beings to communicate in full writing is no more than five thousand years old, and other developments essential to advanced civilization are comparably recent. Hence it is hardly surprising that human societies today exhibit patterns of conduct that are still far short of norms acknowledged by their most enlightened members.

A fitting summary of the costliness of evolutionary creation is provided by Teilhard de Chardin:

> Looked upon experimentally at our own level, the world is an immense groping, an immense search, an immense attack; it can only progress at the cost of many failures and much pain. The sufferers, whatever the reason for their suffering, are the reflection of this austere yet noble condition. They do not constitute elements that are useless or diminished. They are simply the parts that pay for the progress and triumph of the whole. They are soldiers who have fallen on the field of honor.[20]

The struggle, tragedy, and pathos of the evolutionary process must be taken with utmost seriousness in any thinking about God that regards him as Creator and Sustainer of the world we know. On the whole, the evidence does not indicate the design of a placid engineer, who knows in advance exactly what he wants and proceeds with unvarying assurance to actualize it, so that the result is precisely what he intends. There is in the process little to warrant the traditional notion of a God who can bring into existence whatever he wills whenever he wills it, or of a remote Absolute unaffected by the temporal events he sets in motion. Anyone who is sensitively aware of the pain and anguish of the processes that make life possible can hardly fail to respond sympathetically to the judgment of William James: "A God who can relish such superfluities of horror is no God for human beings to appeal to."[21] With full regard for the limitations of human knowledge and perspective, it is difficult to think of the wastefulness and cruelty of the evolutionary process as deliberately chosen by God.

Such an interpretation is of course possible in spite of its difficulties. The evolutionary order may be seen as willed by God as the best means and the unavoidable condition for the creation of free moral persons. It is intended, not as a statically perfect Paradise designed for comfort and unalloyed happiness, but for moral growth, the making of souls. We have examined this interpretation in chapter 7, noting in it positive values but also serious weaknesses. Conceivably an alternative may be found that preserves its advantages while avoiding its defects.

The most hopeful option, it seems to me, is that of attempting to reconceive the meaning and scope of divine power. It is not self-evident that omnipotence as traditionally understood must be attributed to God—especially if the empirical data support modification. We have already suggested that the all-powerfulness of God may be taken to mean that he possesses all the power there is and all he needs to achieve his ends. This need not imply absolute power.

The evolutionary evidence indicates that God is striving to bring into existence a world in which high values can be increasingly realized; moreover, that through vast toil and suffering, he is accomplishing this purpose. The data of experience also suggest that it is impossible for him to attain his goals without strenuous, long-continued effort. Perhaps something in the very structure of his being is at the heart of this impossibility. May we not be here in the presence of something ultimate, a reality that simply is what it is, however much we might wish it were different? Possibly there is in God an eternal aspect or depth of being that corresponds to the ultimate mystery of freedom described by Berdyaev: it is "abysmal, without foundations, inexplicable, non-objectifiable."[22] Implicit in God's very nature is the need to struggle to accomplish his purposes.

He does not and cannot exercise unlimited, absolute power because there is no such power. God is indeed seeking to bring forth a world of persons capable of growing realization of high values in fellowship with one another and with him, but his character—the ultimate nature of reality itself—is such that his creative activity requires arduous, costly, painful effort.

Something like this understanding of God seems implied in the central Christian doctrine of the Incarnation. If God is really embodied in his world, and superlatively in the Man of Nazareth, the life, death, and resurrection of Jesus Christ as recounted in the New Testament disclose something in the nature of God himself. What do they tell us?

For one thing, the New Testament writings make plain that creation is not finished. When criticized for healing on the sabbath, Jesus replied, "My Father has never yet ceased his work, and I am working too" (John 5:17). Work means energy expended to actualize something not yet real, or to modify something that already exists, and the implication here is that God is engaged in a laborious process of creation and salvation that is still going on. That it will continue and find consummation in the future is implied by the eschatological faith of the early church that the Christ would "come again," by the portrayal in Revelation of one who is always making the world anew (Rev. 21:5), and by the expectation of the coming of the kingdom of God. Similar portrayals of a God who is himself on the way are found in the stress laid in the Hebrew Bible on the action of God in delivering his people from bondage and leading them through the wilderness to the land of promise. The God of the sacred writings of Israel is not a static potentate, but one who defines his name to Moses as "I will be who I will be" (Exod. 3:14).

Moreover, the biblical accounts portray the creative and redemptive work of God as requiring sacrificial effort. If Jesus Christ is our model of God, divine power must be thought of, not as omnipotent coercive force, but as the power of suffering love disclosed in the cross. Remembering that Jesus' self-forgetful love was directed toward the reconciliation of sinners with God, we might easily infer that his action reveals a God who suffers only because of moral evil. However, this conclusion was not drawn by Paul, greatest of all the first-century evangelists, who affirms his own incarnational faith in classic manner when he asserts that "God was in Christ reconciling the world to himself" (II Cor. 5:19). He apparently believed that the anguish displayed in God's redemptive action in Christ also enters into God's creative work. Thus he writes to the Christians in Rome, "Up to the present, we know, the whole created universe groans in all its parts as if in the pangs of childbirth" (Rom. 8:22-23). Indeed, the natural order itself needs liberation as well as creation: "The universe itself is to be freed from the shackles of mortality and enter upon the liberty and splendour of the children of God" (Rom. 8:21-22). God's self-revelation in Christ is not an intrusion but a fulfillment of his labor in the natural order, and in both cases his loving concern for his world involves profound travail. Thus L. Charles Birch is making a quite justifiable connection with the New Testament when he writes that evolutionary studies reveal a "cross pattern deeply woven into the very fabric of creation." [23] The nature of reality is such that God himself, its ground and meaning, dies in order to live.

As we survey the costliness of creation, we may be tempted to ask why God does not actualize the possibilities of the universe all at once. Conceivably, he could have done so, but he chose instead the slow, agonizing journey of evolution as the best way to achieve his purpose. Many theologians support this view, but both the divine goodness and the nature of the evolutionary process itself, with its experimental, mutational features and its immense cost, suggest the greater reasonableness of the alternative proposed. Because ultimate reality is what it is, because God is who he is, the world with its potential for value fulfillment does not come into existence ready-made; it can be actualized only through experiences akin to what we know as hazardous, painful striving. [24] If this is true, the following words of Birch offer an accurate description:

> At each stage of the creative process, there are limitations on what can be actualized in the immediate future. The opportunities are limited by what has already been achieved. The existence of man was not a possible immediate step following the origin of the first "living molecule." One stage builds on the previous one to create a continuum. The rivers of creativity do not cut arrows direct to the sea, but wind their way by a long and sure route. As well might we ask why a child does not come into the world as a physically and emotionally mature

man. That would be to deny the very nature of creation which is spontaneity of response, purpose, struggle, and achievement.[25]

Awareness of the need for a dependable natural order functioning according to regular patterns, which a good God will not set aside even though it occasions hardship when orderly processes are violated, contributes substantially to our comprehension of suffering. Especially when nature is seen as a creative evolutionary process that includes the formation of persons for fellowship with God and each other in the realization of values, and when this process is seen to involve travail for God as well as his creatures, important light is shed on the problem of evil. These suggestions are not in themselves adequate, and they need to be supplemented by the exploration of other proposals, but they do help to advance us toward the understanding we seek.

9 Freedom—Perilous Gift

In 1970, twenty-five-year-old Michael Mullen was killed in Vietnam when an American artillery shell fired during night practice fell short of its target and hit him and one other sleeping U.S. soldier.[1] In 1973, a jumbo jet crashed near Paris, killing 345 persons, because the plane became unmanageable when a cargo door blew off; the airline, though amply warned of the danger, had failed to redesign the door. These events, along with the maiming of a child by a reckless driver, the torture of political prisoners, the harassment of Martin Luther King, Jr., by the F.B.I., and the murder of 6 million Jews by the Nazis, have in common the fact that they are traceable to human agency—the errors, carelessness, or malevolence of human beings. They are not attributable to the forces of nature, nor can they be ascribed to the divine will, except to the degree that God creates people capable of such actions. Tom O'Connor, a South Carolina newspaper publisher, wrote of another death in Vietnam:

> I cannot accept my son's death as a matter of God's will. I must reject a God who would create so well and then purposely destroy. The God I reverence is a God of creation. My son was destroyed, I am afraid by me and by you and by man's will, denying the will of God.[2]

Such occurrences call attention to another major proposal for solution of the problem of suffering—recognition of the important part played by freedom. It is widely held that at least limited freedom is essential to the existence and fulfillment of life on a truly personal level, but that this provision inevitably leads to suffering when freedom is deliberately, carelessly, or ignorantly misused. Since the validity of the argument of this chapter depends on the soundness of this double supposition, the question of whether free will is a reality must be faced at the start.

Are Human Beings Really Free?

Few philosophical or theological issues have elicited more controversy or a greater volume of intricate discussion than the problem of human freedom. Philosophically, it has centered in opposition between freedomism and some form of determinism, usually mechanistic or psychological. Theologically, it appears mainly in conflict between those who assert the absolute sovereignty of God and the bondage of the human will to sin and those who affirm that even sinners may exercise some freedom of choice to perform or oppose the divine will. The history of religious thought exhibits many ramifications of these disputes and of the arguments offered to support the contrary theories. In the space here available it is impossible to do justice to a problem so many-sided and complex. However, for our purposes it should suffice to state as clearly as possible what freedom means in the present context, the author's position regarding it, and the grounds of his belief.

By free will I do not mean merely indeterminism, which holds that in some instances volitions are independent of antecedent causation, physiological or psychological. The decisions of the self are always related to its previous character, motives, and situation. A second possibility is to define freedom as autonomy or self-determination, decision not subject to external constraint but depending rather on the inner motives and aims of the agent. This is an important aspect of free will, but it is consistent with a necessitarianism in which the motives that determine acts are dictated by earlier intentions and desires, conscious or unconscious, though without outside interference. Inclusive of self-determination, but going beyond it, is freedom construed as the power of choice, involving the capacity of the agent to choose among possible alternatives. This understanding of free will fully recognizes the strength of environmental influences—physical and social—and the inevitable effects of one's physiological, biological, and psychological constitution, but maintains that the agent is not bound completely by any of these factors. The area of free choice is limited and sometimes nonexistent, but in many situations it is real. When in this chapter we speak of the misuse of free will as contributory to human suffering, it is freedom as alternative or contrary choice that is involved.

Are there good grounds for affirming the reality of freedom so conceived, or is such affirmation itself a delusion not open to rational control? Evidences of restrictions on our freedom are unmistakable. We are all subject to the laws of nature and its causal processes, although their functioning can be modified by human action. Historical and social circumstances drastically narrow our choices. The attitudes and actions of other people powerfully influence our own, and the cumulative effects of our past choices mold habits and characters that permit some decisions and exclude others. Mechanism is constantly at work in ways easily forgotten—in the circulatory, respiratory, and digestive processes of the human body, the motion of the hand and arm in writing, and the automatic operations performed in talking, walking, lifting, or driving a car. This is good, for if we had to control such actions at every point by conscious choice, we should have no time or energy left for more important decisions. Mechanism releases us for pursuit of the values that make life truly human. Yet there are good reasons for affirming a genuine measure of rational choice.

1. First is the plain fact that we do make choices. People express and carry out preferences regarding friends, jobs, clothes, recreation, life-styles, right and wrong, and religious faith. Many of these are largely intuitive, and intuition in itself is not an adequate criterion of truth; yet the experience of choice is real, and in the absence of convincing evidence to the contrary, it must be taken seriously. Moreover, many actions are performed for reasons thought out in advance; though some of these may be unconscious rationalizations, the burden of proof that no free weighing of alternatives occurs is on the person who makes the denial. Further, we experience many of our decisions and those of our neighbors as choices that could have been made differently. If this possibility is ruled out, all regret for unwise decisions and remorse for wrong ones become meaningless.

2. Freedom is presupposed by all intellectual activity that seeks to discover truth. In scientific inquiry, for example, every step assumes freedom of choice on the part of the scientist: as he formulates the problem, gathers data judged to be relevant, advances a hypothesis, tests the hypothesis by experiments carefully contrived, draws conclusions, rejects or modifies the hypothesis if results are negative, and finally attempts to formulate a law that accounts for all the facts. Such investigation depends on the observer's ability to weigh evidence, work out theories, learn by trial and error, retrace steps, and gradually reach results that commend themselves to other investigators. All of this activity presumes a considerable measure of freedom of thought on the part of the scientist. In less precise forms of rational inquiry, the same implication is present. Indeed, without freedom, neither truth nor error would have meaning. If we really *must* think as we do, the conclusions we reach could not properly be called true or false, but only necessary. To discover the truth or falsity of any proposition requires the ability to set up a norm and test the statement in relation to it. If every step is necessitated, we should have no way of applying the norm, hence no way of knowing whether the judgment reached was true or false.

In an incisive essay E. G. Spaulding has shown that the determinist, in the very act of attempting to convince another of the falsity of belief in free will, assumes the freedom he seeks to deny. He imagines a conversation with a psychologist friend who argues for the truth of determinism. "He endeavors to demonstrate—logically, and not psychologically—the correctness of his position, and to get me to think and to reason quite as he does; and not as I not only do think, but also as, by his own philosophy, I cannot help thinking." [3] By trying to convert his opponent, the determinist presupposes, in contradiction to his avowed theory, that the freedomist is more than the causal product of his past, that he can exercise some control over the association of his ideas, that he can perceive the logical cogency of the determinist argument, and that he can therefore reach what to him is a new conclusion. The determinist also assumes that he himself is an agent who by reasoning can change the mind of his friend. The argument is inconsistent with the determinist theory it aims to defend.

3. We confront similar difficulties when we try to make sense of the moral life without presupposing free will. Apart from freedom, our ethical distinctions would be meaningless, since they assume that one kind of conduct is better and more desirable than another and should therefore be preferred. What can *ought* or *obligation* mean if only one course of action is open? If we must act as we do act, what we do cannot accurately be called either good or bad, but simply necessary. The claims of conscience, whatever their content, imply that we have some ability to heed or deny them. The struggle they often lead to makes plain that powerful forces influence our decision, and we can rarely know how free we really are to follow one path or the other. But the guilt we feel when we go against what we regard as good is explicable only on the supposition that we should and could have chosen differently. There seems no point in commending conduct thought good or in censuring the opposite if the course followed is in fact completely determined.

4. The Christian life implies human capacity to respond freely to the love of God. Without entering into the long, involved controversy over predestination, or the doctrines of Paul, Augustine, Calvin, Arminius, and John Wesley, I can only point out the well-nigh universal assumption in Christian circles that God, particularly as disclosed in Jesus Christ, offers to men, women, and children his creative, forgiving, reconciling, life-transforming love, and that he invites them to enter the newness of life that is possible through acceptance of his offer. The evangelical appeal assumes the capacity of people to respond affirmatively or to refuse to do so. Likewise, the promise of the availability of divine strength in our efforts to live the Christian life implies that we are free to accept it and are responsible for our decision. There is here no suggestion that God exercises his sovereignty to enable some to turn to him while denying this ability to others. All are called to a relationship of trust, love, and obedience to him who is their true home. Fortunately, our practice has been more consistent with the character of God as proclaimed in the Gospel than has much of our theology. We are dependent in every moment on divine grace, but in reliance on it we are called to be co-workers with God in fulfilling his will.

There is no basic incongruity between our assertion of freedom of choice and our earlier acknowledgment of the reality of mechanism and uniform law. Dependable mechanical functioning of our bodily processes and the larger natural order is essential to human life, but without the purposive activities of minds it could not account for the most significant personal and social values. Mechanism and freedom are complementary. The relation is nowhere better illustrated than in Plato's classic passage in which Socrates discusses two kinds of causes of his imprisonment for allegedly corrupting the youth of Athens. One account might concentrate on the physiological factors, attributing Socrates' situation to the composition and interrelationships of the bones, muscles, joints, flesh, and skin of his body. He admits that without the movements of his legs and other parts of his body, he would not be there and could not execute his purposes. But to stop with this description would omit

> the true cause, which is, that the Athenians have thought fit to condemn me, and accordingly I have thought it better and more right to remain here and undergo my sentence; for I am inclined to think that these muscles and bones of mine would have gone off long ago to Megara or Boeotia—by the dog; they would, if they had been moved only by their own idea of what is best, and if I had not chosen the better and nobler part, instead of playing truant and running away, of enduring any punishment which the state inflicts.[4]

Finally, says Socrates, to say that his actions are physiologically caused, ''and that this is the way in which mind acts, and not from the choice of the best, is a very careless and idle mode of speaking.''[5]

An illuminating development of the complementarity of mechanism and choice is found in Ian Barbour's theory of levels.[6] In the human quest for knowledge there are different but complementary levels of analysis. From this standpoint, determinism and freedom are concepts in different languages. The scientist, describing a choice in ''spectator-language,'' sees it as determined, whereas first-person ''action-language'' describes it as free. For an adequate account of human experience, both languages are needed, much as in the physics of light the wave theory and the corpuscular theory, though incompatible, can both be shown to be true. However, the two-language methodology fails to account for the unity of the experience of the self.

Barbour goes beyond this methodological approach to suggest also a metaphysical concept involving two levels of organization and activity in reality. There are low-level events that can be interpreted according to the categories of atomic physics or the laws of molecular biology, and there are high-level events involving thought, purpose, and conscious choice. Between these levels there are no gaps or sharp breaks; they are best understood according to the analogy of the color spectrum. The differences they display overlap and shade into each other: indeterminacy may be present even in the atom, and human freedom is often severely restricted. Yet in a limited way the levels reflect the real structure of our world.

In such fashion we can make room for both scientific law and human freedom. Though the strict determinist might prefer a neater and tighter interpretation, he should be reminded that our view of reality must be broad enough to account for the variety and richness we actually find in experience as a whole.

Benefits and Perils of Freedom

The exercise of real freedom of choice is indispensable if men and women are to become true persons, capable of realizing the values that constitute human existence. The growth of moral character can take place only *within* individuals, as they accept responsibility for deciding between alternatives and experience the temptation to reject or ignore acknowledged norms. The intellectual life can develop only to the degree that the mind resists the pull of inertia, undertakes the hard effort required to think clearly, and distinguishes between truth and error by critically examining ideas, testing scientific hypotheses, weighing competing possibilities, and accepting those deemed most cogent. Artistic creation can occur only when the imagination is given free reign and the artist is at liberty to express his own insights in music, sculpture, painting, or words. If, as Hebrew-Christian faith affirms, human beings are made in the image of God, they can fulfill that high relationship only as they are given the capacity to respond to the divine purpose in active, uncompelled acceptance. If they are to grow in love for each other and feel the call to ethical and social responsibility, they must be able to evaluate the claims of various attitudes and modes of action and choose those that seem most in harmony with the demands of conscience. Some degree of freedom is essential for the actualization of these and all other forms of the human experience of value; without it men and women would be merely robots or automata. Freedom is therefore a priceless gift.

However, it is also a perilous gift. The person who can freely elect the right may likewise choose the wrong. The individual who is capable of thinking truly may also fall into error. The artist may fail to develop his or her native talents. The image of God may be badly blurred or distorted. The claims of conscience may be rejected in selfish irresponsibility. All of these misuses of freedom, whether careless or intentional, lead to destructive and sometimes disastrous consequences for all the people involved. We cannot enjoy the benefits of freedom without risking the anguish we ourselves experience when we abuse it as well as the unmerited suffering we cause for others affected by our wrong or unwise choices. In the words of Charles Hartshorne,

> The creaturely freedom from which evils spring, with probability in particular cases and inevitability in the general case, is also an essential aspect of all goods, so that the price of a guaranteed absence of evil would be the equally guaranteed absence of good. . . . Risk of evil and opportunity for good are two aspects of just one thing, multiple freedom.[7]

The same truth is expressed in a different way in a perceptive novel by Hannah Green. The main character, Deborah, is baffled by emotional problems, and enters a mental hospital for therapy. In one session, her psychiatrist, Dr. Fried, calls on her to face reality:

> Look here, I never promised you a rose garden. I never promised you perfect justice, . . . and I never promised you peace or happiness. My help is so that you can be free to fight for all of these things. The only reality I offer is challenge, and being well is being free to accept it or not at whatever level you are capable. I never promise lies, and the rose-garden world of perfection is a lie . . . and a bore, too.[8]

With one exception, the therapist's counsel states accurately the terms on which all human beings are addressed by reality, or by God. The exception is that even a rose garden is not the problem-free paradise envisaged by the metaphor! My own experience in growing roses during the past six years has taught me that though the rewards in fragrance and colorful beauty are great, they occur only as the gardener uses his freedom to fertilize, water, mulch, prune, and combat insects, black spot, and mildew. Thus the rose garden is a better analogy for the benefits and dangers of existence in freedom than it is for the pleasant utopia that Hannah Green wisely warns us not to expect.

It would be easy to overlook another negative aspect of our cherished freedom—what Paul Ricoeur calls its fateful character. Often it involves choices that are neither sinful nor carelessly made, but that inevitably exclude other options of genuine worth. In the process of realizing possibilities, we rule out other possibilities that, if chosen, would become actual; thus we deny existence to, or destroy, the rejected options, which may be in themselves altogether commendable. Thus the intensity of love and close friendship can be enjoyed with only a small number of persons, and it inevitably restricts realization of "the breadth of universal solidarity." Another example cited by Ricoeur is that "it is not possible for me to aim at completeness without running the risk of losing myself in the indefinitely varied abundance of experience or in the niggardly narrowness of a perspective as restricted as it is consistent."[9] Other instances come readily to mind: the choice of a college, a lifework, or a place of residence rules out other alternatives (with the distinctive and perhaps equally rich experiences they might afford), as well as their potentialities to society. This circumstance reminds us that vast numbers of people have almost no opportunity to make such choices, and this absence of freedom carries with it its own brand of anguish.

As in chapter 8, in considering freedom also, we need a sound understanding of the meaning of divine power. From the structure and functioning of the created order we can perhaps justifiably infer that the Creator operates according to ultimate principles broadly consonant with the norms of reason as we know them. If so, the laws of identity, contradiction, and excluded middle hold for him, not because he is bound by rules external to him, but because such criteria are inherent in his very being. Just as he cannot make a spherical cube, he cannot create a world in which his rational creatures are both free to choose the right and incapable of wrong. If he determined their thoughts and actions for them, they would not be moral agents but marionettes possessing no intrinsic worth. God sets the abstract limits within which persons function, but within these limits he sets them free to make their own decisions, incorporating in his universe the results of their actions and thereby giving them permanent meaning. These provisions involve dangerous risks—for God as well as for his creatures. As Leslie Dewart asserts, "History is so free that we can actually crucify God; we can actually deny Him; we can, in a way, make Him not to exist."[10] But only through such risks can God bring into being a fellowship of shared values.

Pertinent here is the distinction between primary and secondary causes made by Thomas Aquinas and others. The God who grants to his creatures a measure of real freedom remains the ultimate cause of all effects, but he works partly through secondary causes. The action of these secondary agents always depends on and utilizes the power given them by God. However, in his great goodness God communicates himself partly by giving things in the created world the capacity to share in causation. On the moral level, this entails freedom. Without it persons would not be able to love God, but it enables them to oppose God as well as serve him. Hence they sometimes fall from goodness. When they do, God regards so highly the freedom he has granted them that, instead of withdrawing it, he actually supports the process that leads from bad choices to evil consequences. In so doing he endures along with his errant creatures the harmful results of the wrong decisions he permits them to make.

Since free will involves the power of alternative choice, its significance for the problem of evil lies primarily in the area of moral evil or sin. However, it also bears on natural evil, because the extent to which events in nature affect human life often depends on human decisions. Some of these are neither right nor wrong, but ethically neutral; they are made without awareness of their bearing on the well-being of the one who makes them or other persons. The choice of one departure time rather than another for a journey may lead to either death or escape from death in a plane crash. Similarly, some of the practices in cattle raising and agriculture that have drastically increased desert areas are due partly to sheer ignorance. But much of the overtilling and overgrazing that have depleted and exposed irreplaceable soil and seriously aggravated the effects of drought is traceable to culpable desire for a quick and maximum gain, without regard for the continuing fertility of the land or the welfare of future generations. The destruction wrought by earthquakes has frequently been multiplied by structural weaknesses in buildings, due to inferior materials or shoddy workmanship. New bridges have collapsed, exacting heavy tolls in deaths and injuries, not as "acts of God," but because builders have placed profits above quality. Children die unnecessarily in fires because of the use of dangerously flammable materials in the manufacture of clothing. Thus abuse of the gift of freedom joins with natural causes to produce much of the havoc that afflicts human life.

Persistent Questions

Broad agreement that the freedom necessary for true personhood may when misused cause extreme harm still leaves questions that press for answers. Two of these must now be examined.

Does Freedom Outweigh Other Values?

Is moral freedom really so worthful that it outweighs other values like life, happiness, aesthetic appreciation, and justice, which are sacrificed when free will is allowed to run its course? This question becomes especially urgent when we realize the extremities to which human evil can go. Why must such vicious sins as those that many human beings are capable of be allowed? Why must there be so much liberty that some individuals can become thoroughly depraved? Would not its curtailment or removal ensure the richer realization of other more important values?

Seldom have the depths to which human beings can sink been more obscenely or boastfully stated than in the words of the Nazi physician to the priest Riccardo in Hochhut's drama *The Deputy:*

> Since July of '42, for fifteen months, weekdays and Sabbath, I've been sending people to God. Do you think He's made the slightest acknowledgement? He has not even directed a bolt of lightning against me. Can you understand that? *You* ought to know. Nine thousand in one day a while back.[11]

Later the doctor reports that though he challenged "the old Gent" to answer, "not a peep came from Heaven, . . . not once since I've been giving tourists tickets to Paradise." Still later he concludes: "The truth is, Auschwitz refutes creator, creation, and the creature. Life as an idea is dead. . . . Only one crime remains: cursed be he who creates life. I cremate life. That is modern humanitarianism— the sole salvation from the future." [12] The existence and power of individuals so totally lacking in moral scruples and respect for life makes unmistakably plain the immense cost of the boon of freedom. Inevitably, sensitive souls ask if the gains are worth so high a price. Even so keen a thinker as Emil L. Fackenheim, though he does not raise the question of the freedom of persons to disobey God, struggles implicitly throughout his work *God's Presence in History* with the question as to why God did not intervene to prevent Hitler's program of extermination of the Jews. The same kind of question might be raised now with regard to the possession by human beings of the power to destroy themselves and their vaunted civilization in a nuclear holocaust.

When we reflect on the bleak existence imposed on millions of people, members of minority groups, by discrimination in housing, education, and job opportunity, and by the stubborn refusal of the white majority to allow the consummation of hopes briefly aroused by the civil rights movement of the 1960s, we may well wonder whether divine action compelling justice for all might not be preferable.

Countee Cullen writes with simple directness of the lynching of a black man:

> A man was lynched last night.
> "Why?" Jim would ask, his eyes star-bright.
> "A white man struck him; he showed fight.
> Maybe God thinks such things are right." [13]

William R. Jones adds, "And God apparently thinks such things are right, because they occur repeatedly, and He does nothing to prevent them or avenge them." [14] At first sight Jones seems to imply that God should have intervened directly to thwart or punish the lynchers—a judgment contradictory to the "humanocentric humanism" he espouses, which affirms "the activity, choice, and freedom of man'' and removes God's "over-ruling sovereignty" in favor of God's functional neutrality in human affairs.[15] But, seen in its context, Jones's comment really states the position of belief in the "white racist God" that he rejects. I cannot share Jones's assertion of God's neutrality in human history. In effect, it denies his deity, divorcing him from the values that make life truly human, excluding any creative or redemptive relationship on his part to human existence as we know it, and leaving him merely a disinterested spectator incapable of either loving or being loved. But Jones's vigorous espousal of human freedom recognizes that the possibilities it affords bring greater worth to human life than would any denial of it, whether by an absolute Sovereign who suppressed it or by a racist God who approved it.

No racism, whether German or American or any other variety, can be justified, and the God who "created every race of men of one stock" (Acts 17:26) must be more adamantly opposed to it than any of his creatures. But we must still ask whether any truly valuable human existence would be possible without the hazardous freedom that permits even wholesale killing. Anyone who, like myself, has never had to face helplessly the cold-blooded genocidal hatred of the Nazis, the blind fury of a lynch mob, or the unbending denial of fundamental rights by the racist attitudes of a powerful majority must speak with diffidence on this issue. Yet many who have themselves borne the full brunt of oppression resulting from tragically abused freedom have not cursed God or demanded a tightly determined existence. Instead, Viktor Frankl discovered that even in the agonies of the concentration camp meaning could still be sought and found. Martin Luther King, Jr., avoided recrimination against his enemies, followed to the end the path of nonviolent love, and demonstrated its power.

It is hard to avoid the conclusion that the withdrawal of freedom to harm other human beings would make impossible the very values it would aim to foster. Without such freedom life would indeed be possible, but it would be purely vegetative existence. Specific experiences of beauty, truth, justice, and concern for other people, which supposedly would be safeguarded by lack of liberty to interfere with them, would actually be vitiated. Norms for appraising them could be neither understood nor applied. Human creativity would be eliminated. Finite persons as we know them are able to share on their level the creative work of God. Yet without the potential for free inventiveness and innovation, they would be quite incapable of truly creative achievements. Life after the pattern of a computerized print-out might conceivably make all the right motions, but it could not be a *good* life. A robot might be programmed to perform certain functions, but not to initiate purposive action. It would be unable to formulate new ideas or combinations of ideas, to propose new goals, to develop and test theories or hypotheses, or to give free rein to the imagination to produce works of art. It could never attain insights like those of Frankl's logotherapy or trailblazing movements like King's "stride toward freedom."

Could God Create Persons Wholly Good?

These latest observations impinge on another question that must now be dealt with: Might not God have created human beings wholly good, so that they would freely and invariably choose the right? Edward H. Madden and Peter H. Hare maintain that God could have given finite persons at least the *disposition* to act rightly, though they still might choose occasionally to do evil. This he has not done. In the view of C. J. Ducasse, an omnipotent and omniscient God could have conferred on all men and women "at the start" the healthy constitution, the wisdom, and the virtue needed for sound choices, so that they would not have to attain moral stature through temptation, struggle, and courageous choice of right over wrong. Antony Flew and J. L. Mackie assert the compatibility of causal determinism and free will: there is no necessary contradiction between free action and behavior that is either predictable or a "result of caused causes" or both. On this basis they argue that "Omnipotence might have, could without contradiction be said to have, created people who would always as a matter of fact freely have chosen to do the right thing." [16] However, Flew points out that this arrangement would conceive God as the Great Hypnotist, whose subjects would unknowingly and irresistibly carry out the commands given them during hypnosis. It would amount to a form of predestination, and when it is combined with the notion that God arraigns and punishes those who "freely" choose the wrong, it is morally outrageous.

Flew is therefore "inclined" to regard the whole idea of an omnipotent Creator as logically vicious.[17]

The notion that God might create all human beings so that they would always freely choose the good has a degree of credibility when it is understood after the analogy of posthypnotic suggestion. However, four considerations argue strongly against its acceptance.

1. The objections raised above because of the inability of computerized behavior to achieve true goodness or any other kind of genuine value apply equally to actions fulfilling the commands of the Great Hypnotist. It strains human imagination and intelligence to conceive of God as devoting his energies to such detailed programming of every individual life. Yet a relationship of this kind, while purely speculative, is theoretically possible. The basic difficulty is that it would destroy true goodness and the free cooperation of persons in the pursuit of shared values. Even though all participants might think they were free, they would not actually be free, and though superficially happy, they would be unable to make their own decisions or to grow in genuinely responsive relations to other persons. They would lack all intrinsic value, since all would be robots unconsciously living out their predetermined destiny in one vast and tightly organized system. They would have no capacity whatever to initiate action or to contribute creatively to society or God. No preprogrammed system could conserve or enhance the worth of the voluntary cooperation of persons in common endeavors deemed by them important. Such an arrangement would be simply the monolithic action of a dictator with many coordinated appendages. A universe of this kind, in which all activity would be in reality that of one all-determining divine will, might conceivably exclude suffering due to sin and error, but it could not approach the true values attainable and attained in the one we now inhabit.

2. True goodness cannot be implanted in persons by their Creator the way a kidney or a retina may be implanted by a skilled surgeon in a human body. Qualities like honesty, courage, strength in temptation, generosity, devotion to truth, and love for others must be forged through free choices, strenuous effort, and struggle. An automatic gearshift can be installed in an automobile by the manufacturer, and a rapid transit system can be devised that functions almost entirely without human operators. Character, however, is of another order. It cannot be bestowed or built in, but only acquired through many choices in widely varying situations. Thus a world without free will might be free of moral evil, but it would also be empty of moral worth.

3. As John Hick points out, the suggestion of Flew and Mackie regarding the creation of persons whose actions would be both free and wholly good is not valid with respect to relations between God and his human creatures. Without contradiction, human beings could be so constituted that they would always act both freely and rightly in relation to each other. But this could not apply to relations between people and the Creator who has so made them. God "cannot without contradiction be conceived to have so constituted men that they could be guaranteed freely to respond to Himself in authentic faith and love and worship." In this situation, men and women would devote themselves in love to God, but God could not value this devotion as a free and genuine response to his love, since he would know that it is the inevitable result of his manipulation of their minds. Thus in the analogy of imagined hypnosis there could be nothing approaching the mutual fellowship between God and human beings that is cherished by Christian faith.[18]

4. Running through the whole idea of free but prearranged goodness, and strengthening all of the preceding objections, is an ambiguity in the Flew-Mackie proposal brought out by Ninian Smart. If we imagine a universe like ours, except that its human inhabitants are supposed to be wholly good, "it is unclear whether the 'men' in such a universe are to be called wholly good or even good," and also "unclear whether they should be called men." If we entertain the possibility of other utopian universes quite unlike ours, these matters are even more unclear. Moral discourse has to do with our cosmic and planetary status quo, a situation in which "men" are beings of a certain kind. For example, they are subject to temptation and fear, potentially courageous and cowardly, and capable of self-centeredness and concern for others. Such experiences would have no clear content in a world where people were created entirely good. To be immunized to evil, men and women would have to be built differently. But then it would be unintelligible to ascribe goodness to them, for good and bad relate to human life as empirically known. It is therefore rational to be agnostic about the possibility of the utopian world envisaged. It is quite unclear whether it would be morally superior to ours, and no antitheistic argument can be built on the supposition that it would.[19]

For these reasons, we conclude that the notion of human beings created so that they would always choose the good is self-contradictory. If they were really free, there could be no guarantee that they would always choose rightly, while if they were so constituted as to exclude wrong choices, they would not be free. Thus we return to the situation in which men and women possessed of real freedom often abuse it, thereby causing widespread suffering.

Nonhuman Indeterminacy

So far in this chapter we have been considering human freedom, particularly in its bearing on moral evil, while assuming free activity in the creative and redemptive work of God. However, also relevant to our effort to understand suffering is the possibility of freedom on the subhuman level, as well as that of the ultimate, "uncreated" freedom postulated by Berdyaev. Both of these should be examined for any light they may shed on our problem.

Atomic Indeterminacy

As far as we know, Epicurus (341–270 B.C.) was the first thinker to affirm the presence of free causality as well as necessity in nature. Basic to his notion was the theory that motion in atoms includes not only that of falling through space in a straight line and that forced by impacts, but a third form involving free declination or swerving from a straight line. In occasional atoms occur swerves that divert the atoms from their ordinary paths; otherwise they would all fall straight downward. Epicurus believed that such movement provided the only explanation of the autonomy he had observed in animals and human beings. This reason for affirming freedom at both levels would find no support today. Nevertheless, Epicurus made an important contribution in refusing to accept a sharp division between animals that are rational and free and those that are subrational mechanisms.

Subhuman animal behavior manifests not only reaction to external stimuli but also varying degrees of internal control—though no high-level rational freedom. As organic life evolves, autonomy increases, and the range of decision widens. Charles E. Raven notes that at roughly the level of the starfish such decisions seem to become conscious and partly purposive. The life of the higher insects exhibits means of communication, learning by trial and error, and conscious coordination of effort. On the vertebrate level appear unpredictable individual variations in behavior patterns, modifications of habits, and primitive forms of value appreciation. Among mammals, conscious choices of individuals contribute significantly to their survival and their total lives.[20] As Charles Hartshorne observes, "Being an individual at all implies some scope for individual action, some freedom to close otherwise open alternatives"[21]—and, we might add, to open alternatives otherwise closed. The significance of this broadening scope of autonomous action for the problem of evil is difficult to assess. However, it obviously affects the well-being—or lack of it—of subhuman animals themselves, and it seems to have much to do with the capacity of both wild and domestic animals to influence human life for good or ill.

In the past half century, research in quantum mechanics has disclosed indeterminacy at the suborganic level. In 1927, Werner Heisenberg made public his principle of uncertainty, which states the theoretical limitations governing the constant effect on each other of certain interrelated pairs of measurable quantities in the atom, like position and momentum. Indeterminacy is such that a quantum mechanical system cannot simultaneously have both an exact position and an exact velocity. An electron is not the kind of entity to which such precise values can be attributed.

Practically all physicists now acknowledge this indeterminacy in the atom. Though some ascribe it either to the limitations of human knowledge or to the imperfection of the observer's measurements, many physicists regard it as an objective characteristic of nature itself. In this interpretation, while observable atomic events are not marked by exact causal connections, they contain many possibilities. "The act of measurement," says H. Margenau, "is a human ingression into the state of a physical system which has the consequence of calling position into being, into actuality."[22]

Similarly, Heisenberg asserts that "the transition from the 'possible' to the 'actual' takes place during the act of observation." [23] Thus the experimentation does not disturb a previously precise or determined situation but actualizes one of many existing potentialities. Atomic events are related in such a way that the range of probabilities is determined, while the particular occurrence is indeterminate and unpredictable.

If this understanding is valid, indeterminacy is objectively real in microphysical nature. However, two words of caution are important. First, uncertainty at the atomic level does not undermine the validity or the statistical accuracy of scientific laws that, as descriptions of uniform operations observed in nature, remain as accurate as before the advent of quantum theory. It is consistent with full recognition of the mechanical aspect of the physical order as well as the stability and regularity noted in chapter 8. However, it helps to account for the randomness also noted; it suggests the presence in things of an inner aspect not completely amenable to mechanical analysis; and it provides a basis for unpredictable novelty.

Second, uncertainty at the atomic and physical level is by no means equivalent to human freedom. The behavior of the electron shows not freedom but randomness. From the standpoint of physics, which one of several quantum probabilities is actualized is wholly a matter of chance, not of responsible choice. Indeterminate chance is not to be identified with free decision. However, indeterminacy in nature may be just as pertinent to consideration of natural evil as freedom is to discussion of moral evil. If real, it may help to explain some natural events that are detrimental to human life but not attributable to the divine will.

From the standpoint of the problem of evil, it is important to ask whether indeterminacy at the atomic or elementary level tends to produce a comparable uncertainty or openness in organic life. On this question the scientific evidence is somewhat ambiguous, but in the main it seems to support the possibility of such a relationship. Aloys Wenzl maintains that life events are not fully explicable in terms of mathematically formulable laws or precise laws of probability: "Perhaps the formative forces of life make use of a wide range of indetermination in the microphysical realm." In support of this view Wenzl cites the experience of decisions that are "not unequivocally determined by the situation," and specifically moral experiences such as those having to do with responsibility, freedom, shame and remorse, and guilt and expiation.[24]

J. Langmuir suggests that atomic events may sometimes lead to biological indeterminacy through a chain reaction that, initiated by an elementary occurrence, results in macrophysical and biological changes, sometimes catastrophic in nature. In such phenomena, "a single discontinuous event (which may depend on a single quantum change) becomes magnified in its effect so that the behavior of the whole aggregate" depends on "something that started from a small beginning."[25] Illustrations cited by Langmuir include freezing of supercooled water triggered by a minor disturbance, the development of a thunder storm or a tornado from a very small beginning, and the origin of species in the evolutionary process. Other biologists, as reported by Ian Barbour, affirm the possibility that at critical neural junctions in the brain a few indeterminate atoms could initiate a switch in pulse-conduction patterns; while one cosmic-ray particle can alone produce an unforeseeable gene mutation, resulting during the process of growth in large-scale changes in an organism.[26]

In contrast, the biologist A. Bachem holds that Heisenberg's principle is not applicable to either physiological or psychological problems. For example, through comparison of the predominantly microphysical events of inorganic nature and the chiefly macro-physical processes on the organic level, he concludes that single elementary events play a prominent role in physics, but are not noticeable in the biology of higher organisms. He believes that even mutations are affected chiefly by properties of the genes rather than changes in genes occurring through spontaneous or artificial mutation; but in his view such a change constitutes "a disturbing event and not a formative force." Further, Bachem points out that the trigger reactions cited by Langmuir are diametrically opposite to the fundamental mechanisms on which life depends; only exception-ally do these latter fail to carry out their compensatory roles.[27]

In their implications for the problem of evil, the opinions of Bachem and those he criticizes are not far apart. All seem to agree that the fundamental life-producing processes are determinate, and Bachem no less than the others acknowledges the occurrence of disturbing and exceptional events and some organic instability traceable to atomic uncertainty. This common recognition of enough spontaneity to produce mutations and other unpredictable incidents is significant for our present discussion. Mutations are a form of indeterminacy, and without their occurrence evolution would be impossible. We are primarily concerned, not with the theoretical merits of determinism or indeterminism, but with the possible effect that even limited indeterminacy in the physical order and organic life may exert on the welfare of sentient beings. Even occasional instances of macrophysical and organic changes related to atomic indeterminacy would be sufficient to account for some of the events that cause suffering on the organic level. So little is known in this area (where uncertainty is at least as great as in the electron!) that no categorical judgments are justified. Yet such evidence as we have suggests at least the possibility that indeterminacy at the suborganic level may contribute to some of the evils to which life is exposed. In particular, it may help us to understand such ills as congenital deformity, idiocy, and susceptibility to certain diseases. Along with our previous findings on human and animal freedom, it sheds some much-needed light on the problem of suffering.

"Uncreated Freedom"

Quite different from the indeterminacy of quantum mechanics is the "uncreated" or uncaused freedom postulated in the mystical thought of Nicolas Berdyaev. Yet the two approaches are mutually supportive. Influenced somewhat by Jacob Boehme, Berdyaev affirms a primordial freedom that is "outside God," that is, prior to all creation and to all determinate being. Irreducibly mysterious, abysmal, and inexplicable, it is the "nonbeing" that has the potentiality of being; out of it God creates the world. Like the darkness in John's Prologue, it is given, but God deals with it creatively and in suffering love, and he is not overcome by it (John 1:5).

For Berdyaev, uncaused freedom comes to a focus in human existence. He attaches decisive importance to the human person, as opposed to all the impersonal aspects of the objective world that threaten it. In the context of the ultimate mystery of freedom, therefore, finite persons as well as God are freed for creative action.

God needs the uncoerced, inventive response of human beings to the divine summons. However, the same freedom that makes possible human creativity offers scope for evil. When human beings actualize the negative potentialities of nonbeing, they lose or distort their creative capacity and fall away from God. Thus evil and suffering enter their existence.[28]

Questions may be raised with respect to the irrationalism and dualistic tendencies of Berdyaev's thought. However, his hypothesis of an ultimate, uncreated, given quality in reality that cannot be further analyzed, but that is inherent in the structure of things, offers an interpretation of evil that aids human thought in its effort to harmonize the power and love of God.

Similar implications are found in contemporary process thought. Interpreting Whitehead, David Ray Griffin ascribes an "inherent power of self-determination" to the "actual entities" that compose our world. Since all entities are related, this capacity for self-causation involves also the power of other-determination. It is not a contingent feature but an ultimate principle of reality. All actualities have a measure of freedom. Hence the "occasions" that constitute the world have the "capacity not to conform to the divine purpose."[29]

If Berdyaev's uncreated freedom is located within the nature of God, and if the self-determination of entities can be kept within the context of Whitehead's "self-creative unity of the universe,"[30] these conceptions can help us to understand the travail of God's creative work as well as the depth and costliness of his love. These implications are examined further in chapter 11.

10 Interdependence, Social and Cosmic

In all that has been said in the past three chapters regarding the potential contributions of suffering to the growth of character, the impact of the regularity of nature on sentient life, and the values and dangers of freedom and atomic indeterminacy, the interconnectedness of the innumerable constituents of our world has been presupposed. This dimension of reality plays so significant a role in human experience that it merits special consideration. It exposes multitudes of persons to pain, hardship, and death, but it also opens the way to some of their highest joys. Without it, life as we know it would be utterly impossible.

Forms and Effects of Interdependence

Three forms of interconnectedness are particularly relevant to our understanding of suffering: the closely intermeshed relationships of human beings with one another, the interaction of all parts of the physical order, and the linkages binding human life to its physical and biological environment. Exploration of each of these should shed further light on our problem.

Intermeshed Human Relationships

"All of us are parts of one body," writes the author of the Letter to the Ephesians (4:25). Carrying further the same motif, the apostle Paul addresses the church at Corinth: "There are many different organs, but one body. . . . If one organ suffers, they all suffer together. If one flourishes, they all rejoice together'' (I Cor. 12:20, 26). Though human society in general does not exhibit the intimacy expected in a normative Christian congregation, it does manifest a comparable interdependence. The metaphor of the bodily organism is essentially true to the human situation.

From early childhood every human being is strongly influenced by parents, siblings, friends, teachers, and, to some degree, even by superficial contacts with others. Every individual in turn influences a myriad of other persons, partly just by existing as a member of society, even more by his or her conscious attitudes and actions. The emergence of self-consciousness, the awareness of oneself as a person, presupposes the existence of something ''other'' that is not the self. In particular it seems to require contrast with other centers of consciousness. We come to recognize ourselves as individuals only as we see ourselves over against an environment, especially a social environment. Those who for whatever reason are denied a variety of communications with other people during growing years develop more or less serious abnormalities that handicap them throughout their lives.

For good or ill, our lives are inextricably interwoven with those of other people. Tennyson's *Ulysses,* looking back over his wide-ranging adventures, recalls:

> Much have I seen and known; cities of men
> And manners, climates, councils, governments.

Then, realizing that all these experiences have helped to form the person he has become, he adds, ''I am a part of all that I have met.'' What we are as persons reflects profoundly what others have contributed to us and what we have given to them. ''No one of us lives, and equally no one of us dies, for himself alone'' (Rom. 14:7).

Moreover, our relations with other individuals and groups are not limited to our own lifetime. The lines of connection run backward into the past and forward into the future. The influence of heredity is unmistakable, and equally clear is the transmission of values from one generation to another, within families and in larger communities and cultures. Even young people who react against the values of their parents are illustrating rather than nullifying parental influence. Each generation affects the destinies of those who follow. Serious interpreters of the meaning and worth of human existence may differ regarding the continuation of personal life beyond physical death, but there can be no question about the immortality of influence.

This social solidarity makes us all vulnerable to the attitudes and deeds of other people. Our membership in communities small and large exposes us to various forms of suffering, some of them extreme. One form of pain familiar to us all is that induced simply by separation from persons for whom we care. Such suffering is inherent in the very existence of interdependent lives in a world of time and space. Whether it is caused by the temporary absence of young lovers from each other, by the finality of death, or by other forms of enforced separation, it precipitates anguish that is sometimes excruciating. The more closely our lives are bound together in mutual affection, the more painful is any event that deprives us of the company of those we love. The separation may be basically psychological or moral, as when longtime friends are parted by the emergence of deep-seated personal, ethical, social, or political differences; when a man and a woman after many years of married life face problems that they feel can be solved only by divorce; or when differences over life-styles drive deep wedges between parents and grown children.

Sometimes we suffer because of the sufferings of others. Parents agonize over children who are seriously handicapped, who do not get along with peers or teachers, become habitual users of drugs, or lose their jobs in a time of economic recession. Young people share the deep hurt endured by parents who face economic setbacks, fail to win deserved professional recognition, or struggle with seemingly incurable marital differences. Friends and relatives share the pain occasioned by illness or injury in the lives of dear ones. The familiar lines of John Fawcett portray truly the experience of all who have been united with other human beings at the deeper levels:

> We share each other's woes,
> Each other's burdens bear,
> And often for each other flows
> The sympathizing tear.

We also share one another's sins. Subtly, often unconsciously, we sometimes come to resemble our close companions. Our own natural tendency toward self-centeredness is strengthened as we observe parents, older relatives and acquaintances, schoolmates, business associates, political leaders, and others advancing their own interests and expressing their will to power. As William Temple declares, "We are, in part, reciprocally determining beings. We make each other what we are." Hence each self-centered person spreads

> an evil infection through all who come within its range of influence. This happens both positively by suggestion and negatively by repulsion. If A is self-centered, B tends to become so by imitation; but also B becomes so in self-defence. The instincts of gregariousness and of fear combine to produce the same result.[1]

Since this process is constantly going on, human society is to a large extent a "network of competing selfishnesses, all kept in check by each one's selfish fear of the others."[2] In this and similar ways we emulate or protect ourselves against the undesirable traits of others by becoming like them, thereby compounding evils that in our best moments we would want to avoid.

Probably the most glaring way in which pain is expanded and intensified through human interdependence is the infliction of suffering on those victimized by the cruelty or carelessness of others. Sometimes the solidarity is intergenerational. The enlightened conscience can no longer regard the hardships of third and fourth generations as punishment by a jealous God for the iniquity of their fathers (Exod. 20:5; 34:7); but the plain fact is that innumerable children begin life grievously handicapped because of inherited physical defects due to alcoholism or drug addiction in their parents, or they grow up intellectually, morally, or culturally deprived because of unworthy patterns of life adopted through the constant influence of families and larger communities.

Innumerable young people, through regular exposure to the perverted sex, violence, and crass materialism of TV programs, movies, and mass-circulation magazines, unconsciously absorb shallow and warped values that may permanently damage their capacity for fully human life.

One of the greatest tragedies of our time is the sufferings of millions due to the callousness of the affluent, the oppression of the powerful, and the injustice of despotic social structures. Many who loudly proclaim their loyalty to ''one nation, indivisible, with liberty and justice for all'' passively accept or actively support policies that deny both freedom and equal treatment to great numbers of blacks, American Indians, and Hispano-Americans. African majorities in Rhodesia and South Africa are kept in poverty and virtual servitude, enforced by the power of white minorities in rigidly segregated societies. In turn, those who exercise power in their own behalf suffer from the constant threat of violent uprisings and the loss of their jealously guarded special privileges. In every war, civil or international, from those which engulfed the Mediterranean world and the Middle East in ancient times to the world wars of the twentieth century, Vietnam, and Lebanon, countless men, women, and children—the little people caught in the maelstrom of events which they did not will and cannot understand—suffer loss of homes, famine, torture, and death.

So real is the oneness of humanity that even high-minded, conscientious acts aimed at the establishment of more just human relations sometimes bring unintended harm to unknown persons. Gandhi's nonviolent campaign for Indian independence brought new self-respect and improved economic status to the poverty-stricken people of his country, partly by teaching them to weave their own cloth on handlooms, but not without a boycott of British-manufactured goods that produced unemployment and hardship for textile workers in Great Britain.

In these and other ways human beings are often injured, sometimes disastrously, by the choices and acts of others to whom they are bound in an intricate network of relationships. Yet the same interconnectedness enables them to benefit immeasurably from the constructive contributions of those who share their world. All the evidence we have indicates that loosening or removing our social solidarity to prevent us from hurting one another would also destroy our ability to help one another, and so destroy the most precious values of life, as well as life itself.

Few persons indeed could survive if abandoned in the wilderness or left alone on a Pacific isle dependent entirely on their own resources. Uncounted thousands of workers have made possible the production and marketing of the materials and services that sustain life in industrialized societies—food, clothing, shelter, education, transportation, recreation, intellectual stimulus, health care, psychological counseling, religious resources. Even in agrarian cultures those who produce the necessities of life depend to a great degree on joint labor that often involves neighbors no less than families. During a year in the Philippines I was able to follow the cultivation of rice from planting to harvesting. At every stage men and women who lived on adjoining plots of land shared the hard work and the rewards, among which was the joy of comradeship and labor lightened by singing to the rhythmic accompaniment of a banjo.

A person's commitment to another in friendship or marriage always runs the risk of encountering disloyalty or infidelity, but without such dangerous commitment life would be deprived of some of its deepest satisfactions. Our close association with others makes us vulnerable to their mistakes and sins, but this very vulnerability is one of the marks of truly human existence. It is costly, but it is the necessary price of the personal and social enrichment of our life together.

Interaction in the Natural Order

The interconnectedness we have noted in human society is equally a characteristic of our natural environment. Here it is perhaps most readily observable on the organic level, particularly in organisms that exist in a mutually helpful relation to one another. The most extreme example is provided by symbiotic relationships like those between termite and protozoa, alga and fungus, or hydra and chlorella in the green hydra, where the intimate association of individuals of two different species is essential to the survival of one or both. Yet the interdependence of the termite and the protozoa in its stomach is hardly more marked than the social interdependence of ants and bees, which rely so completely on other members of their colony that they perish soon if isolated. Other forms of interaction are less crucial but nevertheless important. The pollenization of blossoms by bees that gain food for themselves in the process is well known. Eider ducks often associate with some of the smaller gulls in their nesting locations; the gulls scare off some predators, and since they increase the total of eggs available, they reduce the loss of eider eggs from predation. Ducks also make use of "houses" built by muskrats and of water channels cleared by the muskrats through reedbeds. Instances like these could be multiplied indefinitely. All of them are embraced in local food chains that in turn are intertwined in larger food webs or cycles. These are in turn integrated in aquatic and terrestrial ecosystems in which the biological organisms in a particular region interact with the physical environment to produce a balanced interchange of materials between living and nonliving components.

Such large-scale interrelationships are matched by those operative in the cells of organisms. The division of a single cell to form two cells introduces intercellular relations and leads to more complex organization. Ian Barbour points out that embryological differentiation brings into being "additional patterns of parts and wholes; the genetic endowment of a cell may allow it to develop in various ways depending on its relation to other cells."[3] Each organism exhibits hierarchical levels ranging from atom through molecule, cell, and organ to the organism itself, which is integrated by hormonic, nervous, circulatory, metabolic, and other systems. The properties of any part of the organism are intimately affected by its relation to other parts.

This intricate interconnectedness appears in the process by which the characteristics of parent cells and organisms are passed on to new cells or offspring. For example, each of the approximately one hundred trillion cells in a human body contains about one hundred thousand different genes composed of the amazing chemical, deoxyribonucleic acid (DNA). The double helix of the DNA molecule stores coded information used by the cell to sustain and duplicate itself. When sperm and egg join to form a new organism, or when cells divide, they transmit through the DNA in their genes complete instructions for producing proteins exactly like those of the parent cells. This process occurs at all organic levels, whether plant or animal. Moreover, virtually every cell contains a complete repertoire of the traits to be transmitted.[4]

What is true of organic life also characterizes the physical order as a whole. According to the theories of relativity and quantum mechanics, the universe is one complex system of interdependent factors in which the parts affect the whole and vice versa. So great is the interrelationship that Whitehead can write, "Every particular actual thing lays upon the universe the obligation of conforming to it."[5] Space, time, matter, and energy can be understood only in relation to each other. Causal interdependence is exhibited similarly by the movement of the tides, the rotation of the seasons, electrical networks, and the solar system.

A graphic illustration of ordered relatedness is found in the periodic system of chemical elements. Dmitry L. Mendeleyev's table of the 73 elements he knew in 1861 disclosed an amazing symmetry and order in the chemical constituents of the universe which later inquiry has abundantly confirmed. In the second decade of the twentieth century the order of elements in the system was found to be that of their atomic numbers, and in later years the periodic law came to be explained in terms of the electronic arrangement of atoms and molecules. When the 105 elements now known are arranged in sequence according to their atomic weight and chemical properties, they are found to bear a periodic and cyclic relation to each other. In the progression of the elements of simplest atomic structure to the most complex, the chemical characteristics of the first few are repeated at regular intervals, so that there are families of elements similar in most respects but differing in a few of their properties, depending on the electronic structure of their atoms. So closely knit is the relationship that gaps in the original chart have been filled by the later discovery of elements exactly in accord with predictions based on the periodic table.

Though the entire nonhuman world, organic and inorganic, is marked by causal interdependence, it does not seem to function by rigid mechanical necessity, like an unmanned, electrically controlled urban system of subway trains. The lines of connection are hyphenated rather than solid, and when they cross one another, they often produce important changes. Though the various sectors always influence one another, they seem to have a measure of autonomy, and as a result they sometimes interrupt or impede one another. The freedom and indeterminacy noted in chapter 9 affect significantly the mutual dependence of the entities composing the world, while being also modified by it. Hence interrelatedness may be disruptive as well as constructive.

According to Austin Farrer, there are in the physical realm many flaws that arise because of "the mutual interference of systems." The creation of a physical universe sets in motion "an infinity of forces and a plurality of systems, mostly devoid of intelligence, and acting upon one another in accordance with the limited principle incorporated in each." Such accidental interferences are inevitable in a world like ours, and some of them inflict damage that for sentient beings involved is the essential form of natural evil. Under different circumstances, any single adverse accident could have been averted, but alteration of the circumstances would have produced other accidents. "Accidentality is inseparable from the character of our universe." [6] Hence the interrelationships of the multiple activities in the physical world not only support the advancement of values but also contribute to the evils that occasion suffering. But without the intricate interconnectedness of the physical order life could not exist at all.

Total Interrelatedness and Evil

There is a certain artificiality in the division we have made between human and nonhuman interdependence. The separation is logically and methodologically defensible, but it must not be allowed to obscure the fact that the connections are, as it were, vertical and diagonal as well as horizontal. Our world is one. The lines of relationship evident in all its parts intersect one another in all directions. Just as complex as the interaction of the members of the human community with each other and with other organisms, and as the interconnections of the various parts of the physicochemical world, is the interdependence between all forms of organic life and the nonliving constituents of the physical universe.

Human cells manifest the same chemical reactions—and function according to the same genetic code—as the single-celled algae in a mud puddle. Astronomers have recently found in interstellar space some of the same chemical compounds (e.g., hydrogen cyanide and formaldehyde) as those composing the molecules of organic life on earth. Amino acids, the "building blocks" of proteins, have been identified in a newly fallen meteorite found in Australia in 1969.

Tennyson's familiar lines fitly summarize what we now know of the unity and relatedness of all aspects of living and inanimate reality, while also expressing accurately the sense of mystery evoked in us by such knowledge:

> Flower in the crannied wall,
> I pluck you out of the crannies,
> I hold you here, root and all, in my hand,
> Little flower—but if I could understand
> What you are, root and all, and all in all,
> I should know what God and man is.

Wall, flower, and humanity all belong to one whole, and to the eyes of faith they point to God and derive their sustenance from his creative activity.

However, this complex unity offers no warrant for sentimental cheerfulness. When we focus attention on the interconnections between human and nonhuman existence, we discover the same twofold potentiality that we have noted in each sphere considered separately. The interaction of part and whole—and part and part—is probably less tightly determined than on the physical level alone. But this increases the likelihood of mutual interference at the same time that it enhances the possibilities of cooperation. Utilizing the energy that radiates throughout space, millions of creatures consciously or unconsciously seek their own ends (often at the expense of a myriad of rivals), propagating, competing for nourishment and living room, and inevitably getting in the way of others engaged in the same pursuits.

Harmful as well as helpful consequences flow from the complex interactions of cells. Chance mutations often result in improvement of genes and acceleration of evolution, but abnormalities in the genes that control cell division can free cells from ordinary restraints and lead to the uncontrolled multiplication of cells and their invasion of other cells, producing cancer. Some genes behave differently in different contexts. Thus inhabitants of central Africa with the sickle-cell trait (one gene for normal hemoglobin A and one for abnormal hemoglobin S) are resistant to both malaria and anemia, but black people with the same trait in the United States often contract and die from sickle-cell anemia.[7] Thus human life finds itself both threatened and supported by the physical order and by nonhuman living creatures. Its close connections with other forms of existence provide the needed means for the expression of its creativity but likewise expose it to suffering from natural evils.

At this point our conclusions coincide with those reached in the two preceding chapters. Social and cosmic interdependence exhibits the same twofold character as that previously observed in the regularity and constancy of nature and in the freedom and indeterminacy manifest at various levels of existence. It contributes to the highest values attainable by human beings and is in fact indispensable to their attainment, but it also facilitates the infliction of injuries that impair life and impede the fulfillment of its possibilities for good. We cannot enjoy the benefits of such an order without also being exposed to its risks.

Practical Meanings

Our discussion of interdependence thus far has sought chiefly to offer a partial answer to the *why* questions raised by evil. However, recognition of the interconnectedness of human life with the rest of creation is practically as well as theoretically important. The attitudes and commitments it helps to evoke enable us to deal more effectively with suffering and its causes, and this response itself sometimes tends to diminish the theological problem. Knowledge of our oneness with all other creatures increases our sensitivity to their sufferings and arouses us to try to alleviate them. It also encourages us to see our existence as a whole—an attitude that makes suffering more manageable. Both of these responses deserve brief attention.

The Summons to Reduce Shared Suffering

Though our inescapable involvement with all other forms of existence often increases our suffering, our awareness of this involvement draws us closer to other living things and makes us more sensitive to their needs. Naturally, this result is most apparent in human relations. A major conclusion of MacLeish's drama *J.B.* is that reality offers no evidence of justice, but that human beings may nevertheless find meaning in love for each other. In the closing scene Sarah reminds her husband of their continuing mutual love. When he peers into the darkness and reports, ''It's too dark to see,'' she kisses him and replies,

> Then blow on the coal of the heart, my darling. . . .
> It's all the light now. . . .
>
> Blow on the coal of the heart
> And we'll see by and by. . . .
> We'll see where we are.

James Stephens voices the same persuasion on a broader scale:

> Naught can bind
> Man closer unto man than that he feel
> The trouble of his comrade! So we grope
> Through courage, truth, and kindness, back to Hope.[8]

Probably nothing makes us more acutely aware of our solidarity with other people than knowledge of the anguish of their lives. Moreover, consciousness of our dependence on them and their dependence on us heightens our concern when they, like us, are called on to endure suffering. The sensitive person, whether nontheistic humanist or theistic believer, expresses his identification with others in concrete acts aimed at the reduction of the world's pain. He or she cares deeply enough to struggle side by side with the lonely, the ill, the disinherited, and the oppressed in the effort to lighten their burdens, as well as to remove the causes of human misery.

Some of the most vigorous manifestations of such compassion appear in the lives of nontheistic humanists. There is an added motivation when the ties that bind human beings together are seen as the fabric of the suffering love of God. Such is the faith of Miguel de Unamuno:

There is a vast current of suffering urging living beings toward one another, constraining them to love one another, and to endeavour to complete one another, and to be each himself and others at the same time. In God everything lives, and in His suffering everything suffers, and in loving God we love His creatures in Him, just as in loving and pitying His creatures we love and pity God in them. No single soul can be free so long as there is anything enslaved in God's world.[9]

Though our consciousness of solidarity with all creation is ordinarily keener with reference to other human beings, it is by no means limited to them. Those with seeing eyes perceive their oneness with all that lives. Gratefully aware of their vast and constant debt to subhuman life, they are free of arrogance and indifference toward it. They share rather the deep regard of Wayne Leiser for all living things—itself reminiscent of Schweitzer's "reverence for life:"

> Unto us all,
> all life is given: the darkly growing mold,
> the hidden crab, the red or yellow blaze
> of roses. The bloomless house plant thirsting
> because the novelty is gone, and I grow bored.
>
> All things require
> my constant love, if I would live. The shape
> of a robin is my completion too.
>
> My gently drowsing
> coyote of a dog knows he is part of me, but I
> forget. As though I could move alone through all
> the pathways of this world, a mad and blinded czar.[10]

Most of what we have said in this chapter applies to animal as well as to human suffering. The same is true of our earlier discussions of the regularities of an evolutionary natural order, while the limited degree of freedom exercised by animals sheds further light on animal pain. But whatever theoretical answers we may give to this difficult question, there can be no doubt regarding the practical attitude required of persons who perceive truly their interdependence with the rest of the animal kingdom. Realizing that the taking of animal life is often unavoidable, they will do their utmost to hold killing to a minimum, and they will support all possible measures aimed at the humane treatment of animals, the mitigation of their suffering, and the preservation of endangered species.

We have seen that the dependence of human life on its environment extends to inanimate no less than to animate nature.

Recent advances in ecological knowledge have made unmistakably plain the disastrous results of pollution of air and water and failure to conserve soil and minerals. The unhindered filling in of salt marshes and other wetlands for factories and real estate developments not only cuts off the food supply of fishes and irreplaceably destroys the nesting sites of aquatic and land birds, but, in upsetting the balance of nature, also threatens the stability and quality of human life. Many of the worst evils experienced by human beings in recent decades are in fact traceable to their own disregard for sound conservation practices. The theological problem related to these evils is not that of reconciling their occurrence with the goodness of God, but that of human sin, and hence that of how best to curb selfishness, shortsightedness, and greed. A full recognition of our interdependence with nature therefore lays upon all human beings solemn responsibility for conserving and using wisely rather than squandering the bountiful resources of the good earth.

Our obligation to other human beings is also involved here, with respect to people now alive as well as to generations yet unborn. By what right do nations in which natural deposits of oil, coal, and minerals happen accidentally to be located arrogate to themselves claims to exclusive ownership and control? True understanding of our interrelationships with society and the natural order would lead us to regard the land and the wealth it contains, along with air and water, as part of a total community to which we and other peoples with their resources belong, with appropriate concern for such use as best serves the welfare of all.

Similar responsibility extends to our relation to future generations. They will inevitably be affected by our self-centered ignoring of their need for the same sources of sustenance as those we have enjoyed—and taken for granted. Gratitude for the gifts we have freely received from our ancestors demands that we pass them on untarnished to our descendants.

The Need to See Things Whole

A further implication of social and cosmic interdependence is the importance of seeing evil, as far as possible, in its total context. The interconnectedness of things underlines the element of positive truth in the thought of those philosophers who stress the inadequacy of our partial human perspective and conceive evil as an aspect of the good whole. We have noted the fatal difficulties in the ultimate monism ordinarily assumed in this position, but it contains a valid and valuable insight. The intricately interwoven character of reality makes it imperative that we relate the part to the whole in judging the goodness and evil of our experiences. The more data we consider and the wider our frame of reference, the truer are likely to be the conclusions we reach.

When we examine the impact of a particular event on other persons as well as ourselves, and inquire into the circumstances that caused it and its probable effect on nonhuman life and our physical environment, we may discover that on the whole it is less evil than it first appeared to be. Some years ago I reluctantly declined, for carefully considered reasons that seemed cogent at the time, a position that exerted a strong appeal. Several weeks of anguished regret ensued, though rationally I still regarded the decision as wise. A year later came an invitation to another post much better adapted to my interests and qualifications. It brought many years of deep satisfaction that I could never have had if acceptance of the earlier offer had precluded even consideration of the later one.

Of course it is also true that to see an event in all its present and future connections may disclose it to be *more* evil than we first suspected. However, in either case, the attempt to view it in its total context, including possible future ramifications, will bring us closer to the truth concerning its meaning, and this is presumably what we want.

The effort to see events in the total network of their relations may also enable us to perceive positive factors easily overlooked in experiences that may initially numb or blind us. In a brief essay written in a time of disillusionment and despair, Howard Thurman calls attention to the "little graces" that continue to sustain the dignity of human life. Birds sing; stars still shine (even over battlefields); kind words are uttered; and gracious deeds are performed even amid wartime desolation. We must not shrink, he insists, from acknowledging "the evilness of evil." Yet we must not forget that its real target is not destruction of the body but the corruption and inner disintegration of the human spirit.[11] I would want to recognize that the attacks of evil on the body are as real as those on the spirit. But Thurman's counsel is sound. If we can prevent the evils around us from moving "from without to within," and especially if we remain sensitive to the "little graces" and the amazing grace of the movement of the spirit of God, we may be able to overcome evil instead of being overcome by it.

Postscript: The Principle of Plenitude

Recognition of the interdependence of reality calls to mind an idea that has frequently recurred in Western theology—that of the great chain of being, or the principle of plenitude, given classic historical exposition by Arthur O. Lovejoy.[12] It does not fit harmoniously in the above interpretation of the interconnectedness of the world. However, it has been espoused by great thinkers and has through the centuries exerted considerable influence; it therefore deserves attention before we leave the theme of the present chapter.

The earliest known statement of the principle of plenitude appears in Plato's dialogue *Timaeus*. In Timaeus' account of creation the Demiurge gives to the lower gods, whom he had created, responsibility for creating three kinds of mortal beings. "Without them the universe will be incomplete, for it will not contain every kind of animal which it ought to contain, if it is to be perfect."[13] The Neoplatonists embraced and developed this conception. Plotinus, for example, portrays creation as a flowing out from the One of a series of emanations, "successive grades of being, first, second, third and so on until the last is reached." The best possible world is a "full" world: "the whole earth is full of a diversity of living things, mortal and immortal, and replete with them up to the very heavens." But this means that the best world must contain all possible forms of evil; differences of kind correspond necessarily to differences of excellence and diverse ranks in a hierarchy. It is therefore not possible for everything to be good. A rational world must display all degrees of the imperfections that grow out of the differences among creatures. This provides for Plotinus a ready explanation of animal suffering. The fullness of the cosmos demands the existence of both carniverous animals and those whose "nature" it is to be eaten. The good of the Whole consists mainly in the "variety of its parts," and conflict is only a special instance of, and necessarily implicated in, diversity.[14]

Especially influential in Christian thought has been Augustine's incorporation of the principle of plenitude in his theology of creation. According to him, all things, including those we call evil, contribute to the perfection of God's universe. God creates both great and little things in an orderly arrangement and proportion. "There are some things better than others, and for this purpose they are unequal, in order that they might all exist." A world that contains the greatest possible variety of creatures, including different "gradations according to the order of nature" and "various standards of value," is richer and better than would be one that included only the highest and best. "I reflected that the things above were better than those below, but that all were better than those above alone."[15]

In the Middle Ages the notion of the universe as a great chain of being gained wide currency. Reality, it was held, consists of a vast (theoretically infinite) number of links hierarchically arranged from the poorest existents on the border of nonbeing through every possible grade all the way to the most perfect being. We have already noted Thomas Aquinas' use of this principle in his conception of evil as privation. It is necessary that all possible degrees of goodness be fulfilled. Guided partly by an aesthetic motif, concern for the beauty in things, Thomas holds that the perfection of the universe requires the existence of some things capable of falling from goodness and others incapable of falling. If evil were removed from certain parts of creation, the perfection of the whole would be diminished.[16]

Seventeenth-century rationalists like Matthew Tindal and John Ray differed widely from Augustine and Aquinas in rejecting special revelation, but they partially agreed with their understanding of evil, interpreting it in terms of the great chain of being. In their view there is an ascending ladder of creatures from worm to angel, with no rung missing. Since God did not wish to deny existence to any possible kind of being, he provided a place for destructive insects and animals. The values of a full universe, with every niche occupied, outweigh the disvalues involved in less desirable existents.[17] The Neoplatonic principle of plenitude appears also in the eighteenth century in the theodicies of William King, Alexander Pope, and Gottfried Wilhelm Leibniz. For example, in Leibniz's doctrine that ours is the best of all possible worlds is the belief that the best possible universe is one in which all conceivable forms of being are realized. In the nineteenth century, Friedrich Schelling also accepted the principle, though for him it was necessitated by the love and goodness of God, whereas Leibniz had thought of God as freely choosing the best possible world.[18]

Lovejoy summarizes succinctly the common elements of the principle of plenitude when he describes it as

> the thesis that the universe is a *plenum formarum* in which the range of conceivable diversity of *kinds* of living things is exhaustively exemplified, . . . that no genuine potentiality of being can remain unfulfilled, that the extent and abundance of the creation must be as great as the possibility of existence and commensurate with the productive capacity of a "perfect" and inexhaustible Source, and that the world is the better, the more things it contains.[19]

The idea of the world as a great chain of being is an imposing generalization and a bold hypothesis. However, it fails to qualify as either a coherent interpretation of reality or a defensible account of evil. Four main considerations argue against its acceptance.

1. There is no empirical evidence for its truth. The world does indeed exhibit an immense variety of forms of existence, but there is no basis for claiming that what is must be, that the number of forms might not be greater or smaller, or that the diversity we encounter is better than any other arrangement would be. The notion of a chain necessarily without missing links is a purely speculative venture rooted chiefly in Plato's theory of Ideas or Forms, which regards all specific things as caused by, participating in, or copies of universals, which alone are real. The Forms are external patterns, systematically interrelated; the Demiurge or God uses them to fashion particular things, and logically it can be expected that they will all find manifestation in the created order, which otherwise would lack fullness or perfection. If this view of reality is rejected, the foundation of the conception of the great chain disappears. Indeed, the plenary conception of reality exhibits the same flaw found in Plato's doctrine of Forms—the difficulty, if not the impossibility, of relating the timeless patterns to the concrete flow of life in the physical and historical world. The principle of plenitude implies a static conception of reality determined by a system of necessary and eternal truths. But the world we experience is one of temporality and change. The timeless, motionless realm of the great chain cannot be reconciled with it or account for it.

2. The notion of necessary plenitude is particularly questionable when we consider the vast inequalities manifest in the diverse forms of being. According to the theory, differences in quality are implicated in differences in kind, and all are demanded by the need for fullness. Hence, living beings inevitably vary in their equipment—in size, strength, intelligence, and other qualities. Much injustice seems to be involved, especially to organisms on the lower levels that appear to be chiefly instrumental to the existence of others above them. This circumstance is of course one of the serious difficulties confronting any effort to deal with the problem of natural evil. It appears on the human level in extreme differences of endowment and opportunity and in the disparities between feeble-mindedness and genius and congenital disease and health. However, the great-chain theory is much more vulnerable in this respect than for example an evolutionary interpretation. The latter does not have to assert that the differences and inequalities are necessary, rational, or desirable, but the principle of plenitude makes all of these assertions.

3. The hypothesis of the great chain fails to recognize adequately the unique significance of personality. It does indeed place finite persons at the top of the hierarchy of created being, but the lowest forms are as necessary as the higher. As noted above, subhuman life and the physical order may well have meaning for God other and greater than merely that of providing an environment for the growth of personal life. But we know too little of what this meaning may be to accord to it the same rational necessity as the creation of human persons. Instead of treating moral personality as incidental to a universe packed with the utmost diversity of life forms, we should give precedence to the fashioning of persons capable of fellowship with God and one another in the realization of values. This is especially true from the perspective of Christian faith, which conceives God in personal terms and finds him incomparably disclosed as personal love in the life and work of Jesus Christ.

4. The doctrine of plenitude entails hopeless contradictions. It is basically incongruous to maintain that a universe that contains *evils,* and that must do so in order to include all forms of being, is *better* than one without evils. If moral values are truly valuable, how can evil persons be reasonably regarded as contributory to the goodness or perfection of the whole? So to view them is to substitute abstract completeness for character in defining goodness on the personal plane. It is also contradictory to assume that the continuity implied in plenitude is preserved by the creation of qualitatively different forms of existence on an ascending scale. The emergence of a new kind of thing, rather than simply a greater amount or degree of something characteristic of a whole series, involves a leap, or a disjunction, rather than a continuity.[20]

Because of weaknesses like these, we conclude that the principle of plenitude contributes little of value to our understanding either of evil or of reality as a whole.

11 The Cross at the Heart of Creation

Elie Wiesel, himself a survivor of Auschwitz, tells of the hanging by the Nazi SS of three Jews—two men and a child. The men cried, "Long live liberty!" The boy said nothing. Standing behind Wiesel, another prisoner asked, "Where is God? Where is He?" Though the adults died quickly, the child, being lighter in weight, dangled for a half hour, struggling between life and death. The agonizing question was repeated: "Where is God now?" Wiesel heard a voice behind him answer: "Where is He? Here He is—He is hanging here on this gallows." [1]

This tragic incident introduces us to the most profound of all responses to human anguish—participation by God himself in the pathos and pain of existence. In this instance he suffers with the victims of ruthless human cruelty, but his presence on the gallows—like the cross, it is not too harsh a figure—may also be taken as a symbol of his identification with all who suffer from evils of whatever kind. To examine how this may be true is the purpose of the present chapter. We have already suggested that a cross pattern may be detected in the very structure of creation. What does this mean, and how does it bear on the problem of human anguish in relation to the love of God?

To deal fruitfully with questions like these we must examine critically the notion of divine power. If God himself is agonizing with human beings on the gallows or on the cross, why is he there? Who put him there? Is he there by choice or because he cannot help being there? What is he doing about it? We likewise need to ask,

What is the meaning for him and for his creatures of the suffering he endures? Does his share in human anguish promise release for his victims and offer hope for the victory of his purposes? Such queries fall naturally under two heads, and we shall investigate them in order: the nature and extent of the power of God and the degree and significance of God's participation in the suffering of creation. As always, we shall need to proceed undogmatically, recognizing fully the limitations of our best human understanding, yet searching earnestly for the fullest truth we can discover.

Reconception of the Power of God

Orthodox Christian thought has traditionally asserted the omnipotence as well as the perfect goodness of God. Ordinarily, thinkers who have affirmed both have recognized that the divine power is limited by whatever measure of freedom God has allotted to his creatures. However, this limitation is regarded as willed by God himself in order to facilitate the growth of persons fashioned in his image. Since it is self-imposed, it is under his control and subject to revocation by his own choice. Hence it is felt to be quite consistent with divine omnipotence. It can be maintained also that the regularity and uniformity of the natural order and the social and cosmic interdependence of the created world do not necessarily represent a diminution of God's power, since these provisions may be regarded as chosen by God as the best means of fulfilling his loving purpose.

However, some events are so radically destructive of the values cherished by religious faith that it seems impossible to view them as freely chosen by a God of perfect goodness. Realizing the finiteness of human understanding, we may acknowledge our bafflement and trust the infinite wisdom and love of the God whose purposes we cannot fathom. But there is another alternative. If God is conceived as the ultimate reality viewed from the perspective of religious devotion, it is reasonable to suppose that the basic qualities of his being are what they are because he is who he is, and it is beside the point to ask why he, the ultimate ground of all being and becoming, is not different. Included in the kind of reality he is are the quality and extent of his power. Whether that power is greater or less than human beings might wish, like other facets of his essential character it is eternal and uncreated, neither willed nor chosen by him. Conceivably it is such that some of his purposes can be fulfilled only with great difficulty and over a long period of time. Whether this is true or not cannot be decided arbitrarily. However, if our best evidence suggests that divine power is limited in this way, the sound course is to pursue this possibility with all seriousness. We should be guided by critical interpretation of our experience as a whole, not by preconceived notions of what is appropriate for God or by traditional conceptions of what God must be.

The Temporality of God

Integral to the question of divine power is the relation of God to time. Classical theism, strongly influenced by Aristotle and Neoplatonism, has conceived of God as the changeless Absolute who exists above the world in timeless perfection. The world is a temporal effect of his action, but he is the Unmoved Mover who is not affected by it. For him there can be no before or after. Events experienced by human beings as past, present, and future are grasped by God in one eternal now. There is little empirical basis for such a view. On the contrary, the biblical witness, the evidence of concrete religious experience, and what we know of natural and historical processes all support belief in the temporality of God—a belief that is quite consistent with a defensible notion of his eternity.

It is true that the Hebrew-Christian Scriptures frequently contrast the transitoriness of created things with the permanence of the Creator and stress the changelessness and everlastingness of God (e.g., Ps. 102:26-27; Mal. 3:6; Heb. 13:8; James 1:17). However, such passages aim primarily to affirm that God is not subject to the perishability of finite things, that, unlike vacillating human beings, he is utterly dependable, and that his steadfast love endures forever. His Word is eternal: it is true at all times. The biblical writings assume temporality and historicality as fundamental categories of existence. Creation and redemption are events in time. God makes covenants, fulfills promises, seeks to lead people toward his kingdom, and inspires trust and hope in the fulfillment of his purposes—all time-spanning activities. Noteworthy in the New Testament is the juxtaposition of two conceptions of time. The New

237

Testament assumes the reality of *chronos*—measurable, quantitative, repetitive, or clock time, but it gives special recognition to *kairos*—significant, qualitative, or fulfilled time. The kairoi are creative moments of unique meaning, above all the historical event of Jesus Christ that "in the fulness of time" brings God's self-revelation to special fruition and makes all things new.

Scientific investigation presupposes the reality of the temporal process. Time may indeed be said to be constitutive in the physical world. In quantum physics, for example, the atom is seen as a succession of patterned vibrations, and vibration involves chronological time. Similarly, cosmic and biological evolution exhibit movement and development, hence temporality. But there is also in the natural order something like kairotic time. Atomic vibrations are not merely repetitive; sometimes they present alternative possibilities. Evolution as now understood is marked by the emergence of novelties, new phenomena that could not have been predicted as outgrowths of their antecedents. If we think of this temporal order as manifesting the creative activity of God, it is reasonable to conclude that time has real meaning for God himself. He initiates and guides change, moves forward to new emergents, is involved in the indeterminacy of the physical order, and confronts new situations produced partly by finite persons exercising their freedom.

Contemporary religious experience likewise takes for granted God's involvement in the temporal flow of events. The "will of God" is known to us, not as an abstraction, but as related to concrete circumstances. The sense of divine guidance so prominent in Christian hymnody assumes that God moves with his people through the changing events of their lives to help them realize ends not yet accomplished. Experiences of sin, repentance, and forgiveness imply that God seeks to lead his worshipers from estrangement to reconciliation. Prayers of thanksgiving for past benefits and petitions for strength, healing, deliverance from oppression, and newness of life presuppose that God is really present with those who pray, ministering to their needs and leading them toward futures that involve him as well as them.

Data like these support the judgment that God is temporal as well as eternal. He has neither beginning nor end; he abides and remains himself through all change; he provides the uniformly dependable structure of reality that is our physical environment; and he can always be counted on to act according to his unchanging wisdom and love. But he is also the Pilgrim who is constantly on the way. God did not decide to be temporal; he is, as it were, eternally temporal. To ascribe temporality to him does not mean that time is something external to him to which he must accommodate himself. It means rather that time is inherent in his very being, integral to his nature, ingredient to all his activity. It means therefore that he requires time for the fulfillment of his purposes. Clearly implied in this acknowledgment is the negative judgment that there are some things that even God cannot do at a particular time, however desirable they might be. If time is real for him, he cannot be regarded as unqualifiedly omnipotent. This is one form of limitation on the divine power that has obvious bearing on the problem of evil. It is in no sense demeaning to God, but simply an ultimate aspect of his life that must be reckoned with whenever we ask why he does not instantly change situations that entail pain and hardship for finite beings whom he loves.

Boundless Love, Bounded Power

The qualification of the power of God involved in his temporality is, I am suggesting, an aspect of a broader and similarly ultimate limitation. We should remember, of course, that orthodox affirmations of divine omnipotence have not held that God can do anything whatever, including actions that contradict his rational and moral nature, or that he can make the past never to have been. Traditionally, omnipotence means rather that God has full power to do whatever he wills. In terms of Epicurus' formulation of the problem of evil, divine all-powerfulness would mean that God can remove or prevent evil if he wants to do so.

During the past century and a half, thoughtful voices have been raised questioning such assertions of infinite power. Friedrich Schelling (1775–1854), who wrestled throughout his life with the problem of God and evil, came to espouse a radically evolutionary theology derived largely from his observation of conflict and pain in the natural processes that produce higher forms of life. Influenced also by the mystical thought of Boehme, he held that the "World-Spirit," eternal love, fulfills itself through self-differentiation and the interaction of antagonistic operations, incessantly conquering evil to move toward unity. In Schelling's view, cosmic and human history contain a tragic element, exhibiting an interplay of obstruction and striving. Since the full possibilities of existence are not yet realized, there must be in the nature of things some impediment or retarding principle. It is destined to be overcome, but not without hardship and temporary defeats. God achieves his creative aims only through struggle. Contradictorily, Schelling tried to combine this concept with features of the old Platonic notion of a generativeness seeking the greatest possible fullness of being, but in his mature thought, the emphasis was on movement, dynamic process, and struggle.[2]

Implicit in Berdyaev's notion of uncreated freedom is his conviction that divine power is not only severely limited but only marginally important if the true meaning of deity is grasped. Power is not a religious but a social phenomenon. When we recognize this we see that God has less power than a policeman! The kingdom over which God reigns is incommensurable with the activities ascribed to him by the world. He is not the powerful ruler of the natural order, but is present in "truth, beauty, love, freedom, and creativity." His providence is "to be lived in the depths of the free human spirit."[3]

Though Radoslav A. Tsanoff does not separate the divine activity from the spatio-temporal order, like Berdyaev he relates God to the conservation and advancement of values. However, this process is arduous; worthy goals are attained only as resistance is overcome. Reality throughout manifests unendingly "the urge of the higher and the drag of the lower." God is the Apogee of Value, but his perfection is dynamic, not static. It may be spoken of as infinite, but only in the sense that it is unterminated, open-ended possibility. There is in the cosmic system of things, hence within God, an "evil tug," a "negative moment, the obverse of positive enhancement and ideal activity." God resists the downpulling pressure of the inert and the complacent. "Just this upward-urging, ever more perfectly active character of the cosmos is what we can intelligently mean by God."[4]

The most carefully wrought modern conception of the finiteness of God's power is that of Edgar S. Brightman, whose theistic personalistic idealism has been further developed by Peter A. Bertocci. The major stimulus to Brightman's explorations was his conviction that radical evil cannot be reconciled with divine omnipotence. According to his view, God is limited by eternal, uncreated, unchosen factors within his own nature. He is the ultimate Source and Ground of all creation, unbegun and unending in time, infinite in space by including all nature in his experience, unlimited in his knowledge of all that is, perfect in goodness and love, but limited in power. He is thus the finite-infinite Controller of "the Given"—the term used by Brightman to designate experiences of God not produced by his will. The Given includes both rational and nonrational aspects. The former consists of the norms of reason and other values; the latter, of processes in the divine consciousness that exhibit, by analogy with human experience, "all the ultimate qualities of sense objects (*qualia*), disorderly impulses and desires, such experiences as pain and suffering, the forms of space and time, and whatever in God is the source of surd evil."[5] The nonrational Given is thus a retarding factor that resists the efforts of God's perfectly good will to order reality according to his rational and moral norms.

Bertocci likewise posits "an unwilled Impediment within God's nature." Interpreting and concurring with Brightman, he writes: "God's will cannot overcome all the recalcitrant elements in the nonrational Given, that is, those processes in God which might be compared to the sensory, affective, and emotional life of human beings." To the hampering effect of these elements in God is due excess or nondisciplinary evil—"all evil, whether it be man's fault or not, whose destructive effect, so far as we know, is greater than any good which may come from it."[6]

Brightman and Bertocci affirm that there is nothing contradictory about the relation of the rational and nonrational aspects of the Given, and that they do not involve any ultimate disunity. In personal correspondence Bertocci has stressed that they are no more contradictory than are reason and sense in human experience. Given and non-Given do not divide God's oneness. They point, rather, to distinctions within a dynamic, complex unity. However, Bertocci recognizes that from the standpoint of God's creative aim the two aspects do entail conflict between his willed purpose and his ideal; this conflict results in surplus evil.

Both thinkers find solid grounds for faith in successive triumphs of God's will. In some situations God's utmost endeavors are met by temporary defeat and consequent suffering for him and his creatures. Nevertheless, "no defeat or frustration is final; . . . the will of God, partially thwarted by obstacles in the chaotic Given, finds new avenues of advance, and forever moves on in the cosmic creation of new values." [7]

These efforts to account for evil by qualifying the power of God are not without difficulties of their own. These come to focus primarily in questions regarding the divine unity. Though all of the examples cited repudiate any ultimate or ontological dualism, they postulate opposing tendencies of various kinds that are hard to reconcile with our human experience of a unified cosmos and religious experience of one God. When Berdyaev treats causative and controlling power in the natural order as irrelevant to the true meaning of God, which is confined to our experiences of worth, he introduces a dichotomy that calls in question the very foundations of the values he cherishes. He excludes God from all relation to disease, destruction, and misery, and finds him rather in our experiences of beauty, truth, love, and creative freedom. But can we constructively pursue the latter if we relegate the former, which intimately affect all our endeavors, to a realm of impenetrable mystery where God is not? This is too high a price to pay for keeping God unspotted from the evils of the world.

For the most part, these finitistic theories avoid making the world a battleground of good and evil forces. However, the antagonistic activities posited by Schelling and the "evil tug" that Tsanoff finds opposing the upward urge imply something of the opposition that marks historic ontological dualisms. The nonrational Given is not classically or strictly speaking a dualistic concept, since it is within God and is nonmoral rather than evil. Nevertheless, the notion of an impediment or recalcitrant aspect (Schelling, Bertocci) and that of a retarding factor (Brightman) within the eternal, uncreated nature of God do not readily cohere with the one world known to the sciences and our experience as a whole. Bertocci indeed acknowledges that his view entails a "relative disharmony," but insists that it involves no logical contradiction and no ontic dichotomy within God.

The word *impediment* is derived from the Latin verb *impedire,* which means "to shackle or entangle the feet." Hence an impediment is anything that hinders, obstructs, or blocks normal functioning. The term thus suggests a defect, something abnormal that does not belong where it is. Applied to God, it intimates that because of it he is somewhat at odds with himself, lacking in harmony of aim and execution. The adjective *recalcitrant* comes from the Latin infinitive *recalcitrare,* based on the root *calx,* heel; literally, the verb means "to kick back, or strike with the heels." Hence to be recalcitrant is to be obstinate, disobedient, or stubbornly rebellious; to resist restraint or defy authority. John Stuart Mill in his essay on Comte refers to "a single Deity . . . keeping in recalcitrant subjection an army of devils." Thus the term seems to imply to some degree an actively defiant rebellious tendency, and when applied to God, it suggests an activity that refuses to cooperate with his central purpose. This is certainly not what either Brightman or Bertocci intends, but in spite of all disclaimers, the term has dualistic overtones. A God who must suppress a recalcitrant element in his own being hardly qualifies as the Ground of the universe we experience or the ultimte Source of healing and wholeness in the personal and social life of fragmented human beings.[8]

Nevertheless, the theories examined point in the right direction in rejecting the traditional notion of divine omnipotence and in focusing attention on the nature of God himself rather than on forces external to him. Four considerations argue persuasively for discarding belief in the absolute sovereignty of God.

1. The pain and travail of evolution; the waste and cruelty of the struggle for survival of individuals and species; the accidents, blind alleys, and retracing of steps; and the long, slow processes of a creation still unfinished suggest not the determinations of unlimited power but the hazardous activity of a God who is proceeding experimentally and at immense cost, ever willing and perhaps needing to change courses and explore new possibilities.

2. The phenomena of quantum mechanics, with its disclosures of indeterminacy at the subatomic level; mutation-producing instability and spontaneity in organic life; and the occurrence of events in the physical order marked by randomness, chance, and unpredictable novelty are activities that are not readily attributable to an all-determining divine will or seen as amenable to such a will.

3. The precariousness of human life, threatened as it often is by famine, drought, floods, and other natural disasters; the inequitable distribution of suffering and its disproportionateness to the needs of those who suffer; the seeming purposelessness of much evil and its failure to contribute to good; and the crushing effect that suffering often has on its victims make plain the actuality of "nondisciplinary" evil—evil that exceeds what might conceivably be needed for the character formation of those who suffer. Such events can be attributed partially to the need for a regular, dependable natural order, the functioning of freedom and indeterminacy, and the interconnectedness of existence. But after due recognition has been given to these circumstances, the stunting, warping, and embittering effects of suffering that is not contributory to good undermine the claim that an all-powerful Creator ordains all as means to his holy ends. The occurrence of so much purposeless anguish supports revision of the notion of unlimited divine power.

4. For persons guided by the Hebrew-Christian heritage, further evidence is found in the biblical witness, which portrays God's creative and redemptive work as requiring strenuous, sacrificial, continuing effort. In the Fourth Gospel the Word through whom all things come to be is made known in one who, like a grain of wheat, bears fruit by dying (John 1:1-4; 12:24). In travail God creates the universe (Rom. 8:22), and his saving concern for his people involves a cross.

If we treat data like these with the seriousness they deserve, we shall listen attentively to those thinkers who conceive God to be limited by something within his own nature. However, we can perhaps avoid the difficulties previously noted if we eliminate thought of impediments and recalcitrant elements in God that oppose and obstruct his will, and attempt to speak in more positive terms. It is misleading to use the term *nonrational Given* to designate only hindrances to God's power. What is given—eternal and not produced by his will—is God's power itself.[9] The datum, that which is granted or assumed when we consider nonrational aspects of his experience, is the whole of his energy.

This means that God does not choose how much power to have; it simply is what it is, however immense or limited. Or, rather, since power is not a separate entity but an aspect of the integral wholeness of the divine life, we might better say that God is what he is and who he is. As the ultimate ground of all being and becoming, he acts powerfully to realize his ends. If the evidence of our total experience suggests that the power he exercises is less than infinite, it is sound to regard this limitation as inherent in his eternal nature. Finiteness of power may itself be ultimate. If we can free ourselves of preconceived ideas of what God must be, it should be neither shocking to us nor debasing to God to regard this judgment as affording possibly the truest account of reality.

Empirically, the limitedness of God's power may be manifested in the physical indeterminacy and the genetic mutations discussed in chapters 9 and 10. These can and do function creatively; the spontaneity allowed by indeterminacy may contribute to variety and constructive change, and mutations are essential to evolution. But they also work in ways that are harmful to sentient beings. Conceivably, this may be due to limitations in the power of God. If so, the genetic anomalies that produce deformities, imbecility, and diseases like Johnson's chorea, as well as the abnormalities in cell division involved in cancer, would be better understood.

The view here proposed, obviously related to the thought of Brightman and Bertocci, also has affinities with the views on divine power of thinkers as different in other respects as L. Harold DeWolf, Nicolas Berdyaev, and David Ray Griffin.

DeWolf, upholding a conception that he regards as "in a sense finitistic," states that God's omnipotence is limited not only by his rational nature and his delegation of some power and freedom to his creatures but also "by the bounds of his own being, however unimaginably great." His "will is limited simply by being all that it is and not more." As late as 1968, when a revised edition of his *Theology of the Living Church* appeared, DeWolf apparently did not believe that the bounds of God's power negatively affect the attainment of his aims, permitting more suffering in his creatures than they can use for good. He writes, for example, that "natural evil must be regarded as having a positive place in the purpose of God." By means of it, God's will is being done, and great new good is "coming to pass, good worth much more than all the cost."[10] In private correspondence, DeWolf has stated that within the context provided by the limits of God's being, his voluntary self-limitation, and the creaturely abuse of freedom, in particular situations God's consequential will may be the choice of natural evil "for its possibilities of instrumental good. However, because of the boundedness of divine power, God is not always able to order his particular volitional activity to produce consequences all of which are consistent with his purpose. Some natural evils are not chosen as themselves specific means to good, but result from inherent limitations of God's power to fulfill his purpose perfectly as his acts affect all his human creatures." This interpretation of divine power seems to me to be sound.

In a broad sense, of course, God's choice of creating this world, notwithstanding the risk and even probability of resulting evil, involves his willing indirectly whatever distress that creation entails. As Tennant's "wider theodicy," discussed in chapter 7, maintains, physical ills are often unavoidable but incidental by-products of a natural and moral order that is willed by God in order to develop persons capable of realizing high values. It must be recognized also that the ensuing evils depend ultimately on God's energizing activity, not that of some other power or powers. Yet this does not mean that God specifically wills all the evils that occur. In many particular cases the good attained, as far as we know, is not worth more than it costs. In others, the evil is so debilitating that persons seem to be rendered incapable of value fulfillment. Many evils cannot be turned to good; they far exceed what might contribute to the personal growth of the sufferers, and in fact they tend to demoralize them. We must suppose that a good God opposes such events and does everything possible to prevent them; yet they occur.

The very inevitability of some evil if good is to be won in certain situations may itself be partially due to internal boundaries in the power of God. In some degree, the limitation suggested may be evidenced precisely in the fact that God cannot create a value-fulfilling community without exposing to evil those who compose it.

The notion of an ultimate boundedness in the power of God finds support in Berdyaev's suggestion concerning the irreducible mystery of uncreated or uncaused freedom. This freedom is inexplicable and nonobjectifiable. It has no other foundation than itself; it is simply disclosed as real in existence. "It is a frontier."[11] In similar fashion we may say that in the presence of God we stand before the ultimate reality, which cannot be referred to anything else. The frontier of his action is constituted by or is intrinsic to his nature as God.

There are two additional values in thinking of God as uncaused freedom as Berdyaev does. First, he reminds us that our most painstaking reflection still leaves us confronting profound mystery. There is a depth in existence that we cannot probe, and any claims to detailed knowledge of the inner nature of the divine are suspect. Second, the image of the frontier suggests movement, the possibility of an advancing boundary. Here the thought of Berdyaev broadly parallels that of the unorthodox Marxist Ernst Bloch, for whom reality is a "front." "The real is process." Its nature is to move forward; it proceeds along a changing front from the unfinished past toward a possible future that is not yet determined.[12] May we perhaps think of the frontier of God's power as also moving, so that even he may advance in ability to achieve his goals in difficult situations? An affirmative answer would of course require a dynamic rather than a static interpretation of the God who "is what he is." But it is supported by all the evidence of experimental creativity in the evolutionary process.

Though David Griffin's understanding of reality differs considerably from those of both DeWolf and Berdyaev, his views on the power of God point in the same direction. His process theodicy roots the possibility of evil in the "metaphysical . . . characteristics of the world"—the ultimate principles that function in "the way actual entities become and interact." Following Hartshorne's revision of Whitehead, Griffin locates these categories in "the eternal essence of God." Hence they "are beyond all decision, even God's." In particular, the power of self-determination possessed by the entities that compose reality (already noted in chap. 9) is not a gift of the divine will but an ultimate fact that God cannot control or revoke. Though temporal entities receive from him their "conceptual aims," their actual behavior is not determined by him. God's power is perfect—the greatest he could possibly have over a *created* world—but in the nature of things, it is not unqualified. Therefore he "cannot unilaterally prevent all evil."[13]

Griffin's belief that within the eternal nature of God are ultimate principles that limit God's control of his creatures plays much the same role with respect to evil as the bounds of God's being in DeWolf and the frontier of uncaused freedom in Berdyaev. Such interpretations harmonize with the suggestions I have offered in this chapter, and they shed needed light on the vexing questions of pointless suffering.

Considerations such as those now before us support the judgment that purposeless evil is due in part to the ultimate, unwilled boundedness of the power of God. For God to have any positive nature at all is a form of qualification, since he is this and therefore not that. He is what he is, not something else that is excluded by or contradictory to what he is. With reference to power, this means that God has a kind and degree of power—known to him though not to us—that is prodigious but not unbounded or infinite. Its greatness is attested by the magnitude, orderliness, and marvelous complexity of the cosmos; but its boundaries are such that his creatures must face natural evils that he does not choose, and that sometimes hamper rather than advance the growth of human character, precluding or delaying the fulfillment of his wholly good intent.

It should be borne in mind that to regard divine power as less than infinite does not mean to think of God as weak and puny. His power is not absolute, but it is utterly unparalleled. He is the source, ground, and possessor of all the power there is—and of all he needs for the ultimate attainment of his righteous purposes. Moreover, the unbounded love that animates all his work has its own unique strength. He gains his ends less by coercion than by self-sacrificial effort to lead his creatures toward freely chosen fulfillment of his will. But the reality of boundaries inherent in God's nature means that his creation of a world with high potential for the shared realization of values can occur only through toilsome, hazardous struggle. The best *possible* world, it seems, is a costly world.

The Suffering Love of God

The costliness of God's efforts to attain his purposes implies that he shares deeply the anguish of his creation. Indeed, we are led to this judgment by the whole trend of our previous discussion. We have maintained, for example, that God intimately interpenetrates all aspects of existence. He does not stand over against the world, acting on it from without. Rather, his creative and redemptive activity underlies, permeates, and sustains it. He is the matrix of all its being and becoming, the dynamic personal Spirit who in unbounded love seeks to fashion a community of shared values. Inevitably, therefore, when his creatures suffer for whatever reason, he not only knows about their suffering but concretely experiences it.

Implicit in and consistent with this understanding of God and human anguish are the main positive conclusions of chapters 7 to 10. When finite persons grow in character at the cost of experiences of evil, God shares their agony. When human beings suffer from their own misuse of freedom, he suffers with them, not because he takes part in their evil choices, but because he is grieved by their rejection and loss of the good he wills. When they are exposed to pain through the carelessness or oppressive cruelty of others in an interdependent universe, he feels their misery deeply. When they endure hardships because of the regular functioning of a dependable natural order, he is present in their distress. And when the full exercise of his power does not prevent injury to creatures he loves, he suffers with them. The world's travail is his also.[14]

It must be acknowledged, however, that such assertions confront a long and deeply rooted tradition that summarily rejects the notion of suffering in God as completely contradictory to the divine nature. The Patripassians of the second and third centuries (e.g., Praxeas, Noetus, and Sabellius) were modalistic monarchians who stressed the identity of the Son and the Father. They held that the one God was called Father with reference to his previous relations to the world and Son with respect to his manifestation in human flesh. Hence the redemptive suffering of the Christ was the suffering of the Father as well. They were roundly denounced as heretical—though probably less because they related suffering to God than because they confused the distinctive ministries of Father and Son within the Trinity.

After the Council of Nicaea (325), which condemned the teaching that the Logos was a created being, orthodox doctrine for the most part limited the capacity to suffer, along with other conditions of Christ's earthly existence, to his human nature. Thus Gregory of

Nyssa (*ca.* 332–398) insisted that the Son as God was impassible and incapable of corruption, though as human he was susceptible to suffering. Augustine noted that *passio* connotes "a corruption of the mind contrary to reason"; passion therefore suggests disturbance and changeableness and is incompatible with the blessedness of the transcendent God.[15] Cyril of Alexandria (376–444) likewise linked incapacity to suffer with divine immutability. In his controversy with Nestorius he declared that God the Word "exists in his own nature impassible," but that in the crucifixion he made the sufferings of the flesh his own, though "in an impassible manner." The Definition of Chalcedon (451), with its two-nature doctrine of the one person of Christ, provided a ready rationale for these denials of suffering in the eternal God. Increasingly, it came to be held that the Christ is in his divine nature unchangeable, incorruptible, immortal, and incapable of suffering, though in his human nature he could and did suffer on the cross.

During these early centuries there were of course divergent tendencies. Some Christians saw nothing incompatible with divinity in the notion of the sufferings of Christ as the eternal Word. Even within Chalcedonian orthodoxy there were those who were troubled by the conflict between the official dogmatic formula and both the unity and the real suffering of Christ as portrayed in the Gospels. But throughout the Middle Ages, the Protestant Reformation, and beyond, the doctrine of impassibility remained uppermost. In the thought of Thomas Aquinas, for whom Aristotle's doctrine of the Unmoved Mover was decisive, God "must be pure act, without the admixture of any potentiality." Therefore he is "altogether immutable," hence incapable of passion. Love and joy belong to his nature, but sadness and anger can be attributed to his absolutely perfect being only metaphorically.[16] Except for the Socinians and some Anabaptists, the Reformers followed the dominant tradition. John Calvin declares that God certainly is "not sorrowful or sad, but remains forever like Himself in His celestial and happy repose." When a biblical passage testifies that God, in order to lighten the afflictions of his people, himself bore their burdens, it does not mean that he "can in any way endure anguish," but simply that God is by a customary figure of speech transferring to himself passions that are peculiar to human nature. Likewise, when the Lord is said to be sorry or grieved because he created men and women who have sinned against him, he is merely accommodating himself to our limited human capacity to understand. Actually, God cannot be surprised by any human actions, for his wisdom foresees them all.[17]

These utterances are fairly representative. Until the early nineteenth century the doctrine that God cannot suffer was a postulate of most Christian theology. But while it is still vigorously defended, in more recent decades it has been increasingly questioned and opposed. Mozley lists and briefly expounds the thought of twenty-two theologians, mostly British and American, who explicitly rejected the doctrine during the sixty years preceding 1926. In my own research I have encountered eight others from this period, and forty-two more who during the past half century have either rejected the traditional view or expressed their positive belief in the suffering love of God. But issues of this kind cannot be decided by Gallup polls; critical evaluation is needed.

Viewed in perspective, those who exclude suffering from God find their chief support in five overlapping propositions. (1) Both Judaism and Christianity strongly affirm the transcendence of God; his life is far removed from and other than the life of the world, so it would be inappropriate to apply to him our finite limitations. (2) As we have learned from the Greeks, especially Plato and Aristotle, the eternal God is unmovable, immutable, and unswayed by feeling; if he were involved in variable and often irrational human passions, he would not be the Absolute. (3) God's perfect blessedness is unblemished, unaffected by the pain, sin, and failure of the world. God is full of loving care and sympathy for human beings, but suffering is intrinsically a form of imperfection and evil, and is therefore not to be ascribed to him. (4) Though some biblical passages seem to portray a God who shares our sorrows, these are to be taken as figures of speech; and though the gospel narratives of the passion of Christ point to a God who suffers, these refer only to the human and not to the divine nature of Christ. (5) The enlightened religious consciousness demands an omnipotent, all-knowing Ultimate who can accomplish whatever he wills and before whom it can bow in adoration. Suffering in God would imply that he is subject to sorrow and frustration, and these are not in keeping with the perfection we need in our object of worship.[18]

These arguments properly insist that God immeasurably transcends his creation. They justifiably warn against the anthropomorphism that occurs when human beings make God in their own image. They correctly perceive that there is a nonliteral, symbolic quality in all our statements about God. They rightly take religious experience into account in the search for a sound understanding of God. But they are invalidated by half-truths, oversights, and inconsistencies.

Critical scrutiny discloses the following difficulties in the traditional view and at the same time offers positive support for belief in the reality of divine suffering:

1. Many of those who exclude pain and pathos from the divine life are guided more by *a priori* judgments as to what God's perfection *must* involve than by careful study of the data of concrete experience. Our conception of God, including his perfection, ought to grow out of the most cogent possible interpretation of the available evidence. To conceive of him as without direct acquaintance with suffering is indefensibly to separate him from his creation. In one sense, those who assert that a God who knows anguish cannot be the Absolute are right, but they undermine their own case. Etymologically, the word *absolute* means loosened, free, separate, unrelated, disengaged. There may be such a reality, but if it exists, it is so out of contact with the world we know that it cannot be the God who creates and sustains that world. Moreover, an understanding of perfection revised in the light of our total experience might include the vulnerability to suffering that is involved in loving others. Such sensitivity may be more perfect than its absence.

2. The biblical writings affirm the nearness as well as the otherness of God. Many passages in the Hebrew Bible voice the psalmist's faith in him who is "familiar with all my paths" (Ps. 139:3), and the Holy Spirit in the New Testament dwells in the midst of the congregation. Further, he who is both immanent and transcendent feels deeply the agonies of his people and even suffers for and with them. The God of the prophets of Israel has about him no Aristotelian immutability. To him are ascribed, on the contrary, such traits as anger, joy, repentance, jealousy, grief, and love. When in the servant songs of Second Isaiah (42:1-4; 49:1-6; 50:4-9; 52:13–53:12) the people of Israel are pictured as "tormented and humbled by suffering" (53:3), the character they are called to emulate seems clearly to be that of the servant's Lord. At the heart of both the Pauline and the Johannine traditions in the New Testament is one who was so moved by human need that in love he took on himself the form of a servant, accepted death on a cross, and so manifested the love of God. Whether Jesus' reply to Philip's desire to know the Father represents his own words or the faith of the primitive church, is should set at rest our questions concerning the evangelists' attitude toward divine suffering: "Anyone who has seen me has seen the Father" (John 14:8-9).

3. These affirmations of the New Testament led to faith in the Incarnation, which provides further support for belief in the reality of divine suffering. Based on the witness of John 1:14, II Corinthians 5:19, and other passages, the church came firmly to believe that God had disclosed himself incomparably in Jesus Christ. If the Christ event is truly revelatory—if it really makes God known—what we discern in the life, teachings, death, and resurrection of Jesus Christ must manifest central truth regarding the life and character of God. Then the cross speaks to us decisively of the suffering love of God himself. In this perspective, those who deny that God can suffer implicitly, deny the Incarnation and therefore are closer to heresy than those they censure as "Patripassians."

4. It is a distortion of the intent of the Apostles' Creed to claim that the affirmations of the second article regarding the Son—suffered, crucified, dead, resurrected—give no clue to the Father named in the first article as Creator of heaven and earth. This second-century statement of faith assumes the unity of God and offers no basis for asserting a dichotomy between Son and Father. Similarly, those who distinguish sharply between the human sufferings of Christ and his divine incapacity to suffer seem to overlook that, according to the Definition of Chalcedon, the two natures belong to one Person, without division or separation.

5. If God cannot feel anguish, he cannot love. In human life, to love involves being deeply concerned for others and hence being affected by what happens to them—their agonies as well as their joys. It entails sharing their pains, vulnerability to their suffering. He who cannot suffer is incapable of true love as an outgoing, caring regard for the other. Thus if human love affords dependable intimations of divine love, to exclude suffering from God would eliminate from Christian faith the basic conviction that God is love. According to the New Testament, God's self-sacrificial gift of himself in Christ both proceeded from and manifested his love. The gospel portrayal of the divine character unites love and capacity for suffering. To drive a wedge between them would destroy the meaning of both.

6. If appeal is made, as it should be, to religious experience, the desire of the "religious consciousness" for a powerful God not subject to human frailties must not be allowed to obscure another need, often voiced, for one who knows and shares our deepest distress. It is inappropriate for finite persons to "demand" what God should be or to make human needs or wishes the decisive criterion in their thought of God. But when we turn for guidance to the totality of our experience, we discover that people who hurt most are far more likely to find comfort and strength in the God disclosed on Golgotha than in the almighty potentate, dispassionately seated on a lofty throne. Berdyaev writes perceptively, "God can reconcile man to the sufferings of creation because he himself suffers, not because he reigns."[19]

We are therefore led irresistibly to the conviction that God's loving relation to his creation includes sharing its pain. This does not mean that we naïvely imagine God to suffer precisely as we do. Since he has no nervous system, his endurance of pain cannot be simply equated with ours. In an insightful passage Abraham Heschel suggests that it would be quite fitting to substitute *pathos* for *thoughts* in Second Isaiah's word on the wide difference between God and his people: "My pathos is not your pathos, and your ways are not my ways" (Isa. 55:8).[20] Yet pathos is a central category in the prophetic understanding of the attitude of God toward his people. So it remains. If human experience offers a clue to the ground of our existence, there must be a dimension there akin to what we know as feeling, including feelings of anguish. Something like a cross is an ultimate reality in the universe. Ours is not an easy world, but one that entails struggle, pathos, and suffering for both God and his creatures. As Josiah Royce declares, "The eternal world contains Gethsemane."[21]

Yet the question immediately arises as to whether this imagery applies to natural as well as to moral evil. Gethsemane for Jesus involved a choice. Presumably, he could have turned back and saved his life. Instead he chose the hard way of the cross, convinced that it was God's will in the circumstances that then confronted him. We can affirm that God's redemptive action reflects this kind of choice. The suffering of his creatures due to their own sinfulness and that of others elicits his free self-giving in their behalf. He does not have to save sinners, but at great cost to himself he acts to transform them, to liberate them and their victims from bondage, and to help them all to become new persons. In judgment he opposes those who serve themselves and oppress others, and in love he suffers for and with them to reconcile them to himself and to one another.

But what of the suffering occasioned for God by natural evil and the travail of the evolutionary process? Is this not a necessity? Is there anything voluntary about the anguish he endures because, as suggested above, there are bounds to his power grounded in the given fact that he is what he is and not something else?

The travail is indeed necessary—if God is to call into being such a world as ours. If he is to be involved in nature, life, and human history, his suffering is inevitable. Conceivably, he might have avoided the anguish by creating a different kind of world, and he might reduce the cost by following different processes as he continues to create.[22] But these alternatives, we may believe, would forfeit the positive values made possible by the universe we know. If God is to achieve the goods of this created order, he must experience the risks and negativities of a stable, interdependent, open-ended universe in which persons made in his image may grow in responsible freedom. Embarkation on this costly venture and continuation in it are his own choice.

Light is shed on this combination of necessity and choice if we take together two utterances of Jesus recorded in the Gospels. In the first he tells his disciples, "The Son of Man has to undergo great sufferings" (Luke 9:22; cf. Matt. 16:21; Mark 8:31; Luke 24:7, 26). But the necessity becomes intelligible when—and only when—it is seen as a self-offering, a gift. In the Fourth Gospel he assures his followers that no one has robbed him of his life: "I am laying it down of my own free will" (John 10:18). The anguish of God is not forced on him. God wills to create a world that he knows will involve suffering, but he does so freely and in love, for the sake of the community of shared values that such a world makes possible.

"With His Stripes We Are Healed"

The conviction that there is a cross—or a gallows—at the heart of reality has important implications, both theoretical and practical, for our struggle with evil and suffering. If the power of God has boundaries, and if in limitless love he shares the anguish of his creation, the question of how to affirm both his power and his goodness is at least partially answered. Evils that he does not will and seeks to prevent cannot be charged to his malevolence, indifference, or neglect. They are traceable in part to the fact that the power he wields—though it is all the power that exists and is incomparable—is not infinite.[23] Likewise, the depth and boundless scope of his love is attested by the suffering he willingly endures with and for his creatures as he works for the enhancement of values in the universe.

However, these gains do not come without a price. They make plain the difficulty and precariousness of the struggle for a good life for all persons. For those engaged in that struggle important resources may be found in our understanding of God's relation to human anguish.

1. The awareness that God suffers with us imparts strength to endure the ills that assail us and points the way to healing. In an ancient midrash Rabbi Akiba cites various Scriptures to show that whenever the Israelites were called into exile, such as in Egypt and Babylon, the Shekhinah—the presence of God—went into exile with them. The Rabbi then makes what Fackenheim terms a "breathtaking" assertion applicable even to the Holocaust of the twentieth century—that whenever Israel returns in the future, the Shekhinah "will return with them" (Deut. 30:3).[24] Jews may be in exile, but they will never be cut off from the divine Presence, who will ultimately bring redemption. Surely there is universal meaning here. Faith that the Lord goes with his people when they are exiled to pain, terror, oppression, or misery of any kind brings courage and sustaining power that nothing else can give.

A similar insight came to Albert Camus. Referring to Sisyphus, who was condemned to repeat endlessly the vain effort to roll a huge rock to the top of a mountain, Camus writes, "If man realized that the universe like him can love and suffer, he would be reconciled." [25] Though Camus apparently never got beyond the *if,* Christian faith affirms that just such a universe is actual. For vindication it points to a concrete person and a series of events in history. This disordered world, Jesus believed, is sustained and guided toward its lofty end by the self-giving, transforming love of God, and he backed up this conviction with his life. When we are possessed by this faith and illumined by its disclosure that God himself suffers in our anguish, we are delivered from discouragement and enabled to face life in wholeness and strength.

The integral place of suffering in the Christian understanding of divine love is brought out vividly by the Taiwanese theologian Choan-Seng Song, who points out that in Chinese the words love and pain are interchangeable. They are combined in a term that expresses the highest meaning of human love. Thus a mother is said to "pain-love" her child. "You have not really loved someone else until you feel pain in your love." In "pain-loving" one pours out one's whole being, as did the father of the prodigal son. Jesus Christ is "God's pain-loving enmanned." [26] In him we see a God who does not spare himself but bears our pain with us and gives himself in suffering love for our sake.

What this can mean when people must pass through raging tempests that threaten to overwhelm them was brought home to me several years ago through a married couple who are both dear friends. In a period of despondency following several experiences of extreme difficulty, the young wife attempted to end her life, and lay for many weeks at the brink of death. Supported by the caring ministries of physicians and nurses, and surrounded by a loving community of relatives and friends, she slowly recovered. Looking back on the harrowing events, her husband told me, "From now on, if in public worship 'He descended into hell' is omitted from the Apostles' Creed, I'll get up and walk out. For we have been in hell, and found that Christ was there." These people found that God indeed shared their profoundest agony, upheld them in the midst of it, and led them through it. Perennially, God does descend into the depths of our hells, whether we dig them ourselves or are thrust into them. But he is there with us, and in this consciousness we can find with him the way of healing.

2. It is often through suffering love that God attains his ends. He is not helpless. The fact that he shares our distress does not make him merely a big brother who, like us, is victimized by evil and is too weak to handle it. But the power most characteristic of his action is different from power as we customarily understand it. His kingdom is "not of this world." His power reaches its apex in the compassionate love that takes to itself the agony and tragedy of the world and thereby heals and transforms it. It works primarily, not through fiat or the application of superior physical force, but through the anguished love that seeks the well-being even of those who oppose it. Yet it is the kind of power that the apostle Paul can describe as transcendent, and that enabled him to face all manner of perils with faith and courage: "Hard-pressed on every side, we are never hemmed in; bewildered, we are never at our wits' end; hunted, we are never abandoned to our fate; struck down, we are not left to die" (II Cor. 4:7-9).

In the world we inhabit and the society we belong to, innumerable events can and do occur that are not willed by God and are not subject to his immediate control. Sometimes his utmost efforts meet temporary defeat. There is no absolute guarantee of the outcome; yet no defeat is final. God is constantly exploring and finding new ways of advance and creating new possibilities of value. In everything he works for good with those who love him, and nothing whatever can separate us from his love (Rom. 8:28, 38-39). In our struggles for righteousness and truth we are supported by the Lord of all creation. When he goes into exile with his people, the land of exile is not a foreign country but a part of his own world. In ways that we cannot always trace, through suffering, he fulfills his purposes. The faith of the New Testament—and it can be our faith—is that death and the deadly threats of evil are swallowed up in victory, that amid difficulties we are kept in God's boundless and invincible love, and that we can trust his good will ultimately to prevail.

Such was the faith of Martin Luther King, Jr., who knew intimately the awful power of hate to inflict pain. In a sermon on the deliverance of the Israelites at the Red Sea (Exod. 14:30), he affirms:

God is at work in his universe. He is not outside the world looking on with a sort of cold indifference. Here on all the roads of life, he is striving in our striving. . . . As we struggle to defeat the forces of evil, the God of the universe struggles with us. Evil dies on the seashore, not merely because of man's endless struggle against it, but because of God's power to defeat it.[27]

3. The awareness that God is involved in the struggle against evil to the point of suffering moves concerned human beings to strive with him. The "not merely . . . but" in King's assurance does not denigrate human effort; rather it stimulates and exalts it. When we see all persons held together in the suffering love of God, the springs of our own compassion are released; and, forgetting self, we accept the price of sharing the costly struggle. This should be true especially of professing Christians, who know that Jesus was put to death outside the city wall in "the place of the skull," where the despised outcasts of society were executed. What we know of the sufferings of God deepens our identification with the oppressed and rejected and summons us to labor for their deliverance and their restoration to the human community. Such action not only lightens the burden of suffering; it also blunts the edge of the theological problem of evil, because it diminishes the human anguish that we seek to reconcile with divine goodness.

My cherished friend Paul Johnson found this to be true during his long terminal illness. In his last published utterance, he wrote these words: "At times I am moved to cry with Jesus, 'My God, my God, why hast thou forsaken me?' But then I remember Jesus' word, 'Take my yoke upon you, and learn of me; . . . and you will find rest for your souls.' And, under his yoke, I discover anew his sustaining presence, rejoice in his love, and seek to offer this love to others." [28]

Suppose we acknowledge that the issue posed by evil does stand in doubt. Does this circumstance justify passivity and despair? Does it not rather call us to active, sacrificial effort? In research directed toward the conquest of disease, in attempts to understand and protect our environment, in the struggle against oppression and for just human relations, in personal openness to the Spirit and self-forgetful commitment to his will, in these and related ways we can play a significant role in reducing suffering and heightening the worth and meaning of life. Loving, laboring, and suffering as co-workers with God, we bring ourselves and others into that healing, transforming relationship with him that provides the most convincing answer of all to the problem of human anguish.

PART THREE · PROVIDENCE

12   Of God, Sparrows, and People

Retrospect and Prospect

Our examination of nine responses to the problem of reconciling human anguish with divine love and power has led to several conclusions that heighten our understanding. Basic to all of these is the conviction that the God whose creative activity permeates and sustains our world is seeking to form a community of mutually supportive persons who strive with him and one another for the maximum realization of value. The process through which this venture is being carried on is unfinished; we live in a world in the making.

Four features of this endeavor shed special light on the universality of suffering:

1. The very possibility of life and value fulfillment requires a physical world marked by constancy, regularity, and predictability; but such a determinate natural order entails hardship and pain when sentient creatures fail to observe its provisions, whether intentionally, carelessly, or ignorantly. This stable order is the setting for the changes of the evolutionary process—a vast experiment in which every stage involves incompleteness and deficiency needing to be overcome, hence widespread struggle and suffering. But the resulting ills could be eliminated only by a drastic alteration of the process that would destroy its positive potentialities.

2. Responsible exercise of real freedom of choice is indispensable if men and women are to become true persons rather than automata; yet freedom produces suffering when it is deliberately, thoughtlessly, or ignorantly misused. It is a precious but perilous gift. We cannot enjoy its benefits without risking the distress that our abuse of it occasions in ourselves and others affected, and without causing anguish to God himself when we oppose his righteous will. Also pertinent is a degree of freedom in subhuman animals, which, together with atomic indeterminacy, brings about some organic instability and so contributes to evil as well as development in sentient beings.

3. The interdependence of our world, manifest in intermeshed human relationships, interaction in the physical order, and close interconnections between human life and its total environment, is essential to life and responsible for some of its richest fulfillments; but it makes persons vulnerable to the errors and wrongs of others and the frequently disruptive impact of the natural order.

4. Further comprehension of evil is gained if we discard the traditional notion of divine omnipotence, conceiving the power of God as ultimate and incomparably great, yet less than infinite or absolute. God is who and what he is, not something else that we might prefer. Possibly eternal, uncreated limits are intrinsic to his power. If so, though his love is unbounded, his creative activity involves costly travail over long periods of time, and human beings are exposed to ills that he does not choose, but works ceaselessly to remove and prevent.

Taken together, these considerations go far to render explicable the presence of so much evil in a world created and sustained by a God of unparalleled power, supreme wisdom, and perfect goodness. Vast areas of mystery remain, but we have discovered shafts of light piercing the darkness and illuminating our journey.

Two additional conclusions of our study belong in this synopsis: recognition of the fact that suffering, though not ordained by God, often contributes to the growth of character; and the belief, supported by the travail of evolution and nourished by the concrete historical disclosure of God's suffering love in the cross and resurrection of Jesus Christ, that God intimately shares the pain and pathos of his creation. Strictly speaking, these affirmations are not answers to the theological question of why there is so much suffering. Nevertheless, both of them help us to meet and overcome evil and hence to reduce its terror. To that degree they lessen the theoretical problem also, since they serve to diminish the human anguish that needs to be reconciled with the character of God.

If these conclusions are valid, they support the judgment that God's aid is available to those who must carry on their lives under such promising yet hazardous conditions. He who in love creates moral persons for maturing fellowship with one another and himself can be counted on to do everything possible to reduce misery and strengthen those who must endure it. Thus when Paul admonishes the Philippian Christians, ''You must work out your own salvation in fear and trembling,'' he adds the assurance, ''for it is God who works in you'' (Phil. 2:12-13). But in view of the volume of suffering we encounter, the further question inevitably arises, *How* is he doing this? What does it mean to be in God's care?

In Burma during World War II, acquaintances facing imminent danger of death from bombs or shells often parted with the words, ''God keep you.'' In Paul Geren's interpretation this meant, ''God will keep us from the ultimate evil. . . . To be kept by God means to be in his love whether living or dying. . . . The ultimate evil would be the absence of love. A life outside it would be more evil than a death in it.'' [1] When I cited this understanding of providence in a seminar at Garrett-Evangelical Seminary in 1974, an alert student asked, ''Can we be more specific about this? Concretely, what does it mean to say that we are in God's love? In what ways does he keep us?''

The same query may be raised regarding the persuasion of the apostle Paul that nothing whatever in life or death can separate us from the love of God (Rom. 8:38-39), and the assurance of Jesus that God's care embraces even the falling sparrow and therefore men and women who are worth more than any number of sparrows (Matt. 10:29-31; Luke 12:6). Despite God's concern the sparrow dies, and the believers whom ''nothing in all creation'' can remove from the divine love may still be called on to endure intense physical pain and mental torture. What then does it mean to declare that God is present with them? What implications do the conclusions we have reached have for our concrete existence, when we or our companions face personal suffering in the crises of life or the wearisome afflictions of the daily round?

The cited assertions of Jesus, the apostle Paul, and Paul Geren seem to have primary reference to the mortality of creaturely existence, assuring us that God's care includes provision for life beyond physical death. Unquestionably, the gift of faith and courage in the face of death and the promise of victory over its dark threat constitute a central aspect of any Christian view of providence. But for many people the harshness of life now poses a still more formidable problem. To take just one example, millions of people are condemned to a barren, hungry, diseased existence in abject poverty. Neither government relief programs nor the tender sacrificial ministries of dedicated persons like Mother Teresa of Calcutta can reach them all. We can explain their predicament and preserve faith in the divine goodness by reasoning such as that in the chapters above. Their situation is attributable not to God's lack of concern, but to drought, disease, overpopulation, ignorance, unemployment, human abuse of freedom, the indifference or inhumanity of other people, or boundaries to the power of God inherent in his nature. But their unrelieved suffering goes on.

Suppose we are intellectually convinced that even crushing evils can be harmonized with belief in the love of God. We still must ask what we can do about the deep hurts that we and others are experiencing right now. And we must inquire what faith in God implies regarding his own ministry to anguished men and women. In what ways is he present in the sufferings that he permits or does not prevent? What is he doing to provide for those he loves? How does he "keep" them?

Misleading Views of Providence

At the risk of undue repetition, it should be stressed that God does not keep his own by granting them immunity from harm. Particularly, he does not suspend or violate his established ways of acting in order to save from trouble those who trust in him. Unfortunately, the devotional language of some of the Hebrew psalms lends itself to this interpretation. Psalm 91, for instance, assures us that the Lord provides a "safe retreat" for those who turn to him in faith, guarding them from raging tempests, pestilence, poisonous snakes, and even the dangers of war:

> A thousand may fall at your side,
> ten thousand close at hand,
> but you it shall not touch.

No calamity will befall those who love God. Similarly, Psalm 121 assures Israel:

> The Lord will guard you against all evil;
> he will guard you, body and soul.

These affirmations may be using vivid metaphors and hyperbole to declare the writer's certainty that no evil can remove us from the presence of God, who can be counted upon to strengthen us in every ordeal. So they have been understood by many generations of Jews and Christians, to whose faith calamities are not ultimately calamitous. But if they are interpreted literally, as has also frequently occurred, they run counter to observable facts. There is no evidence that God protects those who trust him from accident, storm, or disease, nor does he exempt them from the universality of death. He provides for human welfare through the constant, dependable functioning of the natural order, but not by delivering a chosen few from the dangers that confront all. He will not suspend the laws of gravity when we lose our balance on the brink of a precipice, or guard from injury a fragile human body struck by a bullet or a speeding automobile, or substitute pure oxygen for deadly carbon monoxide gas given off by a faulty heating unit. We can understand how Eddie Rickenbacker, afloat in the Pacific for many days in World War II, could gratefully attribute the landing of a sea gull on his life raft as God's way of providing the food that saved his life; but we dare not forget that many airmen equally religious perished without benefit of either rafts or gulls, as have thousands of travelers in plane accidents in later years.

Another faulty conception of providence is that which holds that God plans or orders all events, whether they are helpful or hurtful to human life. According to John Calvin's classic formulation of this view, God holds the helm of the universe and regulates all events. "All things happen by the ordination of God," and nothing is "fortuitously contingent." This sweeping judgment applies to inanimate natural forces like winds and storms no less than to "the deliberations and volitions of men." Moreover, providence operates not only through general laws, but through the divine ordering of particular events. "Every year, month, and day is governed by a new and particular providence of God." On the human level "every prosperous and pleasing event" should be ascribed entirely to God, who thereby demonstrates his beneficence. But our adversities and afflictions are likewise "permitted and directed by his righteous dispensation," in order to inculcate patience and self-denial in the faithful and restrain their lower impulses, and to abase the proud and confound the machinations of the wicked. Even robberies and homicides are decreed by God; though the ends he has in view may be concealed from human minds, they are instruments of his providence. Furthermore, providence controls the future as well as the past; "there will be no event which God has not ordained." The faithful may therefore be consoled by the knowledge that their sufferings occur by God's command. They are in the care of him who regulates all things for their good. By his particular providence he sustains, nourishes, and provides for everything he has made. Hence we may in complete trust commit ourselves to his will.[2]

Calvin's interpretation of providence has exerted considerable influence on English hymnody. Thus Isaac Watts affirms:

> Strong is His arm, and shall fulfill
> His great decrees and sovereign will.

The same conception appears fairly frequently in hymns representing the Lutheran tradition. In chapter 3 we have already called attention to Georg Neumark's acceptance of events as "sent" by the gracious will of God. Similarly, Joachim Neander urges the pious Christian to ask,

> Hast thou not seen
> How thy desires e'er have been
> Granted in what he ordaineth?

Watts's hymn was written in the early eighteenth century, and Neumark's and Neander's lines were penned in the seventeenth. Yet the fact that they are often sung in the late twentieth century suggests that Christian congregations today are at least not disturbed by their assertion of absolute divine sovereignty. Whether this acceptance is due more to basic theological agreement or to indifference to the content of what is sung is impossible to judge. The editorial committee of the new *Hymnal of the United Church of Christ* (1974) has altered the translation of "How thy desires e'er have been" in Neander's stanza to read, "All that is needful hath been," but has left unchanged the key verb, "ordaineth."

It is understandable that many people can find comfort in ascribing all that happens to the secret counsels of the divine will. This recourse to mystery and utter trust provides a sense of security amid the bafflements of life, even though it suppresses or evades the difficult questions that many reflective minds cannot help asking. There is good ground for believing that God works in ways unfathomed by us to accomplish his ends; but to maintain that he specifically orders all events in nature and determines all human thoughts and deeds, both good and evil, raises crucial theological and ethical questions.

To portray God as prompting men and women to violate the highest norms of human conduct to fulfill his hidden purposes is to raise anew the ancient query of Abraham, "Shall not the judge of all the earth do what is just?" (Gen. 18:25). Moreover, to regard all natural occurrences and all human choices as locked into a tight system decreed throughout by the divine will excludes all real human freedom and all subhuman indeterminacy, both of which we have found good reasons for affirming. To claim further that this arrangement really works out for our own good runs counter to human experience realistically interpreted. When Neander asks whether we do not perceive that our desires are always granted in what God ordains, an open-eyed observer of human events is likely to respond with a firm negative. Even our noblest desires supported by our best efforts often remain unfulfilled, whether or not the outcome is seen as divinely willed. The moral catastrophes of twentieth-century society, the widespread acceptance of overt and covert violence, and the sensuality and materialism characteristic of much individual life today cannot be regarded as providentially ordained without surrender of belief in the goodness of God or rejection of our keenest ethical insights or both. We must look further for a defensible view of providence with respect to human experience of evil.

The conceptions of providence that we have just discarded bring to mind a third that is equally repugnant—the notion that God keeps us by guarding us safely in the status quo. The verb "keep" readily lends itself to this misunderstanding, since it suggests remaining in a stationary position. One thinks naturally of a jail keeper, an animal keeper in a zoo, the keeper of the grounds. Yet a bee keeper must learn to move with alacrity! The meanings of the Anglo-Saxon root *cepan* include "to desire or seek," both implying change, and to "keep" today may mean to practice or perform, as well as to persevere or continue. Thus one may in walking or driving keep straight ahead, while in attempting to solve a problem one may keep going or proceed in the search for answers. These latter meanings make plain that faith that God keeps us may involve an altogether active relationship. If we are true to the conception of God proposed in the preceding chapters, we shall think of the Spirit who seeks to lead his people toward greater maturity in the realization of their highest potentialities, who is himself on the way in an unfinished venture, and who keeps them by strengthening them for and in the ordeals of the journey. He is less a mighty fortress than a guide who goes before us, sharing our risks and our hardships as we advance into unmapped territory.

Life in the Keeping of God

How, then, does God keep or provide for his people as they attempt to face suffering? In accord with the proposals found most persuasive in the preceding chapters, I suggest five main ways.

1. His presence gives strength and courage to endure hardship and to overcome its devastating effects. Paul the apostle declares, "There is nothing love cannot face; there is no limit to its faith, its hope, and its endurance" (I Cor. 13:7). The love he has in mind is of course that which is a response to the prior love of God. The person who is sustained by active trust in him is never cut off from his fortifying presence. This is the stirring message of Georg Neumark's lines, which is not invalidated by our criticism of his view that God sends the evils that assail us:

> If thou but suffer God to guide thee
>   And hope in him through all thy ways,
> He'll give thee strength what'er betide thee,

      And bear thee through the evil days.
      Who trusts in God's unchanging love
      Builds on the rock that naught can move.

When the Israelites were about to cross the Jordan and enter the Promised Land, a journey still fraught with danger, Moses assured them and their new leader, Joshua: "The Lord himself goes at your head; he will be with you; he will not fail you or forsake you. Do not be discouraged or afraid" (Deut. 31:8; cf. Josh. 1:5). Similarly, when the Hebrew exiles confronted another hazardous journey, the return from Babylon to their homeland, Second Isaiah declared that the Lord would not forsake them. Even in the desert they would find water and growing things, and when they faced the opposite kind of danger, he would provide the needed resources:

> When you pass through deep waters, I am with you,
>   when you pass through rivers,
>   they will not sweep you away. . . .
>
> For I am the Lord your God,
>   the Holy One of Israel, your deliverer.   (Isa. 43:2-3)

Significantly, the prophet does not promise that there will be no turbulent rivers to cross, but rather that those who undertake the crossing will be accompanied by their liberator, and therefore not abandoned or overwhelmed. This is a basic meaning of belief in the care of God. Life itself is a risky pilgrimage. Those who engage in it trusting in him who has called them may expect to be sustained by inner resources more than equal to its demands. His grace is sufficient for their needs.

A related dimension of providence is the inner freedom that comes with the awareness that we are not alone on our journey. A personal consciousness of the Lord's presence releases the author of the Twenty-third Psalm from worry and fear:

> Even though I walk through a valley dark as death
> I fear no evil, for thou art with me.

There is also a positive liberation that springs from the conviction that the Lord of all creation is working ceaselessly for the values he calls on us to seek. It is especially this freedom for resolute action for which Harry Emerson Fosdick prays:

> From the fears that long have bound us,
>   Free our hearts to work and praise.
> Grant us wisdom, grant us courage,
>   For the living of these days.[3]

Our best human plans often go awry. But when we are supported by the divine presence we are freed from nagging fears and enabled to discharge our responsibilities with fortitude and power.

2. God works through human agents to alleviate and prevent suffering. In Christian perspective those who provide food, clothing, and health care are not only serving God, as indicated in Matthew 25:31-40, but through such ministries they become his agents in helping to keep men, women, and children in his love. A chaplain in a mental hospital reports his conversation with a patient in which the chaplain spoke of the love of God. The sick man interrupted: "Don't tell me that God loves me. Show me that you love me." As we share real love and understanding, we make God manifest in the most vivid way possible.

The interdependent world in which we live is permeated by the activity of the God who loves it. We are free to resist his urging, but when we accept responsibility for one another we are responding to the divine reality that binds us together. The spirit of a caring God can be transmitted through people sensitized by their acknowledged relation to him. Thus Mother Teresa and her Sisters of Charity minister to the homeless in the streets of Calcutta, "finding Jesus in the distressing disguise of the poor," including the lepers, the retarded, and the unemployed. Other ministries are provided by persons who have no consciously religious motivation, but are responding to imperatives they cannot ignore. Their sense of accountability springs not from mere tradition or a desire for social approval, but from something more ultimate in the depths of their being. To the eyes of theistic faith they, too, serve the divine purpose.

It would be a serious mistake to think of providence only in relation to needy individuals. God is at work also in organized movements to change social structures that involve oppression and injustice. Thus Martin Luther King, Jr., loses himself in the struggle for the human rights of minorities and the attainment of a just peace in Vietnam; Dorothy Day devotes her energies to the rights of working people through the Catholic Worker movement; and Archbishop Helder Pessoa Camara of Brazil attacks the power of multinational corporations and the advent of a "new nazism," which uses the appeal to anticommunism to subjugate the dispossessed in Latin America. With comparable aims, denominational and ecumenical agencies support the rights of American Indians in South Dakota and elsewhere; the United Methodist Board of Church and Society works for a true allocation of responsibility for the deaths of four students who at Kent State University in Ohio nonviolently protested the U.S. invasion of Cambodia; many religious bodies uphold Cesar Chavez and the United Farm Workers in their courageous attempt to secure the right of workers to determine by secret ballot the union of their choice; and Bread for the World seeks to arouse governments to deal effectively with the causes of world hunger.

The commitment to improving human relations made manifest by these and related groups is deeply religious in rootage. Many others are responding in similar fashion to what for them is an ultimate concern—provision for human beings of maximal opportunity for the free development of their potentialities. Though such bodies may see their work simply as a humanitarian endeavor, their deep regard for human welfare and their conscientious acceptance of social responsibility may be reasonably interpreted as fulfillment of God's purpose. He is able to use their efforts as instruments of his care.

The consequences of our efforts to reduce human anguish are seldom spectacular, but they play an important, indeed indispensable, role in the transformation of human life. One member of an Alcoholics Anonymous group that met in Pennsylvania in 1974 summed up its meaning for him in these words: "None of us is cured of alcoholism, but we just stay with each other, uphold, share, make ourselves present, and we are whole." In our differing networks of relations, we all have opportunities in various ways to bear one another's burdens, and so to help each other to gain wholeness. To the extent that we do this, we demonstrate the love of God. We not only give answers but become answers to the pains, sorrows, and hardships of our fellow travelers.

3. God keeps us by conserving and building on the contributions we make to the ends he seeks. Here the thought of Whitehead provides a useful point of reference. According to him, the values we realize are not merely transient; they are preserved permanently in what he calls the consequent nature of God. No attainment of value ever completely passes away. All aspects of the ongoing life of the world are taken up into the experience of God. All fulfillments of the good, including those wrought through suffering, are transmuted and cumulatively preserved in him, enriching his life. Hence what we do makes a difference to him; our own lives matter ultimately. In a sense, therefore, God grows through the constant actualization by his creatures of experiences of worth. "The image—and it is but an image—the image under which this operative growth of God's nature is best conceived, is that of a tender care that nothing be lost."[4] We dare not forget Whitehead's caution that his language is not to be taken literally. Yet his moving phrase qualifies as an informative if partial definition of providence.

To the degree that the values we cherish and attain are expressions of our personalities, when they are preserved, something of us is carried forward. In this sense God may be said to care for us by preventing the loss of what is dear to us. Our labors do not go for naught. He keeps us by gathering to himself the character, courage, love, and commitment to enduring values that mark our lives, enabling these values to enhance the fulfillment of the aims he prizes. In a solidaristic, interdependent universe in which God invites his creatures to become by their own choice co-creators with him, we can believe that, in ways we cannot fully comprehend, the values we live for are preserved eternally, contributing to the increasing actualization of the goals sought by God himself.

This awareness reinforces the experience of freedom mentioned earlier in this chapter as a by-product of awareness of the divine presence. The conviction that the things that claim our allegiance are in harmony with the deepest tendencies of the universe, and serve to advance those tendencies, helps to release us from doubt and fear. It also liberates us for confident action and a readiness to accept sacrifices and risks for the lasting values that identify us with the movement of existence itself. "The universe is the champion of the upright."[5]

4. God keeps those who trust and serve him by giving them life beyond physical death. Though it is important to recognize that our best efforts to advance God's purposes contribute to his life and that of the world he is fashioning, to stop with this would be to truncate the meaning of providence. We noted near the end of chapter 7 that belief in everlasting life is not in itself a sufficient answer to evil, since no future blessedness can justify the intensity and duration of the terrors that many people must endure here and now. But *without* that belief, the other considerations, however weighty, remain also inadequate.

We have held that God's purpose in creation includes the formation of a fellowship of persons who with him and one another seek the greatest possible realization of values. Persons best fulfill their vocation as they freely undertake the risks of life in a stable, dependable, interdependent, unfinished world in which God shares their travail. Light is shed on human anguish if we think of it in this context. But that light turns to darkness if those whose relation to God imparts to them intrinsic worth are allowed to pass out of existence. Values do not exist abstractly or in a vacuum. They must be experienced by conscious beings, and they can endure only as the persons who cherish them endure. Their status would be precarious in the extreme if those who prize them were constantly coming and going, with no permanence attaching to any. A fellowship of replaceable transients can hardly be the kind of community God seeks, nor could it attain maximal worth or meaning. Hence faith that God really cares for individuals, and is concerned with them for their own sake, implies the belief that he grants to them never-ending opportunity to fulfill the ends for which he created them.

We reach the same conclusion if we start with the redemptive instead of the creative activity of God, as does the New Testament. In sacrificial love, God acts to reconcile men and women to himself, to break down the walls that separate them from one another and from him, to free them from sin and oppression to fullness of life. Life thus healed and renewed goes on forever. This faith was born in the early Christian community through the coming of Jesus, whom they called the Christ. In him, they believed, God had "broken the power of death and brought life and immortality to light" (II Tim. 1:10). The eternal destiny of men and women was assumed in his teachings: "Do not fear those who kill the body, but cannot kill the soul" (Matt. 10:28). "Store up treasure in heaven, where there is no moth and no rust to spoil it, no thieves to break in and steal" (Matt. 6:20). "There are many dwelling-places in my Father's house" (John 14:2). It was attested by his life of self-forgetful love. Most of all it was confirmed by his death and resurrection.

The resurrection narratives in the Gospels and the Pauline Letters contain perplexing ambiguities and contradictions. Yet with all their differences, they speak with one voice in affirming one world-shaking truth: the God disclosed to the disciples in Jesus Christ was victorious over all evil. The suffering love that they had encountered in him had triumphed over sin, pain, and death. The ultimate power in the universe is the love of God, and fulfillment of his righteous will is on the way.

That this is true can be held as an act of reasonable faith by men and women who are fully aware of the evil in today's world. Belief in life following physical death is as strong or as weak as faith in the goodness and the matchless power of God. It does not come with an ironclad, money-back guarantee; and no scientific evidence can prove or disprove it. But it is supported by the richness and inexhaustibility of our experiences of lasting value that point to God as their Source and Conserver, and it is confirmed for Christian faith by the disclosure of God in Jesus the Christ. Those who respond to him with trust and love are freed from gnawing anxiety. Louis B. Russell, who in 1974 died at the age of forty-nine, after living more than six years with a heart transplant, said in an interview two days before his death, "I don't know what the future holds, but I know who holds the future." We can believe that he who keeps us as we enter the future will provide new and enlarging opportunities for sharing experiences of enduring worth.

5. Providence is active not only in the lives of individuals but in social relations and the processes of history. In view of the freedom operative in God's creation, he cannot be said to determine the course of history, but he does seek to guide it toward the actualization of divine values. He may be said to act negatively as Judge and Destroyer of the evil, and positively as Creator and Redeemer of the good.

When James Weldon Johnson begins his poem "The Prodigal Son" with the lines

> Young man—
> Young man—
> Your arm's too short to box with God,[6]

he states in simple imagery a profound truth: operative in human life is a value structure that tends to make evil self-defeating. There are limits beyond which wickedness cannot go without destroying itself. The message of doom so frequently heard in the great Hebrew prophets is grounded in their recognition of this moral constitution of reality, of which Yahweh is the concrete embodiment. Amos and Isaiah see a nation marked by bribery in court, dishonesty in business, luxury for the few, appalling poverty for the many, ruthless oppression of the poor and the weak, and over all a veil of ceremonial religion. Such a people, they declare, stands under the judgment of God (Amos 5:11; 2:9-10; 5:18-20; 6:11; 9:8; Isa. 1:20; 5:7-30; 10:1-4).

Reinhold Niebuhr makes plain the applicability of this insight on a much broader scale:

> The predatory character of every social system is the ultimate cause of its own dissolution. History is the oft-repeated tale of a once robust life coming to an ignominious death. Civilizations, like men and beasts, perish partly because they grow old and feeble and partly because they are slain by those whose enmity they have deserved by their ruthlessness.[7]

The truth of Niebuhr's observation is illustrated by the overthrow of successive powers in world history, and it is abundantly confirmed by events in the twentieth century. It is demonstrated in the downfall of the Italian fascist and Nazi regimes in 1945; in the collapse of colonial and imperialistic regimes as subject peoples have become conscious of their rights as human beings; in the effective demand by blacks and other minorities, aware of their own inherent dignity, for the end of white exploitation; in the humiliating failure of American armed might to control the destiny of southeast Asia; and in the forced resignation of an American president following revelations of conniving deceit, suppression of truth, and unscrupulous disregard of basic rights connected with the Watergate break-in. It is true that some individuals and groups find ways to profit from such debacles, and that new injustices are engineered by cynical individuals and powerful organizations. But when such machinations succeed, they gain only the limited ends opted for, forfeiting the opportunity for higher values. There seems to be a moral fabric in reality that sets the conditions within which humanity may realize the deeper satisfactions; those policies and movements that violate it compass their own defeat. In the words of Friedrich von Logau,

> Though the mills of God grind slowly,
> yet they grind exceeding small.[8]

Also discernible in society are tendencies working positively for the conservation and enhancement of values. It is illuminating to regard these as indications that God is acting creatively and redemptively in the historical process. He is not only a consuming fire but a spirit of reconciling and transforming love. In the words of Jeremiah, as the Lord watched over his people "with intent to pull down and to uproot, to demolish and destroy," so he will "watch over them to build and to plant" (Jer. 31:28). Though the author of the book of Revelation probably wrote in the midst of the persecutions of Domitian, he dared to affirm that God was working for the coming of "a new heaven and a new earth" (Rev. 21:1).

Hebrew-Christian faith conceives God as empowering, stimulating, and guiding those activities that aim to reduce suffering and enrich life. It also perceives in him the ability to influence the outcome of activities that have the opposite intent, and so to use even evil itself as a means to good. Through a certain subtlety and artfulness, he incorporates into larger patterns the energies of those who seek only their own selfish ends, so that they contribute ultimately more to his goals than their own.

Leslie Weatherhead tells of a conversation with a Persian student about Persian rug-making, in which boys work on the wrong side of a rug while the artist directs their labors from the right side. "What happens," asked Weatherhead, "when a boy makes a mistake?" "If the artist is great enough," replied the student, "he weaves the mistake into the pattern.'' [9] This understanding of the relation of God to human events appears often in Hebrew biblical interpretations of history. Thus the Elohistic narrative in Genesis connects the jealousy of Joseph's brothers, which led to his slavery in Egypt, with the opportunity he gained through his later rise to power to save the Hebrews as well as the Egyptians from famine: "It was God who sent me ahead of you to save men's lives. . . . You meant to do me harm; but God meant to bring good out of it by preserving the lives of many people, as we see today" (Gen. 45:5, 8; 50:20).

Isaiah voices a similar view of the relations between Assyria and Judah. In a variety of figures he declares that the Lord, no more in sympathy with the despotic cruelty of Sennacherib than with the sinfulness of Judah, nevertheless uses the Assyrian invasion to discipline the Hebrew people and arouse in them a keener awareness of their ethical and religious obligations. Assyria is the rod of Yahweh's anger, the razor he uses to shave Judah, the axe with which he hews away the rotten wood in the land. Sennacherib is unconscious of the use to which he is being put. Filled with arrogant pride and lust for power, he follows his own devices and goes forth to conquer. But in that very process, he contributes to purposes quite foreign to his intention (Isa. 7:20; 8:7,8; 10:5,7,12-15; 14:24-27; cf. Amos 6:14; Jer. 21:8-10; 38:2,3; Isa. 44:28; 45:1; 54:16).

This conception of God's use of evil appears in the apostle Paul, Augustine, Luther, and others in the history of Christian thought. It reaches its clearest philosophical expression in Hegel, who calls it the cunning of (divine) reason:

> Reason is as cunning as it is powerful. Cunning may be said to lie in the inter-mediative action which, while it permits the objects to follow their own bent and act upon one another till they waste away, and does not itself directly interfere in the process, is nevertheless only working out its own aims. With this explanation, Divine Providence may be said to stand in the world and its process in the capacity of absolute cunning. God lets men do as they please with their particular passions and interests; but the result is the accomplishment of—not their plans, but His, and these differ decidedly from the ends primarily sought by those whom He employs. [10]

A pious claim that evil is always turned to good would not be justified by the empirical data. The interpretation so eloquently stated by Hegel does not clearly apply to all situations. As far as we can tell, much evil has not contributed to the fulfillment of divine purposes. Though its long-range by-products often do so, these are little comfort to the immediate victims of human arrogance and exploitation. Yet there is sufficient evidence to indicate that Providence sometimes functions in the manner suggested. Like a sailing vessel that by tacking uses contrary winds to drive it forward, God does often convert to his own purposes the very energies which oppose him.

For the Hebrew people the fall of Jerusalem in 586 B.C. was a disaster. Yet through the resulting captivity in Babylon they encountered Persian belief in one principle of light or goodness in the world. So stimulated, they searched their own writings with new interest, and found there, clearly taught, the message that God is one. For centuries the prophets had sought with little success to instill ethical monotheism into the nation. It was the Exile and the resulting influence of a politically dominant foreign people that finally opened the eyes of the Hebrews to the meaning of their own heritage. Polytheism and idol worship were then no longer a threat.

The crucifixion of Jesus seemed to his enemies to finish him and his revolutionary teachings. Yet in fact his power and influence were vastly extended by his death. Whatever the explanation, his apostles, emboldened by the resurrection experience, were soon going to all parts of the Roman Empire propagating the new faith. Thus the crucifixion became, despite its agony and defeat, the occasion for one of the most momentous movements of world history. The executioners of Jesus became unwitting instruments in spreading the very teaching they sought above all else to suppress.

World War II, with its staggering carnage, was so monstrous a calamity that it cannot be justified by any of its consequences. Yet it did lead to the formation of the United Nations, which, despite its glaring weaknesses, has for thirty years provided a valuable world forum for the expression of grievances and demands for justice; while in many cases it has served to prevent, contain, or end hostilities that without it might have engulfed wide areas of the world. It has given new and developing countries an opportunity to participate responsibly in the family of nations and has taken important steps toward a world community.

The colossal destructive power of nuclear weapons and the proliferation of the capacity to manufacture and use them constitute a grim threat to world peace and civilization itself. Yet the sheer gravity of the danger, while it has not prevented the stockpiling of weapons and the search for more deadly devices, has been an effective deterrent to the actual use of atomic armaments by the superpowers and a goad to détente and cooperative action. Such instances as these confirm the faith that God sometimes turns even evil to his own advantage.

Looking back on the various ways in which God sustains his people amid the anguish of their earthly journey, we are reminded again that the venture is not an easy one for any of its participants. But there is firm basis for belief in the sustaining power of God's sacrificial love and in the future toward which he leads us. The created universe not only groans in travail; it also "waits with eager longing" for the appearance of God's mature sons and daughters (Rom. 8:19). The long, painful processes of evolution in the natural order and the arduous endeavors of human history have been aptly called the eighth day of creation—an ongoing, never-ending activity in which men and women are summoned to be co-laborers with God.[11] Frustration and anguish will often beset us, but creative and healing energies far surpassing our own are quietly and effectively working in individuals, in peoples, and in all creation to actualize a true community of shared and inexhaustible values.

Each person must decide how he will respond to existence as it touches him, with all its evil: in rebellion, in passive resignation, or in trustful, active affirmation of the loving purpose of God. We have found ample support for the third of these choices. We can declare with John Calvin—though without his determinism—that God is at the helm of the universe. Such confidence does not bring all storms to an end, but it assures us that our frail craft can, with his guidance, avert shipwreck and be kept on course.

Notes

Chapter 1

1. T. S. Eliot, *Murder in the Cathedral, The Complete Poems and Plays* (New York: Harcourt, Brace and Co. [1930], 1952), p. 180.

2. Michael J. Arlen, *Passage to Ararat* (New York: Farrar, Strauss & Giroux, 1975), pp. 176, 183-94, 232, 239-40.

3. *Encyclopaedia Britannica,* 15th ed., *Micropaedia,* IX, 517; *Macropaedia,* 17, 578.

4. Arlen lists the following peoples who have undergone massacre and attempted genocide: the Ibos of Nigeria; the Communists of Indonesia; the Hindus in Bangladesh; the Incas of South America; the Indians of North America; the Ukrainian peasants of the U.S.S.R.; the black slaves of Haiti and Guadaloupe; Protestants, Catholics, and Muslims at various times and places; and the Cappadocians, whom Tigran of Armenia marched across the wilderness to his new capital. Arlen defines genocide as "an expression of generalized hate, a hate so wide and encompassing that it included everyone—man, woman, child—within a certain national or racial group" *(Passage to Ararat,* pp. 188, 189-90).

5. Ibid., pp. 279-80.

6. Arthur Simon, *Bread for the World* (New York: Paulist Press; Grand Rapids: William B. Eerdmans Publishing Co., 1975), p. 10.

7. C. J. Ducasse, *A Philosophical Scrutiny of Religion* (New York: Ronald Press, 1953), pp. 356-57.

8. Langdon Gilkey, *Maker of Heaven and Earth* (Garden City, N.Y.: Doubleday & Co. [1959], 1965), pp. 240-46.

9. Aquinas, *Summa Theologica,* I, Ques. 49, Art. 3, Reply Obj. 5; John Hick, *Evil and the God of Love* (London: Macmillan & Co., 1966), p. 299; C. S. Lewis, *The Problem of Pain* (New York: The Macmillan Co., 1944), p. 77; Radoslav A. Tsanoff, *Religious Crossroads* (New York: E. P. Dutton, 1942), p. 306.

10. Lewis, *The Problem of Pain,* p. 77.

Chapter 2

1. Langdon Gilkey, *Maker of Heaven and Earth (Garden City, N.Y.: Doubleday & Co., 1959), p. 246.*

2. Alan Paton, *Instrument of Thy Peace* (New York: The Seabury Press, 1968), p. 26.

3. T. S. Eliot, *Murder in the Cathedral, The Complete Poems and Plays* (New York: Harcourt, Brace and Co. [1930], 1952), p. 212.

4. David Hume, *Dialogues Concerning Natural Religion,* Parts V, X, XI, in Charles W. Hendel, Jr., ed., *Hume: Selections* (New York: Charles Scribner's Sons, 1927), pp. 327-33, 364-70, 380-81.

5. Frederick Sontag, *The God of Evil: An Argument for the Existence of the Devil* (New York: Harper & Row, 1970).

6. Michael J. Arlen, *Passage to Ararat* (New York: Farrar, Strauss & Giroux, 1975), pp. 177, 119-21. See Avedis K. Sanjian, ed. and trans., *Colophons of Armenian Manuscripts, 1301–1480: A Source for Middle Eastern History* (Cambridge: Harvard University Press, 1969).

7. Erich Kellner, ed., *Christentum und Marxismus–Heute* (Wien, Frankfurt, Zürich: Europa Verlag, 1966), p. 96.

8. Elie Wiesel, "Jewish Values in the Post-Holocaust Future," *Judaism,* 16 (1967), 281.

9. Peter DeVries, *The Blood of the Lamb* (Boston: Little, Brown, 1962), p. 104.

10. Ibid., pp. 224-37; cf. pp. 241, 246.

11. Alfred de Vigny, "The Mount of Olivet," quoted by Radoslav A. Tsanoff, *Religious Crossroads* (New York: E. P. Dutton, 1942), p. 326.

12. W. E. B. DuBois, "A Litany of Atlanta," in *Black Voices,* ed. Abraham Chapman (New York: Mentor Books, New American Library, 1968), pp. 372-73.

13. Langston Hughes, "A New Song," in Jean Wagner, *Black Poets of the United States,* trans. Kenneth Douglass (Urbana, Ill.: University of Illinois Press, 1973), p. 438.

14. It is worth noting that the index of the authoritative symposium edited by Yervant K. Krikorian, *Naturalism and the Human Spirit* (New York: Columbia University Press, 1944), contains no entries for either "evil" or "suffering."

15. Harry Emerson Fosdick, *Living Under Tension* (New York: Harper & Brothers, 1941), pp. 215-16.

16. Lactantius, *A Treatise on the Anger of God,* chap. 13; cf. chaps. 12, 15, 16, 17, 21.

17. Augustine, *Confessions,* VII, 5.

18. Ibid., VII, 5.

19. John Stuart Mill, *Three Essays on Religion* (New York: Henry Holt & Co., 1874), pp. 186-87.

20. In the *Enchiridion,* Augustine declares that if the existence of evil were not a good, it "would not be permitted by the omnipotent God" (XCVI).

21. For critical examination of proposals that the ultimately real be conceived as dualistic, or as including evil as well as good in one supreme reality, see below, chapter 5.

22. C. J. Ducasse, *A Philosophical Scrutiny of Religion* (New York: Ronald Press, 1953), p. 352.

23. Cited in Benjamin E. Mays, *The Negro's God* (Boston: Chapman and Grimes, 1938), p. 49.

24. Martin Luther King, Jr., *Letter from Birmingham City Jail* (Philadelphia: American Friends Service Committee, 1963), p. 6.

25. James H. Cone, *God of the Oppressed* (New York: The Seabury Press, 1975), p. 163.

26. Augustine, *Enchiridion,* I, 673.

27. Augustine, *Confessions,* VII, 5.

28. Highlighted by John Hick in his definitive study *Evil and the God of Love* (London: Macmillan & Co., 1966). See below, pp. 148-51, 161-64.

29. Cone, *God of the Oppressed,* pp. 178-81. A similar demand for involvement by Christians in the sufferings of people is vigorously expressed by Dorothee Soelle in her book *Suffering,* trans. Everette R. Kalin (Philadelphia: Fortress Press, 1975). She does not dismiss the theological problem: "Not retreat from the problem, but its conquest, is necessary" (p. 144). However, her work is primarily a critique of apathy and an impassioned call for personal concern, manifested in active opposition to all forms of human oppression, for those who suffer.

30. Fosdick, *Living Under Tension,* p. 221.

31. E. Stanley Jones, *The Divine Yes* (Nashville: Abingdon, 1975), p. 98.

32. O. Fielding Clarke, *God and Suffering: An Essay in Theodicy, or the Justification of God in the Face of Evil* (Derby: Peter Smith, 1964), p. 160. See also Michael J. Taylor, S.J., ed., *The Mystery of Suffering and Death* (Staten Island, New York: Alba House, 1973), p. 79.

33. Clarke, *God and Suffering,* pp. 141, 126, 127.

34. George A. Buttrick, *God, Pain, and Evil* (Nashville: Abingdon, 1966), pp. 168-69, 229, 8, 226, 193. The books cited by Buttrick are Austin Farrer's *Freedom of the Will* (London: A. & C. Black, 1958) and M. C. D'Arcy's *Pain of This World and the Providence of God* (London: Longmans, Green & Co.). Both are painstaking critical investigations of basic aspects of the problem of evil.

35. Buttrick, *God, Pain, and Evil,* p. 227.

36. Obviously, philosophical discussion would not suffice either, but in a case like this the declaration of faith to one outside the faith is not demonstrably superior.

37. Archibald MacLeish, "The Book of Job," *The Christian Century,* 76 (1959), 419; *J.B.* (Boston: Houghton Mifflin Co., 1956), p. 11.

38. Cited in Buttrick, *God, Pain, and Evil,* p. 183.

39. *Evangelisches Kirchengesangbuch,* Ausgabe für die Evangelische Landeskirche in Württemberg, Mit Predigttexten (Stuttgart: Verlagskontor des Evangelischen Gesangbuchs, 1953), pp. 447-48 (author's translation).

40. *Boston Globe,* 17 November 1975.

41. Cone, *God of the Oppressed,* pp. 184, 165.

42. Cited by S. H. Bergman in "God and Man in Modern Thought: Man as the Heir of God," *Arguments and Doctrines: A Reader of Jewish Thinking in the Aftermath of the Holocaust,* ed. Arthur A. Cohen (New York: Harper & Row, 1970), p. 211.

43. Indeed, this possibility was almost inevitably entertained during my research in atheistic thought a decade ago, which resulted in *God in an Age of Atheism* (Abingdon, 1966).

44. Cited in L. Charles Birch, *Nature and God* (London: SCM Press; Philadelphia: Westminster Press, 1965), p. 34.

Chapter 3

1. Cited in L. Charles Birch, *Nature and God* (London: SCM Press; Philadelphia: Westminster Press, 1965), p. 50.

2. Wolfgang Trillhaas, "Theodizee. III. Systematisch," *Die Religion in Geschichte und Gegenwart,* 3rd ed., VI, 745-46.

3. T. B. Kilpatrick, "Suffering," in *Hastings Encyclopaedia of Religion and Ethics,* XII, 9.

4. *New York Times,* 13 April 1973, p. 4.

5. *Westminster* (Md.) *Times,* 5 May 1949.

6. *Beacon,* newsletter of Mason United Methodist Church, Tacoma, Washington, 2 August 1973.

7. *Washington Post,* 8 May 1974.

8. Artur Buchenau, ed., *Vorkritische Schriften,* vol. I, *Immanuel Kants Werke,* ed. Ernst Cassirer (Berlin: Bruno Cassirer, 1922), pp. 429-84, especially 441, 471-72.

9. Cited in Benjamin E. Mays, *The Negro's God as Reflected in His Literature,* Studies in American Negro Life, no. 11 (New York: Atheneum, 1968), p. 49.

10. D. C. Stange, "Bishop Daniel Alexander Payne's Protestation of American Slavery," *Journal of Negro History,* 52 (1967), 60.

11. Nathaniel Paul, "An Address Delivered on the Celebration of the Abolition of Slavery in the State of New York, July 5, 1827," cited in Carter G. Woodson, *Negro Orators and Their Orations* (New York: Atheneum, Russell & Russell, 1969), p. 69.

12. James H. Cone, *God of the Oppressed* (New York: The Seabury Press, 1975), p. 191.

13. Ibid., p. 192.

14. For a vivid interpretation of the role of Christocentric faith in the black experience see Cone, in ibid., pp. 191-93. A noteworthy parallel to Cone's account is the view of John Bowker that the central response to suffering in Christian thought as a whole is based on the faith that the life and resurrection of Jesus Christ disclose God's victorious power over evil. See Bowker's *Problems of Suffering in Religions of the World* (London: Cambridge University Press, 1970), p. 93.

15. Associated Press despatch by John Barbour, *Boston Sunday Globe,* 21 December 1975.

16. Kilpatrick, "Suffering," XII, 7.

17. In the King James Version the admonition is as follows: "Be ready always to give an answer to every man that asketh you a reason of the hope that is in you."

18. For consideration of the relation to evil of the structure of natural law, see chapter 8.

19. For further examination of the bearing of human freedom on evil see chapter 9.

Chapter 4

1. Mary Baker Eddy, *Science and Health with Key to the Scriptures* (Boston: Trustees Under the Will of Mary Baker G. Eddy [1875], 1934), pp. 107-115; cf. p. 465.

2. Ibid., pp. 103, 102; cf. pp. 110, 469, 71, 205, 346, 450, 480. At the beginning of *Science and Health,* Mrs. Eddy quotes as a basic maxim the words of Shakespeare's *Hamlet:* "There is nothing either good or bad, but thinking makes it so" (act II, sc. 2, lines 251-52).

3. Eddy, *Science and Health,* p. 472. In another passage, she writes that her recognition that "matter cannot be actual" enabled her to "behold, as never before, the awful unreality called evil" (p. 110).

4. Henry Clarke Warren, ed. and trans., *Buddhism in Translations. Passages Selected from the Buddhist Sacred Books* (Cambridge: Harvard University Press [1896], 1922); see pp. 84, 166, 204, 177, 155, 148-49, 208, 132-33. On *karma* and the related concept of *samsara,* see below, chapter 6.

5. Pope, *An Essay on Man,* Epistle I, lines 289-94.

6. Ibid., lines 258-59.

7. Bernard Bosanquet, *The Value and Destiny of the Individual* (London: Macon & Co. [1918], 1968), p. 158.

8. Josiah Royce, *The Religious Aspect of Philosophy: A Critique of the Bases of Conduct and of Faith* (Boston: Houghton Mifflin Co. [1885], 1913), pp. 451, 454.

9. Ibid., pp. 452-53, 456.

10. Ibid., pp. 455-56, 457, 459.

11. Pope, *An Essay on Man,* Epistle I, line 17.

12. Augustine, *Confessions,* VII, 12; cf. *Enchiridion,* XI, XII; *City of God,* XII, 6.

13. See Augustine, *Enchiridion,* XI, XII, XIII; *City of God,* XI, 9; XII, 6; *Confessions,* III, 7; VII, 12.

14. Augustine, *City of God,* XIV, 13; XII, 6, 7; *Confessions,* VII, 16. It should be borne in mind that in Augustine the will's capacity to oppose the divine will does not mean freedom of choice, but ability to act according to the nature and disposition of the agent, without external compulsion.

15. Augustine, *City of God,* XII, 6, 7. Augustine supports the closing question by citing Ps. 19:12: "Who is aware of his unwitting sins?/Cleanse me of any secret fault."

16. Augustine, *City of God,* XI, 22.

17. It is important to note that the distinction is not the same as that between physical and mental being. A person is marked by both matter and form; thus a female child is the matter for the form of the adult woman. A block of marble is the matter which is "formed" to produce a statue, but a collection of ideas may be the matter that is actualized in the form of a speech or a document.

18. Aquinas, *Compendium of Theology,* trans. Cyril Vollert (St. Louis: B. Herder Book Co., 1947), pp. 119-20; *Summa Theologica,* I, Ques. 48, Art. 3; Ques. 5, Art. 3.

19. Aquinas, *Summa Theologica,* I, Ques. 49, Art. 3; *Compendium of Theology,* pp. 119. Cf. *Compendium of Theology,* p. 123; *Summa Theologica,* I, Ques. 48, Art. 3.

20. Aquinas, *Compendium of Theology,* p. 122; *Summa Theologica,* I, Ques. 49, Art. 3.

21. Aquinas, *Summa Contra Gentiles,* III, 71.

22. Ibid.

23. Aquinas, *Summa Contra Gentiles,* III, 66, 70-71; cf. *Compendium of Theology,* chap. 141.

24. Aquinas, *Compendium of Theology,* chap. 142; *Summa Contra Gentiles,* III, 71; *Summa Theologica,* I, Ques. 49, Art. 3.

25. Jacques Maritain, *God and the Permission of Evil,* trans. Joseph W. Evans (Milwaukee: Bruce Publishing Co., 1966), p. 9.

26. Karl Barth, *Church Dogmatics,* trans. G. W. Bromiley and T. F. Torrance (Edinburgh: T. & T. Clark, 1936–62), I, 1–IV, 3. For an incisive critique of Barth's conception of evil, see John Hick, *Evil and the God of Love* (London: Macmillan & Co., 1966), pp. 141-50. Further contemporary statements of the doctrine of evil as privation may be found in Charles Journet, *The Meaning of Evil,* trans. Michael Barry (New York: P. J. Kenedy & Sons, 1963); and Paul Siwek, *The Philosophy of Evil* (New York: Ronald Press, 1956).

27. Paul Ricoeur, *The Symbolism of Evil,* trans. Emerson Buchanan (New York: Harper & Row, 1967), pp. 156-57.

28. See chapters 5 and 10.

29. See chapter 9.

30. Austin Farrer, *Love Almighty and Ills Unlimited: An Essay on Providence and Evil* (New York: Doubleday & Co., 1961; London: Collins, 1962), p. 30.

31. The principle of plenitude espoused by both Augustine and Aquinas also calls for critical evaluation. This is deferred until the postscript to chapter 10, where the concept is discussed more fully than was necessary in the present chapter.

Chapter 5

1. *Boston Globe,* 27 January 1976.

2. *Encyclopaedia Britannica,* 15th ed., *Macropaedia,* V, 1066-70.

3. C. E. M. Joad, *God and Evil* (London: Faber & Faber, 1942), 108-9; cf. pp. 92, 359

4. Edwin Lewis, *The Creator and the Adversary* (Nashville: Abingdon, 1948), pp. 19-20.

5. Ibid., pp. 143, 138, 133, 146.

6. Ibid. See pp. 24-26, 140-46, 210, 237, for further background on this discussion.

7. Augustine, *City of God,* XIX, 13.

8. Aquinas, *Summa Contra Gentiles,* III, 71.

9. This is a large body of Jewish writings, composed between 200 B.C. and A.D. 200, which are not found in either the Hebrew Bible or the Apocrypha. They are misleadingly named, since many of them are anonymous rather than pseudonymous, and since pseudonymous works are also found in both the canonical and the apocryphal writings.

10. The heightened influence of belief in Satan in Judaism during the Greco-Roman period was no doubt due not only to contact with Iranian dualism but to the bitterness and frustration of hopes experienced by Jews during successive foreign occupations and finally in the Diaspora. Belief in the malicious work of Satan helped them to understand both the sinfulness that occasioned God's judgment on Israel and the viciousness of her oppressors.

11.   How you have fallen from heaven, bright morning star,
        felled to the earth, sprawling helpless across the nations!
          You thought in your own mind,
            I will scale the heavens;
        I will set my throne high above the stars of God. . . .
          Yet you shall be brought down to Sheol,
            to the depths of the abyss.

12. See Arturo Graf, *Story of the Devil,* trans. Edward N. Stone (New York: The Macmillan Co., 1931).

13. Gustav Aulén, *Christus Victor,* trans. A. G. Hebert (New York: The Macmillan Co. [1931], 1951).

14. Gustaf Wingren, *The Living Word: A Theological Study of Preaching and the Church,* trans. Victor C. Pogue (Philadelphia: Muhlenberg Press, 1960), pp. 49, 112-13, 53, 91; *Creation and Law,* trans. Ross Mackenzie (Philadelphia: Muhlenberg Press, 1961), p. 114; *Gospel and Church,* trans. Ross Mackenzie (Philadelphia: Fortress Press, 1964), pp. 48-50.

15. Augustine, *City of God,* XIV, 13; cf. James 1:14.

16. Alan M. Olson, ed., *Disguises of the Demonic: Perspectives on the Power of Evil* (New York: Association Press, 1974), p. 124; see also pp. 110, 118.

17. Paul Ricoeur, *The Symbolism of Evil,* trans. Emerson Buchanan (New York: Harper & Row, 1967), pp. 177, 191, 198, 214, 327.

18. Jakob Boehme, *Morgenröte,* XIV, 72.

19. Frederick Sontag, *The God of Evil: An Argument for the Existence of the Devil* (New York: Harper & Row, 1970), pp. 129, 135; cf. pp. 3, 14, 25, 30.

20. Ibid., p. 21; Sontag, *God Why Did You Do That?* (Philadelphia: The Westminster Press, 1970), p. 37. Cf. *The God of Evil,* pp. 37-38, 132-34, 136; *God, Why Did You Do That?,* pp. 27, 35-36.

21. Sontag, *The God of Evil,* p. 140; cf. pp. 111-12; 150-52.

22. For discussion of this issue see chapter 11.

23. See Sontag, *God, Why Did You Do That?,* pp. 27, 35-37, 109-10, 127, and *The God of Evil,* pp. 17, 22-24, 41, 44, 132, for the background of this discussion.

Chapter 6

1. Associated Press report by Kernan Turner, *Boston Globe,* 15 February 1976.

2. The strong influence of this narrative on later thought leads Paul Ricoeur to designate the penal understanding of evil as "the Adamic myth" (*The Symbolism of Evil,* trans. Emerson Buchanan [New York: Harper & Row, 1967], pp. 309-17).

3. See Amos 1:2-15; 2:4-8; 3:9-11; 4:6-10; 5:7, 10-12, 17, 27; 6:1-8, 14; 8:1-5.

4. See Isaiah 9:8-10:4; 5:24*b*-30; 30:1-18; 31:1-3; 1:1-17; 2:6-22; 10:5-18.

5. Cf. Jeremiah 2:19, 26-29; 7:21-26, 31; 11:2-10; 25:3.

6. Cf. Ricoeur, *The Symbolism of Evil,* p. 321.

7. For other New Testament passages in which physical evil is regarded as God's judgment on sin, see Luke 1:20; Acts 12:22-23; 13:10-11.

8. Augustine, *Confessions,* VII, 3; *Against Adimantus,* chap. 26, quoted in *Confessions,* trans. E. B. Pusey, Everyman's Library (London: J. M. Dent & Sons; New York: E. P. Dutton [1907], 1926), p. 121 n.l.

9. Augustine, *Enchiridion,* XCVIII.

10. Augustine, *City of God,* XI, 22; XIX, 28.

11. Ibid., XXII, 30.

12. Calvin, *Forms of Prayer for the Church,* in Henry Beveridge, trans., *Tracts and Treatises on the Doctrine and Worship of the Church* (Grand Rapids: William B. Eerdmans Publishing Co., 1958), I, 106, 108-110.

13. Calvin, *Institutes, of the Christian Religion,* I, xvi, 4-5.

14. Ibid., I, xvii, 1; cf. II, vii, 6-12.

15. Ibid., I, xvii, 1.

16. William King, *Essay on the Origin of Evil,* 3rd ed., trans. Edmund Law (Cambridge, 1739).

17. Thomas Downing Kendrick, *The Lisbon Earthquake* (J. B. Lippincott Co., 1957), pp. 137-39.

18. Ibid., pp. 232-33.

19. Ibid., pp. 51-52, 225.

20. Ibid., pp. 127-29, 168-69.

21. Ibid., pp. 241-42.

22. T. B. Kilpatrick, "Suffering," in *Hastings Encyclopaedia of Religion and Ethics,* XII, 6.

23. Archibald MacLeish, *J.B.* (Boston: Houghton Mifflin Co., 1956), pp. 109-12.

24. Sarvepalli Radhakrishnan, *The Principal Upanishads* (New York: Harper & Brothers, 1953), pp. 113-14.

25. *Chandogya Upanishad,* vi, 9; see also *Brihadaranyaka Upanishad,* IV, 3, 21-22. These translations by Radhakrishnan appear in John Bowker, *Problems of Suffering in the Religions of the World* (London: Cambridge University Press, 1970), pp. 215, 214. A helpful discussion of *karma* and *samsara* is found on pp. 193-216.

26. *Dharmapada, Karmavarga,* vi, 5, 8, 19 (Sanskrit version, trans. Conze).

27. See Bowker, *Problems of Suffering,* p. 250.

28. Hesiod, *Works and Days,* lines 1-105, 181-99, 230-31, 238-40 in *Hesiod: The Homeric Hymns and Homerica,* with an English translation by Hugh C. Evelyn-White (London: William Heinemann; New York: The Macmillan Co., 1914), pp. 4-9, 16-17, 20-21.

29. Examples are disturbances created by heavy vehicular traffic, machinery, underground nuclear explosions, and the construction of dams and reservoirs. A destructive earthquake at Koynanagar, India, in 1967 was correlated with the filling of a large reservoir, and in 1962 damage was caused in Denver by a series of shocks clearly associated with the pumping of liquid wastes into a deep well.

30. Kendrick, *The Lisbon Earthquake,* p. 228.

31. Ibid., p. 186.

32. Immanuel Kant, *Kritik der praktischen Vernunft,* ed. Karl Vorländer (Leipzig: Felix Meiner, 1929), pp. 131-33, 137, 140-42. Also see Theodore Meyer Greene, ed., *Kant: Selections* (New York: Charles Scribner's Sons, 1929), pp. 352-55, 358-60.

33. Macleish, *J.B.,* p. 70.

34. Richard L. Rubenstein, *After Auschwitz: Radical Theology and Contemporary Judaism* (Indianapolis: Bobbs-Merrill, 1966), pp. 151-52, 224-25.

35. Emil L. Fackenheim, *God's Presence in History: Jewish Affirmations and Philosophical Reflections* (New York: Harper & Row, 1970), p. 73; see also pp. 30, 34.

36. John Hick, *Evil and the God of Love* (London: Macmillan & Co., 1966), p. 95.

Chapter 7

1. M. B. Forman, ed., *The Letters of John Keats,* 4th ed. (London: Oxford University Press, 1952), pp. 334-35.

2. The modifying clause is significant because of the way in which it presents creation and redemption as the work of one God, who is manifested in one who suffers. See chapter 11.

3. John Hick, *Evil and the God of Love* (London: Macmillan & Co., 1966), pp. 220-21, 223, 262-66, 285.

4. Irenaeus, *Against Heresies,* IV, xxxix, 1; cf. V., vi, 1.

5. Ibid., IV, xxxix, 2.

6. Augustine, *Enchiridion,* XXVII.

7. See Book 12, lines 462-78, especially lines 473-78.

8. Arthur O. Lovejoy, "Milton and the Paradox of the Fortunate Fall," *Essays in the History of Ideas* (New York: Capricorn Books, G. P. Putnam's Sons, 1960), p. 282; see also p. 284.

9. Hick, *Evil and the God of Love,* pp. 116-17, 182, 400.

10. Friedrich Schleiermacher, *The Christian Faith,* ed. H. R. Mackintosh and J. B. Stewart (Edinburgh: T. & T. Clark, 1928), p. 338.

11. Nicolas Berdyaev, *Spirit and Reality,* trans. George Reavey (London: Geoffrey Bles, 1939), pp. 114-15; see also *Dream and Reality: An Essay in Autobiography,* trans. Katharine Lampert (London: Geoffrey Bles, 1959), pp. 178-79.

12. Berdyaev, *Spirit and Reality,* p. 117; see also *Freedom and the Spirit* (New York: Charles Scribner's Sons, 1939), pp. 309-10.

13. Berdyaev, *Spirit and Reality,* pp. 112-13.

14. Ibid., p. 102; see also Berdyaev, *Dream and Reality,* p. 73; *Freedom and the Spirit,* pp. 309-10.

15. Berdyaev, *Spirit and Reality,* pp. 105-6, 116-17.

16. Berdyaev, *The Divine and the Human,* trans. R. M. French (London: Geoffrey Bles, 1949), p. 164; see also pp. 156-57.

17. Berdyaev, *Spirit and Reality,* p. 124.

18. Ibid., p. 117.

19. Bernard Bosanquet, *The Value and Destiny of the Individual* (London: Macmillan & Co. [1918], 1968), pp. 89-92, 194.

20. Ibid., pp. 68-69, 89, 203.

21. Ibid., pp. 158, 181, 221.

22. Ibid., p. 202.

23. Radoslav A. Tsanoff, *The Nature of Evil* (New York: The Macmillan Co., 1931), pp. 392-93, 398-400.

24. Ibid., pp. 392-94, 400; cf. Tsanoff, *Religious Crossroads* (New York: E. P. Dutton, 1942), pp. 336-37, 346-49.

25. Tsanoff, *The Nature of Evil,* p. 401.

26. F. R. Tennant, *Philosophical Theology,* 2 vols. (Cambridge: The University Press, 1930), II, 181. See also "The Problem of the Existence of Moral Evil," in

W. R. Sorley et al., *The Elements of Pain and Conflict in Human Life Considered from a Christian Point of View* (Cambridge: The University Press, 1916), pp. 89-90.

27. Tennant, "The Problem of Suffering," in Sorley, *Elements of Pain and Conflict in Human Life,* pp. 99-100.

28. Ibid., pp. 109-10; see also Tennant, *Philosophical Theology,* II, 198.

29. Tennant, "The Problem of Suffering," pp. 108, 111-13; see also *Philosophical Theology,* II, 197.

30. Tennant, *Philosophical Theology,* II, 205; see also "The Problem of Suffering," pp. 113-16.

31. Austin Farrer, *Love Almighty and Ills Unlimited: An Essay on Providence and Evil* (New York: Doubleday & Co., 1961; London: Collins, 1962), pp. 151, 164.

32. Augustine, *Enchiridion,* XI.

33. Farrer, *Love Almighty and Ills Unlimited,* p. 163.

34. Ibid., pp. 87-88, 94.

35. Ibid., pp. 69-70. See chapter 10 below.

36. Austin Farrer, *The Freedom of the Will* (London: A. & C. Black, 1958).

37. Hick, *Evil and the God of Love,* pp. xii, 201, 204.

38. Ibid., pp. 201-3, 290-95, 319, 344.

39. Ibid., pp. 358-59.

40. Ibid., pp. 344-45, 359-60.

41. Ibid., pp. 296-97, 371-72, 375-77.

42. Ibid., p. 399.

43. Additional thinkers who are broadly representative of this type of theodicy include these whose approach is primarily philosophical: Andrew Seth Pringle-Pattison, *The Idea of God in the Light of Recent Philosophy* (New York: Oxford University Press, 1920), pp. 386-417; Sorley et al., *The Elements of Pain and Conflict in Human Life,* opening lecture; John Wisdom, "God and Evil," *Mind,* 44 (1935), 1-20; and the following whose emphasis is mainly theological, especially christological: Paul F. Andrus, *Why Me? Why Mine?* (Nashville: Abingdon, 1975); Herbert H. Farmer, *Towards Belief in God* (London: Student Volunteer Movement Press, 1942), pp. 231-49; Leonard Hodgson, *For Faith and Freedom* (Oxford: Basil Blackwell, 1956), I, 192-217; II, 47-67; J. S. Whale, *The Christian Answer to the Problem of Evil* (London: SCM Press [1936], 1957).

44. Johann Wolfgang von Goethe, *Faust: A Tragedy,* trans. Bayard Taylor (Boston: Houghton Mifflin Co. [1870], 1912), II, 294.

45. William E. Hulme, "Our Daughter Need Not Have Died," *The Christian Century,* 91 (1974), 1147.

46. "Death at Sea," five articles by David J. Rosenthal, *Boston Globe,* 25-30 January 1976.

47. Paul Ricoeur, *The Symbolism of Evil,* trans. Emerson Buchanan (New York: Harper & Row, 1967) p. 254; see also Ernst Bloch, *Man on His Own; Essays in the Philosophy of Man,* trans. E. B. Ashton (New York: Herder & Herder, 1970), pp. 79-80, 88-92; and *Philosophische Grundfragen: Zur Ontologie des Noch-Nicht-Seins* (Frankfurt am Main: Suhrkamp Verlag, 1961), pp. 8-9, 25, 39-40.

48. George Pickering, *Creative Malady* (New York: Oxford University Press, 1974), pp. 71-94, 179.

49. Pickering, *Creative Malady,* pp. 23, 98, 118, 165-77.

50. Eugene Debs, "Statement to the Court," *Writings and Speeches of Eugene V. Debs,* with an introduction by Arthur M. Schlesinger, Jr. (New York: Hermitage Press, 1948), p. 437. This statement was made at the close of Debs's trial on charges of violating the espionage law. He was convicted on September 12, 1918.

51. Alfred North Whitehead, *Process and Reality* (New York: The Macmillan Co., 1929), p. 531.

52. C. J. Ducasse, *A Philosophical Scrutiny of Religion* (New York: Ronald Press, 1953), p. 364.

53. W. R. Jones, *Is God a White Racist? A Preamble to Black Theology* (Garden City, N.Y.: Doubleday Anchor, 1973), p. 198.

54. Hick, *Evil and the God of Love,* p. 292.

55. Albert Camus, *The Plague,* trans. Stuart Gilbert (New York: Alfred A. Knopf, 1958); Fyodor Dostoyevsky, *The Brothers Karamazov,* trans. Constance Garnett (New York: Random House, The Modern Library, 1950), pp. 250-51.

56. "Souffrir passe, avoir souffert ne passe jamais" (Bloy, *Le Pèlerin de l'Absolu).* See Berdyaev, *Freedom and the Spirit,* pp. vii, 309-10.

Chapter 8

1. F. R. Tennant, *Philosophical Theology* (Cambridge: The University Press, 1930), II, 201; see also "The Problem of Suffering" in W. R. Sorley et al., *The Elements of Pain and Conflict in Human Life Considered from a Christian Point of View* (Cambridge: The University Press, 1916), pp. 104-5.

2. C. S. Lewis, *The Problem of Pain* (New York: The Macmillan Co., 1944), p. 59.

3. Austin Farrer, *The Freedom of the Will* (London: A & C Black, 1958), p. 178. Cf. Tennant, *Philosophical Theology,* II, 199-200; "The Problem of Suffering," p. 102.

4. Ronald W. Hepburn, *Christianity and Paradox* (London: Franklin Watts, 1958), p. 200.

5. Paul F. Andrus, *Why Me? Why Mine?* (Nashville: Abingdon, 1975), pp. 63-64, 65-66, 68-69.

6. Ian Ramsey, *Religious Language* (New York: The Macmillan Co., 1963), pp. 85-87.

7. David Hume, *Dialogues Concerning Natural Religion;* in *Hume: Selections,* ed. Charles W. Hendel, Jr. (New York: Charles Scribner's Sons, 1927), pp. 373-74.

8. John Hick, *Evil and the God of Love* (London: Macmillan & Co., 1966), pp. 344-45. The evaluation of the soul-making view in chapter 7 above is pertinent here.

9. George F. Thomas, *Philosophy and Religious Belief* (New York: Charles Scribner's Sons, 1970), p. 242.

10. Alfred Noyes, *The Unknown God* (New York: Sheed & Ward, 1949), p. 227.

11. See chapter 11.

12. Thomas, *Philosophy and Religious Belief,* pp. 342-43.

13. Charles Hartshorne, *The Divine Relativity* (New Haven: Yale University Press, 1948), p. 152; *The Logic of Perfection and Other Essays* (La Salle, Ill.: Open Court Publishing Co., 1962), p. 297.

14. Alfred North Whitehead, *Process and Reality* (New York: The Macmillan Co., 1929), pp. 521-24.

15. Alfred North Whitehead, *Religion in the Making* (New York: The Macmillan Co., 1926), p. 156.

16. Origen, *De Principiis,* II, 9, in *The Ante-Nicene Fathers,* ed. Alexander Roberts and James Donaldson, American Reprint of the Edinburgh Edition (Grand Rapids, Mich.: William B. Eerdmans Publishing Co., 1965), IV, 239-384.

17. It may be recalled that Tsanoff, Tennant, Farrer, and Hick assume an evolutionary order in their discussions of the relation of evil to the growth of character.

18. *Encyclopaedia Britannica,* 15th ed., *Micropaedia,* IV, 219.

19. See L. Charles Birch, *Nature and God,* (London: SCM Press; Philadelphia: Westminster Press, 1965) pp. 42-44; "Creation and the Creator," *Science and Religion: New Perspectives in Dialogue,* ed. Ian G. Barbour (New York: Harper Torchbooks, 1968), pp. 213-15.

20. Teilhard de Chardin, "Le Signification et le valeur constructrice de la souffrance" (1933), *Oeuvres,* VI, 63.

21. William James, *Pragmatism* (New York: Longmans, Green, & Co., 1907), p. 143.

22. See above, p. 152. Berdyaev begins this series of adjectives with *irrational.* The context indicates that he has in mind a reality that is not opposed to rationality but beyond it. However, I am not at liberty to substitute *nonrational;* and since *irrational,* ordinarily defined as unreasonable or void of understanding, is not what I mean, I am omitting it. I am trying to suggest the presence in God of a factor that in human terms is neither rational nor irrational but simply nonrational. Edgar S. Brightman calls it the "nonrational Given" *(A Philosophy of Religion* [New York: Prentice-Hall, 1940], pp. 336-37).

23. Birch, "Creation and the Creator," p. 214.

24. For further examination of this possibility see chapter 11.

25. Birch, *Nature and God,* pp. 103-4.

Chapter 9

1. See C. D. B. Bryan, *Friendly Fire* (New York: G. P. Putnam's Sons, 1976).

2. *Congressional Record,* 29 January 1968; submitted by Mendel Rivers, Chairman, House Armed Services Committee.

3. E. G. Spaulding, "The Walls of the Past," *What Am I?* (New York: Charles Scribner's Sons, 1928), p. 42; cf. pp. 43-46.

4. Plato, *Phaedo,* 98-99.

5. Ibid., 99.

6. See Ian Barbour, *Issues in Science and Religion* (Englewood Cliffs, N.J.: Prentice-Hall, 1966), pp. 310-15, 331-33, 335-37, 359-60, for the background of this discussion.

7. Charles Hartshorne, *A Natural Theology for Our Time* (La Salle, Ill.: Open Court Publishing, Co., 1967), p. 81.

8. Hannah Green [Joanne Greenberg], *I Never Promised You a Rose Garden* (New York: Holt, Rinehart and Winston, 1964), p. 122.

9. Paul Ricoeur, *The Symbolism of Evil,* trans. Emerson Buchanan (New York: Harper & Row, 1967), p. 312.

10. Leslie Dewart, in *Initiatives in History: A Christian-Marxist Exchange* (Cambridge, Mass.: The Church Society for College Work, 1967), p. 14.

11. Rolf Hochhuth, *The Deputy,* adapt. Jerome Rothenberg (London: Samuel French, 1964), pp. 247-48.

12. Ibid., p. 248.

13. William R. Jones, *Is God a White Racist?* (Garden City, N.Y.: Doubleday Anchor, 1974), p. 30.

14. Ibid.

15. Ibid., pp. 193-97.

16. Madden and Hare, *Evil and the Concept of God* (Springfield, Ill.: Charles C. Thomas, 1968), pp. 74-75; C. J. Ducasse, *A Philosophical Scrutiny of Religion* (New

York: Ronald Press, 1953), pp. 364-65; Flew, "Divine Omnipotence and Human
Freedom," Flew and MacIntyre, eds., *New Essays in Philosophical Theology,* p. 152;
Mackie, "Evil and Omnipotence," *Mind,* 64 (1955), 200-212.

17. Flew, *New Essays in Philosophical Theology,* pp. 162-69.

18. John Hick, *Evil and the God of Love* (London: Macmillan & Co., 1966), p.
311.

19. Ninian Smart, "Omnipotence, Evil and Supermen," *Philosophy,* 36 (1961),
188-95.

20. Charles E. Raven, *Natural Religion and Christian Theology,* second series,
Experience and Interpretation (Cambridge: The University Press, 1953), p. 125.

21. Charles Hartshorne, "A New Look at the Problem of Evil," in *Current
Philosophical Issues,* ed. F. C. Dommeyer (Springfield, Ill.: Charles C. Thomas,
1966), p. 204.

22. H. Margenau, "Advantages and Disadvantages of Various Interpretations of
the Quantum Theory," *Physics Today,* 7 (1954), 6-7.

23. Werner Heisenberg, *Physics and Philosophy: The Revolution in Modern
Science* (New York: Harper & Brothers, 1958), p. 54.

24. Aloys Wenzl, "Einstein's Theory of Relativity Viewed from the Standpoint of
Critical Realism, and Its Significance for Philosophy," *Albert Einstein: Philosopher-
Scientist,* ed. Paul Arthur Schilpp (Evanston, Ill.: Library of Living Philosophers,
1949), pp. 599-600.

25. J. Langmuir, "Science, Common Sense, and Decency," *Science,* 97 (1943),
1.

26. Barbour, *Issues in Science and Religion,* p. 309.

27. A. Bachem, "Heisenberg's Indeterminacy and Life," *Philosophy of Science,*
19 (1952), 264-66.

28. Berdyaev, *The Divine and the Human,* trans. R. M. French (London: Geoffrey
Bles, 1949), pp. 90-91; *Spirit and Reality,* trans. George Reavey (London: Geoffrey
Bles, 1939), pp. 114-15; *Dream and Reality,* pp. 99, 178-81, 288, 299-300; *The
Destiny of Man,* trans. N. Duddington (New York: Charles Scribner's Sons [1933],
1937), p. 34.

29. David Ray Griffin, *God, Power, and Evil: A Process Theodicy* (Philadelphia:
Westminster Press, 1976), pp. 278, 280, 292. Cf. Alfred North Whitehead, *Process
and Reality* (New York: The Macmillan Co., 1929), pp. 68, 75, 130, 135.

30. Whitehead, *Process and Reality,* p. 75.

Chapter 10

1. William Temple, *Nature, Man, and God* (London: Macmillan & Co. [1934],
1951), pp. 366-67.

2. Ibid., p. 367.

3. Barbour, *Issues in Science and Religion* (Englewood Cliffs, N.J.: Prentice-Hall,
1966), p. 330.

4. Rick Gore, "The Awesome Worlds Within a Cell," *National Geographic
Magazine,* 150 (1976/77), 355-57.

5. Alfred North Whitehead, *Symbolism* (New York: The Macmillan Co., 1927), p.
39.

6. Austin Farrer, *Love Almighty and Ills Unlimited: An Essay on Providence and
Evil* (New York: Doubleday & Co., 1961; London: Collins, 1962), pp. 59-60, 75-76.

7. Robert F. Weaver, "The Cancer Puzzle," *National Geographic Magazine,* 150
(1976/77), 390; *Encyclopaedia Britannica, Micropaedia,* 15th ed., IX, 182.

8. James Stephens, "Optimist," in Robert C. Baldwin and James A.S. McPeek, *An Introduction to Philosophy Through Literature* (New York: The Ronald Press, 1950), p. 344.

9. Miguet de Unamuno, *The Tragic Sense of Life in Men and in Peoples,* trans. J. E. Crawford Flitch (London: Macmillan & Co., 1931), p. 209.

10. Wayne Leiser, "And, Behold, It Was Very Good," *The Christian Century,* 92 (1965), 706.

11. Howard Thurman, *Meditations of the Heart* (New York: Harper & Brothers, 1953), pp. 110-11.

12. Arthur O. Lovejoy, *The Great Chain of Being* (Cambridge: Harvard University Press [1936], 1966).

13. Plato, *Timaeus,* 41, B-C.

14. Plotinus, *Enneads,* II, 9, 13; III, 2, 3, 7, 11, 15, 16.

15. Augustine, *City of God,* XI, 16, 22; *Confessions,* VII, 13; cf. *Soliloquies,* I, 2; *Nature of the Good,* VIII.

16. Aquinas, *Summa Contra Gentiles,* III, 71; *Summa Theologica,* I, Ques. 48, Art. 2; Ques. 49, Arts. 2, 3; *Compendium of Theology,* trans. Cyril Vollert (St. Louis: B. Herder Book Co., 1947), chaps. 141-42.

17. Barbour, *Issues in Science and Religion,* p. 60.

18. Lovejoy, *The Great Chain of Being,* pp. 65, 118.

19. Ibid., p. 52.

20. This evaluation is in part indebted to the criticisms of Lovejoy in *The Great Chain of Being,* pp. 315, 329-33, and John Hick, *Evil and the God of Love* (London: Macmillan & Co., 1966), pp. 201-4.

Chapter 11

1. Elie Wiesel, *Night,* trans. Stella Rodway (New York: Avon Books [1960], 1969), p. 76.

2. See F. W. J. Schelling, *Werke,* ed. Manfred Schröter (München: Beck, 1927/28), I, 8, 70, 77; *Denkmal der Schrift von den göttlichen Dingen* (Tübingen: Cotta, 1812); Arthur O. Lovejoy, *The Great Chain of Being* (Cambridge: Harvard University Press [1936], 1966), pp. 317-26; Frederick O. Keil, *Die theologischen Grundlagen von Schellings Philosophie der Freiheit* (Leiden: Brill, 1965), pp. 16-17; Kurt Lüthi, *Gott und das Böse* (Zürich: Zwingli Verlag, 1961), pp. 8, 15, 43, 282-84. In important respects Schelling's thought parallels that of his contemporary G. W. F. Hegel (1770–1831), for whom the suffering of the world reflects dialectical tension and opposition within the very nature of God. The Spirit fulfills itself through self-negation and self-differentiation, which are eternally overcome. Severity, pain, and struggle characterize the nature of reality. See G. W. F. Hegel, *Sämtliche Werke,* ed. Georg Lasson (Leipzig: Felix Meiner, 1907–1933), II, 13, 140, 523, 545; IX, 937; XIV, 149, 156-58, 161, 165, 167, 178-79.

3. Nicolas Berdyaev, *Dream and Reality: An Essay in Autobiography,* trans. Katharine Lampert (London: Geoffrey Bles, 1950), pp. 179, 299-300; cf. *Spirit and Reality,* trans. George Reavey (London: Geoffrey Bles, 1939), pp. 114-15.

4. Radoslav Tsanoff, *The Nature of Evil* (New York: The Macmillan Co., 1931), pp. 398-401; *Religious Crossroads* (New York: E. P. Dutton, 1942), pp. 337, 346-49.

5. Edgar S. Brightman, *A Philosophy of Religion* (New York: Prentice-Hall, 1940), pp. 336-37; cf. *The Problem of God* (New York: Abingdon, 1930), pp. 113, 192. By "surd" evil Brightman means "evil that is inherently and irreducibly evil and contains within itself no principle of development or improvement." As an example,

he cites the intrinsic worthlessness of an imbecile's existence. He regards it as debatable whether there are "dysteleological surds," but "their existence is at least conceivable" (*A Philosophy of Religion*, p. 246).

6. Peter A. Bertocci "Theistic Personalistic Idealism and the Problem of Good-and-Evil," a paper presented to the Personalistic Discussion Group, Eastern Division, American Philosophical Association, Statler-Hilton Hotel, New York, December 28, 1975, p. 7 (cf. pp. 8, 10, 12-13); *Introduction to the Philosophy of Religion* (New York: Prentice-Hall, 1951), pp. 435, 398 (cf. pp. 430, 433).

7. Brightman, *A Philosophy of Religion*, p. 338; cf. Bertocci, *Introduction to the Philosophy of Religion*, pp. 435, 437.

8. This argument does not simply *assume* a cosmic unity without regard to the evidence, or *presuppose* that moral and religious experience are wholly dominated by good. On these issues see the discussions of dualism and the unity and interdependence of the natural order in chapters 5, 8, and 10.

9. There are also what might be called temporal givens. Every past act of God becomes part of the context within which he works. Moreover, his energy is constantly being expressed in innumerable finite centers of energy, each with a form and a boundary; these provide both channels and temporal frontiers for his activity. The creation of a single biological cell, for example, becomes a frontier that bounds the nature and scope of his future creative action.

10. L. Harold DeWolf, *A Theology of the Living Church* (New York: Harper & Row [1935], 1968), pp. 141-42.

11. Berdyaev, *Spirit and Reality*, pp. 114-15.

12. Ernst Bloch, *Man on His Own: Essays in the Philosophy of Religion* (New York: Herder & Herder, 1970), pp. 73-92.

13. David Ray Griffin, *God, Power, and Evil: A Process Theodicy* (Philadelphia: Westminster Press, 1976), pp. 276, 297-98, 281; cf. pp. 269, 273, 278-80, 248-49.

14. For careful historical surveys of the doctrine that God is incapable of suffering, see Bertrand R. Brasnett, *The Suffering of the Impassible God* (London: S.P.C.K., 1928); and J. K. Mozley, *The Impassibility of God* (Cambridge: The University Press, 1926).

15. Gregory of Nyssa, *Adversus Eunomius*, VI, 1; Augustine, *City of God*, VIII, 17.

16. Aquinas, *Summa Theologica*, I, Ques. 9, Art. 1; II, Ques. 25, Art. 1; *Summa Contra Gentiles*, II, 25.

17. Calvin, *Commentaries*, on Isaiah 53:4-8; Genesis 6:6.

18. See Brasnett, *The Suffering of the Impassible God*, pp. 10-11, 152, 155; Friedrich von Hügel, *Essays and Addresses*, second series (London: J. M. Dent & Co., 1923), pp. 179, 186, 199-210; Hans Küng, "Kann Gott leiden?", *Menschwerdung Gottes* (Freiburg, Basel, Wien: Herder, 1970), p. 631; Mozley, *The Impassibility of God*, pp. 46, 116, 173-74.

19. Berdyaev, *Dream and Reality*, p. 179.

20. Abraham Heschel, *The Prophets* (New York: Harper & Row, 1962), p. 276.

21. Josiah Royce, *Studies of Good and Evil* (New York: D. Appleton & Co., 1898), p. 27.

22. In view of the difficulty, if not the impossibility, of conceiving of God as not creating at all, it seems to me sound to think of him as inherently creative—by his very nature as God. Would not a wholly noncreative God be a meaningless abstraction? But it is reasonable to suppose that within the bounds of his divine character various options are open to him.

23. For example, evils related to physical indeterminacy and the occurrence of

mutations in evolution may be attributed to the bounds of God's power inherent in his nature.

24. Emil L. Fackenheim, *God's Presence in History: Jewish Affirmations and Philosophical Reflections* (New York: Harper & Row, 1970), pp. 18-29.

25. Albert Camus, *The Myth of Sisyphus and Other Essays* (New York: Alfred A. Knopf [1955], 1964), p. 17.

26. Choan-Seng Song, "The Role of Christology in the Christian Encounter with Eastern Religions," *South East Asia Journal of Theology,* 5 (January 1964), 29-30.

27. Martin Luther King, Jr., *Strength to Love* (New York: Harper & Row, 1963), p. 64.

28. Paul E. Johnson, "New Light on a Christian Vocation," *The Christian Century,* 91 (1974), 174.

Chapter 12

1. Paul Geren, *Burma Diary* (New York: Harper & Brothers, 1943), pp. 30-31.

2. Calvin, *Institutes of the Christian Religion,* I, xvi, 1-9; xvii, 1, 5-8, 10.

3. Harry Emerson Fosdick, "God of Grace and God of Glory," in the *Hymnal of the United Church of Christ* (Philadelphia: United Church Press, 1974), no. 198.

4. Alfred North Whitehead, *Process and Reality* (New York: The Macmillan Co., 1929), p. 525.

5. The Wisdom of Solomon 16:17c (Goodspeed).

6. James Weldon Johnson, *God's Trombones* (New York: Viking Press, 1927), p. 21.

7. Reinhold Niebuhr, *Reflections on the End of an Era* (New York: Charles Scribner's Sons, 1934), p. 31.

8. Friedrich von Logau, "Retribution," *Poetic Aphorisms* (1654).

9. Leslie Weatherhead, *Why Do Men Suffer?* (New York: Abingdon, 1936), p. 134.

10. G. W. F. Hegel, *The Logic of Hegel,* trans. William Wallace (Oxford: Clarendon Press, 1892), p. 350.

11. In Thornton Wilder's novel *The Eighth Day* (New York: Harper & Row, 1967), Dr. Gillies declares during a New Year's celebration: "Man is not an end but a beginning. We are at the beginning of the second week. We are children of the eighth day!" (p. 16).

Index of Persons

Index of Subjects

Index of Biblical References